THE KOSHER PALETTE

Joseph Kushner Hebrew Academy
Kushner Yeshiva High School
Livingston, New Jersey

Joseph Kushner Hebrew Academy/Kushner Yeshiva High School

Library of Congress Card Catalog Number: 99097181

ISBN: 0-9676638-0-6

First Printing   April 2000   6,000 copies
Second Printing   August 2000   10,000 copies
Third Printing   December 2000   10,000 copies
Fourth Printing   December 2001   10,000 copies

For additional copies, use the order form in the back of the book.

Printed in the USA by

WIMMER
COOKBOOKS
Memphis
1-800-548-2537

TABLE OF CONTENTS

FOREWORD

Few of us today have the time or the inclination to spend hours in the kitchen putting together the same kinds of kosher meals we were served as children. What we want instead is a repertoire of elegant, healthful dishes that taste as sensational as they look-and don't take forever to prepare.

And that's exactly what you'll find in *The Kosher Palette*.

Compiled by parents at the Joseph Kushner Hebrew Academy in Livingston, New Jersey, *The Kosher Palette* celebrates the most original-and delectable-dishes emerging from today's kosher kitchens.

Emphasizing fresh, seasonal ingredients, all of the recipes featured here are certain to stir your senses. Even the photographs are mouth-watering!

What's more, *The Kosher Palette* features the healthful yet sophisticated recipes preferred by America's most innovative cooks, as well as selected specialties from today's most popular international cuisines. You'll find extraordinary recipes for everyday dining, along with unforgettable treats for Jewish holidays and other special occasions. Carefully edited and clearly presented, more than 300 recipes have been double- or triple-tested to ensure ease of preparation and elegant presentation, as well as quality, consistency and adherence to *kashrut*.

But *The Kosher Palette* is more than an indispensable cookbook. It's a celebration of kosher hospitality, an enduring hallmark of Jewish life.

Here you'll find funny, nostalgic and inspiring personal anecdotes from our contributors, along with practical suggestions for creating your own, unique celebrations any day of the year. In addition, you'll find tips for enhancing every aspect of at-home entertaining-from selecting complementary menus and wines, to fashioning dazzling table decorations and centerpieces. And like our recipes, all of these special features emphasize ease, elegance, and expressive personal style.

For us, *The Kosher Palette* has been a labor of love. More than 200 kosher cooks from eight local communities helped us create this cookbook, contributing an enormous amount of time, energy, and skill. We hope you will be as impressed as we are by the breadth and depth of their expertise and that their recipes, menus, stories, and suggestions will help you nourish and entertain all the wonderful people who enrich your life every day.

Hearty Appetite!
Susie Fishbein
Sandra Blank
Editors, The Kosher Palette

JOSEPH KUSHNER HEBREW ACADEMY
KUSHNER YESHIVA HIGH SCHOOL

From a small house on 13th Street and Clinton Avenue, Newark…

…to an impressive building on the corner of Seymour and Clinton Avenues, Newark…

…to a merger with the Hebrew Institute in the Young Israel building on Lyons Avenue, Newark…

…to a facility on Maple Avenue, Hillside…

…to Centre Street, South Orange…

…to Henderson Drive, West Caldwell…

…to its present location on South Orange Avenue, Livingston.

The history of the Joseph Kushner Hebrew Academy has followed a path of growth.

Our school was founded in 1942, in a small house in Newark, by a handful of individuals, who understood that the chain of Jewish continuity is directly linked to a Torah education. Such an education must be simultaneously innovative and superb as well as affordable and thus accessible to all. This vision strengthened with time, and today we are recognized as one of the finest Modern Orthodox day schools in the United States.

Located in Livingston, New Jersey, on a sprawling eleven-acre campus that boasts an unparalleled state-of-the-arts facility, our school today educates 800 children from pre-kindergarten through twelfth grade and is continually growing. Our students come from numerous communities attracted by our small class sizes and myriad of extracurricular activities taught by a staff of dedicated teachers.

We also house a unique program, the SINAI Institute. It is the metropolitan area's only Yeshiva program that caters to the special needs of developmentally challenged children. In addition, our campus is home to the Jewish Education Association of MetroWest wherein 350 teenagers and young adults are educated in afternoon and evening programs.

Distinguished by a professional and lay leadership committed to the pursuit of lofty educational goals, our children thrive in a nurturing learning environment that focuses on the intellectual, emotional and physical needs of every student. The guiding force behind our educational philosophy is our heritage– a heritage founded on timeless Torah values and love of Israel. This philosophy is interwoven with the ideals of western civilization and the American democratic way of life.

We invite you to visit our school and meet with our administrators and teachers who are preparing our children to face the challenges of future leadership and productive citizenship with wisdom, dignity and care. To schedule an appointment please call the school office at (973) 597-1115. You may also visit our website at www.jkha.org.

The Kosher Palette Sponsors

Diamond Level
Barbara & George Gellert
Robin & Brad Klatt
Lee & Murray Kushner
Rae Kushner
Seryl & Charles Kushner
Barbara & Alan Listhaus
Marisa & Richard Stadtmauer
Sherry & Henry Stein

· · · · ·

Gold Level
Hattie & Arthur Dubroff
Alice & Jacob Klein

· · · ·

Corporate Sponsors
Lucent Technologies
Mandelbaum & Mandelbaum
M&M® Mars
Nabisco
NorCrown Bank
Zurich Reinsurance

· · · · ·

Silver Level
Eva & Arie Halpern
Cynthia & Harold Kestenbaum
Linda & Murray Laulicht
Sharon & Jonathan Sherman

· · · · ·

Bronze Level

Shari & Robert Alter
Bonnie & David Anfang
Mira Barnea
Debbie & Harvey Bell
Suzanne & Miles Berger
Marilyn & Leonard Bielroy
Andrea & Bryan Bier
Sandra & Howard Blank
Tita & Paul Celler
Barbara & Larry Ellberger
Myrna Fishbein
Susie & Kalman Fishbein

Maralyn & Isidore Friedman
Audrey & Norbert Gaelen
Pepa & Meyer Gold
Avivah & Michael Gottlieb
Cheryl & Fred Halpern
Joanne & Jeffrey Ingerman
Milly & Herbert Iris
Barrie & Simon Jacob
Judith & Irwin Kallman
Rebecca & Douglas Kuber
Marci & Jeffrey Lefkovits

Linda & David Lewinter
Eva & Irving Miller
Dara & David Orbach
Malkie & Paul Ratzker
Janet & Sheldon Rosenberg
Robin & Joseph Sabbagh
Esther & William Schulder
Fran & Arie Schwartz
Daryl & Edward Shapiro
Linda & Leonard Spector
Rita & Jerome Waldor
Debbie & Wayne Zuckerman

Cookbook Committee

Editors-In-Chief
Susie Fishbein
Sandra Blank

· · · · ·

Founding Committee
Sandra Blank
Debbie Finkelstein
Susie Fishbein
Robin Klatt
Alice Klein
Pepi Kolb
Sherry Stein

Recipe Testing Coordinator
Dorene Richman

· · · · ·

Copy Editors
Diane Covkin
Leah Levy
Judy Sandman

Assistant Copy Editors
Ellen Arian
Robin Klatt
Alice Klein
Nancy Perlmutter
Dorene Richman
Sherry Stein
Stacey Ullman

· · · · ·

Judaic Writer
Belle A. Dardik Kronisch

Judaic Advisor

Rabbi Scot Berman

. . . . .

Fundraising

Shari Alter
Sandra Blank
Susie Fishbein
Robin Klatt
Alice Klein

. . . . .

Writers

Diane Covkin
Malkie Ratzker

. . . . .

Treasurer

Sharon Sherman

. . . . .

Public Relations

Diane Covkin
Debby Klein

. . . . .

Artistic Presentation Committee

Bonnie Anfang
Debbie Bell
Annette Gross
Frank Russo
Sherry Stein

. . . . .

Wine & Beverage Advisors

Larry Gross

Skyview Liquors
of Riverdale, NY

. . . . .

A Special Thank You

Robin Klatt
Alice Klein

*Our true and constant friends,
for helping us every step of the way.*

Kalman, Kate, Danielle,
& Jodi Fishbein
Howard, Jessica, Adam,
Joshua, & Daniel Blank

*Our heartfelt thanks and love
must go to our wonderful
families for all of their endless
sacrifices and constant support
and encouragement for this
seemingly neverending project.*

. . . . .

Special Friends

*The Kosher Palette wishes
to thank the friends and businesses
who by their participation have
made possible this cookbook. We
are grateful for your time, expertise,
support and generosity.*

. . . . .

Annette Gross
Lee Kushner
Barbara Listhaus
Dorene Richman

*A special thank you for all
of your help in elevating this
book to a higher level.*

. . . . .

Michael Grad
Beth Aron
Sheree Bohbot
Eileen Collins
Chaya Felzenberg
Anita Panas
Nicole Sperduto

*For your assistance on
behalf of the school office.*

. . . . .

Jan Press of
Jan Press Photomedia
Scott Laperruque of
G2 Productions

*For your patience and expertise
in creating the perfect photos for
this book. You really went that
extra mile to strive for perfection.*

Carl Mink of
Livingston Camera

*For your generosity in developing the
photos that helped promote the book.*

. . . . .

Randy and Angie Zablo of
Foremost Caterers

*For your abounding
generosity and guidance.*

. . . . .

Abby Sussman, Wali Alidad,
Donald Koedyker and the
entire kitchen staff at
Foremost Caterers

*For allowing us into your kitchen to
experience some of your magic.*

. . . . .

Robert Holland of
Spitz & Peck Florists

*For providing us with the exquisite
flowers and arrangements that make
our book truly special.*

. . . . .

B.G., Floral Designer of
Spitz & Peck Florists

*A special thank you for your
creativity and enthusiasm.*

. . . . .

Shelly Golombeck of
Morris J. Golombeck Spices

For your donation of spices.

. . . . .

The Kitchen Store

*For loaning us your
merchandise to photograph.*

. . . . .

Melissa Singer of
Victorian Seasons

*For your expert floral advice
and the donation of incredible
flowers for our kick-off event.*

The Kosher Palette gratefully acknowledges the energy and dedicated efforts of the men and women who tested and perfected the recipes in this book. Our sincere gratitude for your time, money, advice and discerning taste, ensuring our recipes are fabulous.

Appetizer and Hors d'Oeuvres Testers

Bonnie Anfang
Debbie Bell
Marilyn Bielroy
Freda Cochavi
Diane Covkin
Beverly Cytto
Connie Edelman
Micky Hirsch
Fran Kadosh
Yuda Kadosh
Vivian Kandel
Batsheva Mehl
Sarah Lachs
Hal Robinson
Michal Robinson
Debbie Rosenwein
Giulianna Ross
Laraine Rubin
Judy Sandman
Sylvia Stark
Sherry Stein*

Soup Testers

Amy Braun
Lisa Ben-Haim
Chana Erbst
Rosalyn Farkas
Batya Karmi
Pepi Kolb*
Judith Krauss
Marcia Roth
Heidi Schwartz
Shulamit Zenou

Salad Testers

Deena Altman
Debbie Buechler
Linda Cohen
Hattie Dubroff
Emily Faiwiszewski*
Debbie Finkelstein*
Carol Goldberg
Gail Hausdorff
Judy Israeli
Loraine Langer
Eileen Levitt
Bobbi Luxenberg
Susan Moskowitz
Dorene Richman
Deena Rubin

Mindy Saibel
Mali Schwartz
Sharon Sherman
Sandy Small
Dori Sobin
Debbi Weintraub
Tova Weiser

Poultry Testers

Deena Altman
Shani Blenden
Debbie Brody
Abbie Cohen
Emily Faiwiszewski
Debbie Finkelstein
Cheryl Furer
Gail Hausdorff
Judy Israeli
Ellie Langer
Loraine Langer
Paul Langer
Linda Laub
Bobbi Luxenberg
Susan Moskowitz
Ron Richman
Sharon Sherman*
Debra Silverman
Sharon Zughaft

Meat Testers

Judy Epstein*
Cheryl Friedman
Michele Homa
Robin Klatt
Alice Klein
Sue Leibovich
Barbara Listhaus
Karen Lyman
Lauren Mayer
Edith Michaely
Malkie Ratzker
Rachelle Safar
Jayne Sayowitz

Fish & Pasta Testers

Susie Fishbein
Brenda Freeman
Debby Friedman
Elissa Gorkowitz
Miriam Greenberg
Stanley Greenberg
Robyn Krieger

Nancy Lefkowitz
Amy Ruderman
Fern Steinberg
Helene Wengrofsky*
Lori Zucker

Brunch & Dairy Testers

Nancy Caplan
Tita Celler*
Francine Glick
Elissa Gorkowitz
Avivah Gottlieb
Michelle Levine
Mairav Pascheles
Barbara Zohar
Debbie Zuckerman

Side Dish Testers

Shari Alter
Anna Dickstein*
Michele Homa
Belle Kronisch
Barbara Listhaus
Lauren Mayer
Malkie Ratzker
Dalila Rosenstrauch
Amy Ruderman
Marisa Stadtmauer
Hope Tafet
Stacey Ullman
Lori Zucker

Cake & Dessert Testers

Shari Alter
Deena Altman
Robin Bellicha
Helene Benzel
Jonathan Blank
Shani Blenden
Emily Faiwiszewski
Debbie Fine
Debbie Finkelstein
Cheryl Friedman
Fran Friedman
Jill Geiger
Gail Hausdorf
Gladys Hirschorn
Anne Homa
Judy Israeli
Susan Kahnowitz
Robyn Krieger
Belle Kronisch

Barbara Listhaus*
Bobbi Luxenberg
Karen Lyman
Martha Maik
Lauren Mayer
Cammuna Meghnagi
Edith Michaely
Nancy Perlmutter
Malkie Ratzker
Amy Ruderman
Rachelle Safar
Marsha Sanders
Monica Schwartzbach
Dori Sobin
Esther Stock
Hope Tafet
Lilli Tammam
Stacy Ullman
Jeanne Waxman
Helene Wengrofsky
Karen Weiss

Cookies & Bars Testers

Deena Altman
Amy Bitton
Shani Blenden
Emily Faiwiszewski
Loraine Langer
Bobbi Luxenberg
Marcia Sanders
Esther Schulder*
Mali Schwartz
Dori Sobin

Recipe Development Committee

A second helping of thanks to those who did additional testings and recipe consultation for *The Kosher Palette*:

Deena Altman
Shani Blenden
Seryl Kushner
Bobbi Luxenberg
Dori Sobin
Tova Weiser

We gratefully acknowledge those who opened their homes for testing parties.

The Kosher Palette thanks all of the cooks and storytellers who generously contributed their treasured recipes and food memories to this book. We regret that we were unable to include all of the stories and recipes which were submitted due to similarity or availability of space. We also hope that we have not inadvertently overlooked any contributors.

Tammy Abramowitz
Joy Abramson
Shari Alter
Deena Altman
Beth Aron
Shira Baruch
Debra Bassan
Ilene Bayar
Harriet Blank
Sandra Blank
Marie Blau
Kathy Brody
Randi Brokman
Debbie Buechler
Al Bukiet
Nancy Caplan
Tita Celler
Rhoda Chait
Sherry Chernofsky
Linda Cohen
Karen Dachs
Sheila Dardik
Alisa David
Eileen David
Limor Decter
Deborah Druce
Hattie Dubroff
Connie Edelman
Beth Eidman
Allen Eisenberg
Estee Eisenberg
Andrea Elstein
Emily Faiwiszewski
Harriet Fettner
Debbie Finkelstein
Karen Finkelstein
Myrna Fishbein
Susie Fishbein
Marcy Fox
Brenda Freeman
Erica Freilich
Kaye Freireich
Ada Friedler
Debby Friedman
Fran Friedman
Karen Friedman

Maralyn Friedman
Melissa Friedman
Rena Fuchs
Lenore M. Gaire
Dianne Gindi
Francine Glick
Billy Goldberg
Debra Goldberg
Lauren Goldman
Gitty Goldschmidt
Anne Golombeck
Shelly Golombeck
Marvin Gorodetzer
Shimona Gotlieb
Edith Grauer
Elisa Greenbaum
Miriam Greenberg
Stanley Greenberg
Chaya Edda Raiza Greenfeld
Annette Gross
Toba Leah Grossbaum
Gail Hausdorff
Libby Hendler
Fern Herschfus
Elisa Hertzan
Michele Homa
Marsha Horowitz
Roberta Horowitz
Ilana Houten
Chana Hove
Joanne Ingerman
Sylvia Irwin
Judy Israeli
Batya Jacob
Susan Kahnowitz
Betty Keller
Robin Klatt
Alice Klein
Midge Kra
Faigy Krausz
Belle Kronisch
Lee Kushner
Seryl Kushner
Ellie Langer
Loraine Langer

Aleeza Lauer
Ruth Borgen Lauer
Jill Lasman
Eta Levenson
Adina Levine
Nancy Robinson Levine
Connie Levitt
Linda Libby
Estee Lichter
Helen Lichtman
Natalie Lichtman
Barbara Listhaus
Bobbi Luxenberg
Karen Lyman
Martha Maik
Lauren Mayer
Jennifer Miller
Julie Miller
Leslie Mink
Debbie Moed
Julia Moed
Leon Moed
Marilyn Moed
Iris Moskowitz
Lori Moskowitz
Susan Moskowitz
Walter Nachtigall
Leslie Nbostrin
Gayle Newman
Lynda Novick
Mairav Pascheles
Florence Passner
Eve Pasternak
Shlomis Peikes
Ahava Podhorcer
Jolly Raiss
Linda Ramos
Helen Ratzker
Malkie Ratzker
Dorene Richman
Sharon Ronan
Renee Rose
Lisa Rosenberg
Dalila Rosenstrauch
Leah Rottenberg
Deena Rubin

Amy Ruderman
Julia Rutland
Mindy Saibel
Teena Samter
Judy Sandman
Annette Schabes
Bonnie Schertz
Bambi Schleider
Esther Schulder
Mali Schwartz
Marla Scott
Howard Shapiro
Sharon Sherman
Galina Shenfeld
Robin Shulman
Sandy Small
Dori Sobin
Marilyn Sokol
Linda Spector
Marisa Stadtmauer
Rhonda Starr
Carol Stein
Sherry Stein
Fern Steinberg
Carol Sufian
Andrea Sultan
Hope Tafet
Sondra Tammam
Edith Tersch
Elissa Titen
Stacey Ullman
Malva Ulrich
Joyce Weinberger
Debbi Weintraub
Pearl Weisberger
Miriam Weisblum
Tova Weiser
Yael Weil
Helene Wengrofsky
Debra Wenig
Rosie Wilensky
Nadine Wruble
Shulamit Zenoli
Sherry Zimmerman
Lori Zucker

A Note About Kosher Cooking

The word kosher means "proper" or "fit." It refers not only to foods that the Torah declares fit to eat, but also to the ways in which food is prepared according to Jewish religious law.

Kosher food can be divided into three categories: meat, dairy, and parve. Meat and dairy foods are never eaten together, but parve foods may be eaten with either meat or dairy.

Meat: Only animals that chew their cud and have cloven hoofs are permitted. Pork is forbidden. Poultry-turkey, chicken, duck, goose, dove-is permitted, but birds of prey are forbidden. Permitted animals must be slaughtered by those specially trained in the Jewish ritual. The humane treatment of animals is an important consideration in kosher slaughtering.

Meat is made kosher–"kashered"–through the process of soaking (in water) and salting to draw out the blood. Many kosher butchers sell meat that has already been kashered. Meat that will be broiled need not be kashered since the process of broiling itself draws out the blood. Liver that is saturated in blood may only be broiled to "kasher" it.

Dairy: In this category are milk and milk products, such as cheese, butter, cream, yogurt, and ice cream.

Parve: Parve foods are neither meat nor dairy. All fresh fruits, vegetables, and nuts are parve, as are all spices, salt, sugar, coffee, and tea. All grains are parve. Parve foods may be served with either meat or dairy foods. Insects are not kosher; therefore, special care must be taken to examine and wash fresh produce.

Chicken eggs are parve, but because it is not permissible to consume blood, eggs that contain blood spots must be discarded.

Fish is parve. Only fish with fins and scales are kosher. Salmon, flounder, sole, trout, whitefish, and cod are examples of kosher fish. All shellfish are prohibited. Other kinds of fish that are forbidden include catfish, swordfish, and eel. Though fish have blood, no special kashering is required.

When buying packaged foods, one should look for symbols indicating that the food was prepared under proper rabbinical supervision to assure its kashrut.

Keeping a kosher home requires having at least two sets of dishes, utensils, and pots and pans, one for meat, and the other for dairy. Meat and dairy products cannot be prepared in the same pots or bowls or with the same utensils. Different sponges, one designated for meat, the other for dairy, are required. Two additional sets of dishes and accoutrements are required for Passover use.

Special Equipment

Meat Thermometers

Correct temperature is very important for proper cooking, so this utensil is really a kitchen must. Poke the metal shaft into the food or liquid, and the temperature should register within about 30 seconds.

Garlic Press

A garlic press is a quick and easy way to mince garlic cloves. It allows you to benefit from the flavor and juices of the garlic without having the odor remain on your hands.

Mini Ice Cream Scoop

This 1-inch ice cream scoop is ideal for garnishing a plate by serving a small amount in a perfect round shape. It is also the correct size for measuring cookie dough to be placed on a baking sheet.

Pastry Brush

A pastry brush is a small soft-bristled brush which can be used for applying glaze, greasing pans, and brushing off crumbs on a cake before icing. This brush comes in different sizes for these multiple applications.

Ginger Grater

A ginger grater takes the ginger from its original state, which resembles knobby fingers, and grates it to a finer consistency.

Tart Pan

This pan makes a beautiful presentation. The sides of this pan are fluted and the bottom of the pan is removable. When your tart is baked and cooled, gently push the bottom up and remove from the outer ring. This pan is also available with a nonstick surface.

Springform Pan

The sides of this deep, round baking pan are separate from the bottom and expand so that you can remove the sides of the cake from the pan. The ring is held together with a strong clamp. This pan is ideal for cheesecake and is also used in our Tricolor Soufflé. It comes in three sizes: 8-inch, 9-inch, and 10-inch.

Salad Spinner

The quickest and easiest way to dry washed greens is by using this device. It consists of a rotating basket that fits into a plastic bowl and a crank handle or pull cord, which makes the basket spin, throwing off the excess water.

Poultry Frills

These decorative frills help to garnish and "dress up" any bird or chops. They are perfect for baby lamb chops. Simply slide one on each leg or chop.

Whisk

A whisk is a teardrop shaped "cage" made of wire loops attached to a long handle. This kitchen tool is made for blending, beating, and whipping ingredients.

Meat Pounder

This mallet-like tool is for flattening or tenderizing meat or poultry. Ideally this tool should have both a flat side and a ridged or toothed side. A rolling pin or a small heavy skillet can stand in for a meat pounder.

Immersion Blender

This hand-held appliance consists of a rotary blade on a shaft; the shaft is attached to an upright handle, which houses a small motor. An immersion blender allows you to blend food directly in the pot in which it was cooked. This appliance is very inexpensive and tremendously helpful in the kitchen. We call for it in almost all of our soups.

DUTCH OVEN

This large pot or kettle is usually made of cast iron. This versatile cooking pot is large (at least 4 quarts) with a close fitting cover and two side handles. It is designed so that it can be used on the stovetop as well as in the oven. A Dutch oven is useful for soups, stews, braises and casseroles.

TUBE PAN

This is a popular pan for baking cakes. It has tall sides and a center tube, which is removable. When cake is cooled lift center tube, removing from sides. If desired turn over onto a plate and remove tube.

BUNDT PAN

This cake pan is ideal for larger cakes. It is fluted in shape and when cakes are baked, cooled and removed they make a beautiful crownlike presentation. We call for it in our Pecan Noodle Ring and Black and White Rice Mold.

GRILL PAN

A grill pan is a perfect answer to stovetop grilling. The raised ridges in the pan provide a professional grilled look. It is perfect for searing fish, meat, and chicken.

DOUBLE BOILER

This is a combination of two pots where one sits partially inside the other. The lower pot is used to hold simmering water, which gently heats the mixture in the upper pot. Double boilers are used to melt chocolate or warm heat-sensitive foods like delicate sauces.

The Kosher Palette is about the many pleasures that food and cooking can bring. This includes the details and ambiance of the dining environment and presentation of the dishes. Throughout the book you will find artistic tips in the sidebars that highlight various ways to prepare or put the finishing touches on your meals.

The tips are broken down into five categories, each with a different icon to represent it:

 Wine and Beverage: drinks that complement the dish & beverage tips

 Preparation: Hints or shortcuts for an aspect of preparing the dish

 Tablesettings: Ways to dress up your table

 Accompaniments: Side dishes that go nicely with the recipe, usually drawn from another part of the book

 Garnishing: The little extra something to bring your presentation of the plate or platter to an extraordinary level

**APPETIZERS &
HORS D'OEUVRES**

*Salmon Spinach Bonnet,
page 15*

This optional sauce goes very nicely with the Veal and Spinach Roll.

Mustard Sauce

1 cup mayonnaise

¼ cup Dijon mustard

2 tablespoons Worcestershire sauce (see note page 112)

2 tablespoons lemon juice

Mix all in a bowl and serve.

An elegant way to present an accompanying sauce is to place it in individual Cucumber Wells. Cut the ends off of a large cucumber. Cut the cucumber into 3 inch pieces. You can use a vegetable peeler to make designs with the skin like removing a few strips to make eye-catching stripes. Stand the cucumber pieces on your work surface. Trim the bottoms if necessary to make sure they stand. Carefully scoop out the seeds, making a well but leaving the bottoms intact so the sauce won't run out. Fill each with sauce and place one on each plate.

Elegant Meat Pie

Meat

1   teaspoon vegetable oil
1   onion, chopped
2   pounds lean ground beef
1   (15-ounce) jar marinara sauce

1   (17.3-ounce) package frozen puff pastry, thawed
1   large egg, lightly beaten
    Sesame seeds
    Garnish: fresh basil leaves

Preheat oven to 350°.

Heat oil in a large skillet over medium-high heat. Add onion and sauté until translucent. Add ground beef and cook until brown; drain.

Stir in marinara sauce.

Place one sheet of puff pastry into a lightly greased 13- x 9-inch glass baking dish. (Dough may have to be trimmed.) Spoon meat mixture on pastry.

Place remaining puff pastry sheet over meat mixture. Trim any excess pastry. Brush with egg and sprinkle lightly with sesame seeds.

Bake for 30 to 45 minutes or until golden brown. Cut into squares and garnish each piece with a fresh basil leaf.

Yield: 8 servings.

Veal and Spinach Roll

Meat

1   tablespoon oil
1   medium onion, chopped
1½   pounds ground veal
     Salt
     Freshly ground black pepper
     Garlic powder
½   cup bread crumbs
1   large egg, lightly beaten

1   (10-ounce) package frozen chopped spinach, thawed and drained
1   (17.3-ounce) package frozen puff pastry, thawed
1   egg yolk
     Sesame seeds

Preheat oven to 350°.

Heat oil in a large skillet over medium-high heat. Add veal, onions, salt, pepper, and garlic powder; sauté until meat is browned.

Stir in bread crumbs, egg, and spinach; remove from heat.

Roll out one pastry sheet on a lightly floured surface. Spread half of meat mixture on pastry, leaving a ½-inch border on all sides. Roll up jelly roll style. Repeat with remaining ingredients.

Place each roll, seam side down, in a lightly greased baking dish. Brush with yolk and sprinkle with sesame seeds.

Bake for 45 minutes to 1 hour or until veal is cooked through and pastry is golden brown.

Yield: 4 to 6 servings.

Salmon Spinach Bonnet

Parve

1 tablespoon vegetable oil
6 ounces fresh spinach
   leaves
2 shallots, chopped
   Kosher salt
   Pepper
2 tablespoons margarine
½ (14-ounce) can artichoke
   hearts, drained and cut
   into slivers

½ tablespoon fresh chopped
   parsley
1 (17.3-ounce) package
   frozen puff pastry,
   thawed
1 (8-ounce) salmon fillet,
   skinned, boned and cut
   into 4 equal pieces
1 large egg, lightly beaten

Preheat oven to 375°.

Heat oil in a large skillet over medium-high heat. Add the spinach and shallots; sauté 3 to 4 minutes or until spinach wilts. Season to taste with salt and pepper. Transfer to a bowl.

Heat margarine in the skillet. Add artichokes and sauté for 3 minutes. Stir in parsley and season to taste with salt and pepper; set aside.

Roll out pastry onto a floured surface. Cut each pastry in half crosswise to form a total of four rectangles and turn each piece vertically on the work surface.

Place salmon in the bottom half of each pastry rectangle. Top each salmon piece evenly with artichoke mixture and spinach mixture.

Combine egg and a pinch of kosher salt; brush around salmon in a circle. Fold pastry over salmon to cover completely. Press pastry around salmon to seal. Cut a 4-inch circle around filled pastry with a cookie cutter, discarding excess pastry. Crimp the edges of the pastry with a fork. Snip decoratively around the edges of pastry with kitchen scissors. Brush with egg mixture.

Bake for 10 to 15 minutes or until golden brown.

Yield: 4 servings.

Flower Garden Plates

Turn plain glass plates into a stunning table setting by using two plates per setting and pressing fresh flowers and petals between them.

Chicken and Beef Saté

Meat

1 pound boneless, skinless chicken breasts	2 teaspoons sugar
1 (1-inch thick) boneless steak (about 1¼ pounds)	2 cloves garlic, crushed
2 limes	24 (10-inch) wooden skewers
¼ cup soy sauce	Spicy Peanut Dipping Sauce
1 tablespoon peeled and grated fresh ginger	

Slice chicken breasts lengthwise into ¾-inch wide strips and place in a medium mixing bowl. Slice steak diagonally at a 45-degree angle into ¼-inch strips and place in another mixing bowl.

Grate 2 teaspoons of lime peel and place in a small mixing bowl. Cut limes in half and squeeze 2 tablespoons of juice into the bowl. Add soy sauce, fresh ginger, sugar, and garlic, stirring well.

Pour half of marinade mixture on chicken strips and half on steak strips, tossing to coat. Cover and refrigerate both bowls 30 minutes.

Soak wooden skewers in water 15 to 20 minutes to prevent burning.

Preheat grill to medium heat.

Remove the chicken and steak strips from marinade, discarding marinade. Thread the chicken and beef strips, accordion style, separately on the prepared skewers. Pull meat flat against skewers so meat will cook quickly and evenly. Grill 3 to 7 minutes, turning once, until just cooked through.

Yield: 12 appetizer servings.

Spicy Peanut Dipping Sauce:

Parve

¼ cup creamy peanut butter	4 teaspoons rice wine vinegar
¼ cup very hot tap water	⅛ teaspoon cayenne pepper
1 tablespoon soy sauce	
1 tablespoon light molasses	

Combine all ingredients in a medium bowl and beat with a wire whisk until blended and smooth.

Yield: ⅓ cup.

Asparagus Chicken Hors d'oeuvres

Meat

The pretty green and white spirals are both colorful and delicious. They look beautiful piled in a basket or served over couscous.

3-4 boneless, skinless chicken breasts, cut into ¼-inch strips
1 pound thin asparagus spears

¼ cup Dijon mustard
2 tablespoons vegetable oil
2 tablespoons lemon juice

Preheat oven to 350°.

Blanch asparagus in salted boiling water 2 to 3 minutes until bright green and slightly tender; drain and cool slightly. Cut asparagus into 5-inch pieces, discarding bottom pieces. Spiral chicken strips around asparagus; secure ends with toothpicks. Place on a lightly greased baking sheet.

Combine mustard, oil, and lemon juice; stir with wire whisk until blended. Brush mustard mixture on chicken.

Bake 20 to 25 minutes until chicken is done. Do not overbake or asparagus will darken and wilt. Remove toothpicks before serving.

Yield: 6 to 8 appetizer servings.

Turkey Terrine

Meat

2 tablespoons vegetable oil
3 stalks celery, chopped
1 large onion, chopped
1½ pounds ground turkey
2 large eggs, lightly beaten
1½ cups fresh bread crumbs or seasoned, dry bread crumbs

⅔ cup sun-dried tomatoes in oil, drained and chopped
½ cup non-dairy creamer
1 tablespoon water
2 teaspoons dried oregano
2 teaspoons rubbed sage
1-2 teaspoons freshly ground pepper
  Ketchup

Preheat oven to 350°.

Heat oil in a medium skillet over medium-high heat. Add celery and onion and sauté 3 to 5 minutes or until tender; drain.

Combine sautéed vegetables, turkey, eggs, bread crumbs, dried tomatoes, creamer, water, oregano, sage, and pepper, blending well. Place turkey mixture in a lightly greased 9- x 5-inch loaf pan and flatten top. Brush top of terrine with ketchup to cover.

Bake for 1 hour; cool in pan on a wire rack. Gently turn terrine out onto a cutting board. Slice and serve on a bed of parsley or greens.

Yield: 12 to 15 servings.

Serving Platters for Hors d'oeuvres and Buffet Tables

Prepare two serving platters for each dish being served. While one is on the table or being passed around, the other can be readied in the kitchen. It is best not to wait until the platter is completely empty. By removing and replacing serving dishes, you ensure that the food stays fresh and appealing.

CHICKEN LIVERS AND PEAS ON RISOTTO

Meat

6 cups chicken stock
   (page 39) or broth
7 tablespoons margarine,
   divided
1 onion, chopped
2½ cups Arborio rice
⅔ cup dry white wine
  Salt
  Freshly ground pepper

2 cups shelled fresh peas or
   frozen peas, thawed
4 shallots, thinly sliced
½ teaspoon dried sage
⅔ cup Marsala wine
1½ pounds kashered chicken
   livers, trimmed and cut
   into 1-inch pieces

Heat broth in a large saucepan over low heat; keep warm.

Heat 2 tablespoons margarine in a large saucepan over medium heat. Add onion and sauté 8 minutes or until translucent.

Stir in rice; cook 1 minute or until translucent. Add wine and cook, stirring constantly, until the liquid almost evaporates.

Stir in three-fourths of the hot broth; cook over medium heat, stirring occasionally, until almost all of the broth is absorbed.

Add remaining broth, stirring constantly, for 20 minutes or until rice is creamy and tender. Season with salt and pepper.

Blanch peas in boiling water for 8 minutes or until tender; drain.

Heat 3 tablespoons margarine in a skillet; add shallot and sauté 5 minutes, stirring frequently, or until golden brown.

Stir in sage and Marsala; cook over high heat, scraping up browned bits from bottom of pan, for 4 minutes until thickened and syrupy. Add peas and liver pieces, stirring until thoroughly heated. Add remaining 2 tablespoons margarine, stirring until blended.

Spoon risotto on serving plates. Top with liver mixture and serve immediately.

Yield: 6 servings.

Procedure for Kashering Liver:
Thoroughly wash off all of the outside blood and remove all visible blood clots. If the liver is whole, make an incision across its length and width. Salt both sides with kosher salt and place it, cut side down, on a broiling rack. Broil on both sides until liver is cooked through; discard pan drippings. After broiling, liver should be rinsed three times under water.

Twisted Knish

Parve

"During a recent charity cooking demonstration, the chef presented this recipe. The aroma was wonderful! All of the guests clamored to get a taste of the dish. I was one of the lucky ones. One bite and I knew we needed to include this recipe."

5-6 tablespoons oil, divided	3 tablespoons chopped scallions
¼ cup chopped onion	Salt
Whole grain mustard	Pepper
2 (10-inch) flour tortillas	2 tablespoons oil
1 cup mashed potato	Mustard Vinaigrette
½ cup kasha, cooked according to package directions, or chopped sautéed mushrooms	

Heat 3 to 4 tablespoons oil in a small skillet over low heat. Add onion and sauté 20 minutes, stirring constantly and scraping caramelized bits from the bottom of the skillet. Drain excess oil.

Spread mustard on one side of the tortillas; set aside.

Combine cooked onion, potato, kasha or mushrooms, and scallions in a medium bowl. Season to taste with salt and pepper.

Place half of the onion mixture on the bottom half of each tortilla. Fold in half and press firmly to seal.

Heat remaining 2 tablespoons oil in a skillet over medium-high heat. Fry tortillas until golden brown on each side. Cut into wedges and drizzle with Mustard Vinaigrette.

Yield: 2 to 4 servings.

Mustard Vinaigrette:

Parve

¼ cup oil	1 tablespoon champagne (optional)
2 tablespoons whole grain mustard	Salt
1 tablespoon apple cider vinegar	Pepper

Whisk together oil, mustard, vinegar, and champagne in a small bowl. Season to taste with salt and pepper.

Yield: ½ cup.

Fresh Tuna Kabobs
with Ginger–Soy Marinade

Parve

¼ cup soy sauce	3 scallions, finely chopped
2 tablespoons rice vinegar	2 cloves garlic, crushed
2 tablespoons canola or vegetable oil	2 tablespoons peeled and grated fresh ginger
2 tablespoons water	1 pound fresh tuna, cut into 1-inch cubes
1 tablespoon dark sesame oil	1 red bell pepper, seeded and cut into ½-inch cubes
¼ teaspoon sugar	24 (10-inch) wooden skewers

Combine soy sauce, vinegar, canola oil, water, sesame oil, and sugar in a large bowl, whisking until blended. Whisk in scallions, garlic, and ginger.

Add tuna and red bell pepper, tossing to coat. Cover and chill 30 minutes.

Soak skewers in water for 15 to 20 minutes to prevent burning.

Preheat oven to broil, with rack 5 to 6 inches from heat.

Remove tuna from marinade, reserving marinade. Thread 2 pieces of tuna and 1 piece of pepper on each skewer and place in a broiler pan.

Broil (with electric oven door partially open) 1 minute on each side, basting and turning 1 time. Tuna should be slightly pink on the inside. Serve immediately.

Yield: 2 dozen.

Turn plain ice cubes into a visual treat with the addition of colorful edible flowers and leaves. Fill an ice tray halfway with water (distilled water will make the clearest cubes) and place a variety of flowers and herb leaves in each compartment. Freeze several hours or until solid. Pour additional water over cubes and freeze to keep the flowers and leaves centered in the cubes.

GRAVLAX
Parve

1 (3-3½ pound) salmon
 fillet, scaled and boned
¼ cup kosher salt
¼ cup firmly packed dark
 brown sugar
2 tablespoons black
 peppercorns, crushed

2 tablespoons vodka
1 bunch fresh dill, snipped
 Honey Mustard Sauce
 Garnishes: capers, lemon
 wedges

Place salmon, skin side down, in 13- x 9-inch glass or enamel baking dish.

Combine salt, sugar, peppercorns, and vodka. Rub the mixture over the salmon and top with chopped dill. Cover with plastic wrap and chill 2 to 3 days to cure, turning salmon twice a day.

Slice gravlax thinly on a diagonal. Serve with Honey Mustard Sauce and garnish with capers and lemon wedges.

Yield: 10 to 15 servings.

HONEY MUSTARD SAUCE:
Parve

⅓ cup vegetable oil
3 tablespoons Dijon mustard
1 tablespoon vinegar
1 tablespoon fresh dill sprigs
2 teaspoons honey
1½ teaspoons sugar
¼ teaspoon freshly ground black pepper

Combine all of the ingredients in a blender or food processor; process until smooth. Recipe may be doubled.

Yield: ⅓ cup.

PARVE STUFFED MUSHROOMS

Parve

It is hard to imagine a stuffed mushroom recipe without traditional ingredients like cheese or cream. Try this recipe – we know it will quickly become a favorite to serve at your non-dairy meals or to those who do not eat dairy products.

12	large mushrooms	1	large egg, lightly beaten
1	small onion, quartered		Salt
1	clove garlic		Pepper
2	tablespoons margarine	2-3	tablespoons seasoned dry
1	teaspoon dried parsley		bread crumbs

Preheat oven to 400°.

Remove stems from mushrooms and place stems in the container of a food processor fitted with knife blade. Add onion and garlic; process until finely chopped.

Melt margarine in a large skillet over medium-high heat. Add mushroom mixture and sauté for 5 minutes or until liquid begins to evaporate.

Remove from heat and stir in egg and parsley. Season to taste with salt and pepper.

Stir in bread crumbs until mixture holds together. Stuff each mushroom cap with bread crumb mixture and place on a lightly greased baking sheet.

Bake 15 minutes or until stuffing is puffy.

Yield: 1 dozen.

Rosemary Breadsticks

Parve

Nothing compares to the aroma of fresh breadsticks before a meal or salad. For variety, try this recipe with different kinds of herbs.

¼ cup warm water (105° to 115°)	1 teaspoon salt
1 (¼-ounce) package active dry yeast	¾ cup cold water
	2 tablespoons olive oil
1 teaspoon sugar	Cornmeal
1½ cups all-purpose flour	1 egg white, lightly beaten
¾ cup whole wheat flour	Pinch salt
1½ teaspoons fresh rosemary	Kosher salt, sesame seeds, or poppy seeds

Stir together water, yeast, and sugar in a large bowl; let stand 5 minutes.

Combine flour, whole wheat flour, rosemary, and salt in the container of a food processor bowl fitted with a plastic dough blade; pulse 5 seconds.

Stir water and oil into yeast mixture.

With processor running, pour yeast mixture through food chute. Process until dough forms a ball, adding flour, 1 tablespoon at a time, if necessary.

Place dough in a lightly greased bowl, turning to grease top. Cover; let rise in a warm place for 1½ hours.

Divide dough in half. Roll each piece into a 12-inch log. Cut each log into 1-inch pieces. Roll each piece into a long log. Fold log in half, twist, and place on a lightly greased baking sheet. Sprinkle breadsticks with cornmeal. Let rise 15 minutes.

Preheat oven to 300°.

Combine egg white with a pinch of salt. Brush egg mixture on breadsticks and sprinkle with salt, sesame seeds, or poppy seeds.

Bake for 30 minutes. Increase heat to 350° and bake 5 minutes or until golden brown.

Yield: 2 dozen.

PORTOBELLO MUSHROOM NAPOLEONS

Parve

*T*his very beautiful appetizer can be served alone, on a bed of wild rice, or on top of salad greens with a light dressing. Raspberry vinaigrette is a good choice. The mushrooms have an especially good flavor when grilled, but they can also be broiled, if desired. The presentation of this dish works best if the mushrooms and tomatoes are the same diameter.

¾ cup olive oil
2 teaspoons balsamic vinegar
6 cloves garlic, crushed in garlic press
8 small portobello mushroom caps, stems removed

2 firm tomatoes, cut into ¼-inch thick slices (4 slices per tomato)
8 fresh basil leaves
4 frozen puff pastry squares (4- x 4-inches), thawed
1 large egg, lightly beaten
Kosher salt

Combine olive oil, vinegar, and garlic in a large bowl. Add mushroom caps and tomato slices, tossing to coat. Cover and marinate at least 30 minutes.

Preheat grill to medium-hot heat.

Remove mushrooms and tomatoes, discarding marinade. Place the mushroom caps in a grill basket or on a sheet of aluminum foil. Grill the mushrooms until tender. Place tomato slices in a grill basket or on a sheet of aluminum foil. Grill tomatoes 1 minute. Do not overcook or tomatoes will fall apart. (The marinating and grilling can be done a day or two ahead.) Cover and refrigerate until ready to assemble.

Preheat oven to 375°.

Layer 1 mushroom cap (stem side up), 1 tomato slice, 1 or 2 basil leaves, 1 tomato slice, and one mushroom cap (stem side down).

Wrap a square of puff pastry around the mound, tucking the ends underneath to form a rounded, covered mound. If puff pastry squares are unavailable, cut puff pastry sheets large enough to cover the layered ingredients. Repeat with remaining mushrooms, tomatoes, basil, and pastry squares.

Combine egg and a pinch of salt; brush on bottom of the napoleons to keep seams together.

Place napoleons, seam side down, on a lightly greased baking sheet. Repeat with remaining ingredients. Bake for 20 minutes or until pastry is puffed and golden brown.

Yield: 4 servings.

SUN–DRIED TOMATO STUFFED MUSHROOMS

Dairy

These tasty bites are a colorful and different spin on traditional stuffed mushrooms.

5 ounces sun-dried tomatoes, packed in oil	3 cloves garlic, minced
	Pinch dried thyme
16 cremini or button mushrooms	Pinch salt
	Pepper
¼ cup finely chopped shallots	3 tablespoons heavy whipping cream

Preheat oven to broil with rack 6 inches from heat.

Drain tomatoes, reserving oil. Mince tomatoes; set aside. Remove mushroom stems from caps and coarsely chop stems; set aside.

Brush mushroom caps with some of the reserved oil and place them on a baking sheet, stem side down.

Broil (with electric oven door partially open) 2 to 3 minutes. Remove from heat and turn caps over, stem side up.

Preheat oven to bake at 350° with rack in center of oven.

Heat remaining oil in a large skillet over medium-low heat. Add shallots and garlic; sauté until soft.

Stir in mushroom stems, minced tomatoes, thyme, salt, and pepper to taste. Sauté 5 to 10 minutes, stirring occasionally, until liquid evaporates. Stir in cream.

Stuff each mushroom cap with tomato mixture. Bake for 15 to 18 minutes or until thoroughly heated.

Yield: 6 to 8 servings.

Variation

To make elegant small Napoleon hors d'oeuvres, use cremini mushrooms about 2 inches in diameter. Choose tomatoes that have a similar diameter to the mushrooms, such as plum tomatoes. Cut thawed puff pastry sheets large enough to cover layered ingredients and follow same procedure to assemble and bake. These bite-size appetizers are easy to pass on an hors d'oeuvre tray.

MUSHROOM PUFFS
. . . .
Dairy

"When we did the food shoot for the appetizer and hors d'oeuvres section, we were a little intimidated to 'talk food' with the food stylist. We figured she must create the most incredible and complicated dishes – recipes way over our heads. We worked up the nerve to ask her what hors d'oeuvres she likes to serve and were delighted to hear her response. With all of the fancy and intricate recipes she makes, these easy Mushroom Puffs are a must at all of her private events."

4 tablespoons butter	½ cup heavy whipping cream
1 small onion, chopped	Salt
¾ pound mushrooms, chopped	Pepper
2 tablespoons all-purpose flour	1 (17.3 ounce) package frozen puff pastry, thawed
½ teaspoon lemon juice	

Melt butter in a large skillet over medium heat. Add onion and mushrooms; sauté until liquid evaporates.

Add flour, whisking until smooth. Cook 1 minute, stirring constantly. Add lemon juice, stirring constantly. Add cream and cook over medium heat, stirring constantly until mixture is thickened and bubbly. Stir in salt and pepper, to taste. Remove from heat.

Roll out puff pastry on a floured surface to ⅛-inch thick. Cut into 2½-inch squares. Place a heaping teaspoon of the filling in the center of each square. Grasp all 4 corners and pinch the four seams to form a bundle; drop into the cup of a mini muffin pan. (Do not force them down.) Repeat with remaining pastry and filling. Cover and chill.

Preheat oven to 400°. Bake for 20 to 25 minutes or until sides and bottoms are browned.

Yield: 2 dozen.

CHEESE STRAWS

Dairy

1 (17.3-ounce) package
   frozen puff pastry,
   thawed
1 egg white, lightly beaten
   and divided

¾ cup grated Parmesan
   cheese, divided
2 cups (8 ounces) shredded
   cheddar cheese, divided
   Cayenne pepper
   Parchment paper

Preheat oven to 400°.

Roll out pastry on a floured surface into a 20- x 24-inch rectangle. Brush lightly with half of egg white.

Sprinkle half of the Parmesan cheese and half of the cheddar cheese over the dough. Sprinkle lightly with cayenne pepper. Press cheese into the dough with a rolling pin.

Fold dough in half and roll into a rectangle. Brush dough with remaining egg white and sprinkle with remaining cheeses. Press cheese into the dough with a rolling pin.

Cut the dough into ⅓-inch wide strips. Twist each strip into a corkscrew shape. Place cheese straws on a parchment lined sheet, just touching each other (to prevent untwisting).

Bake 15 to 20 minutes or until golden brown. Remove immediately and place on a wire cooling rack. (If straws are left to cool on baking sheet, they will be difficult to remove without breaking them.)

Yield: 18 to 20 straws.

ZUCCHINI FRITTERS

Dairy

5 tablespoons olive oil, divided	¼ teaspoon crushed red pepper
2 zucchini, unpeeled and cut into scant ½-inch pieces	1 cup all-purpose flour
	1½ teaspoons baking powder
1 yellow squash, unpeeled and cut into scant ½-inch pieces	1¼ teaspoons dried oregano
	¾ teaspoon salt
	¼ teaspoon pepper
3 cloves garlic, chopped	¾ cup whole milk

Heat 2 tablespoons oil in a large skillet over medium heat. Add zucchini, squash, garlic, and crushed red pepper; sauté 8 minutes or until lightly browned.

Combine flour, baking powder, oregano, salt, and pepper in a medium bowl. Add milk, whisking until smooth (batter will be thick). Stir in zucchini mixture.

Heat 1½ tablespoons oil in skillet over medium heat. Spoon half of batter by rounded tablespoons into skillet. Cook fritters, 4 minutes on each side, until browned and cooked through. Transfer to a platter and keep warm. Repeat with remaining oil and batter.

Yield: 4 to 6 servings.

ZUCCHINI STICKS

Dairy

1½ pounds zucchini	1¼ cups seasoned dry bread crumbs
½ cup all-purpose flour	
½ teaspoon salt	Vegetable oil
2 large eggs	Marinara or spaghetti sauce
¼ cup milk	

Cut zucchini into 2½-inch long x ½-inch wide sticks; set aside.

Combine flour and salt on a large piece of waxed paper; set aside. Combine eggs and milk in a small bowl; set aside. Place bread crumbs on a large piece of waxed paper.

Coat zucchini with flour mixture, dip in egg mixture, and coat with bread crumbs. Place on a baking sheet and repeat with remaining zucchini. Place zucchini in freezer for 10 minutes.

Heat 1½-inches oil in a frying pan or skillet to 375° over medium-high heat.

Remove zucchini from freezer and fry in batches 3 to 5 minutes or until golden brown. Drain on paper towels. Serve immediately with warm marinara sauce.

Yield: 6 to 8 servings.

SALMON LOAF EN CROÛTE WITH CUCUMBER-DILL SAUCE

Parve

1   (16-ounce) can red or
    pink salmon, boned,
    skinned, and drained
¾   cup dry bread crumbs
    (plain or seasoned)
¾   cup mayonnaise
½   cup chopped onion

½   teaspoon salt
½   teaspoon pepper
½   (17.3-ounce) package
    frozen puff pastry,
    thawed
1   large egg, lightly beaten
    Cucumber-Dill Sauce

Preheat oven to 350°.

Combine salmon, bread crumbs, mayonnaise, onion, salt, and pepper in a large bowl, mixing well.

Place puff pastry sheet on a lightly floured surface and spoon salmon mixture down middle section. Fold the right side over salmon; then fold left side, overlapping puff pastry. Seal edges.

Place loaf, seam side down, on an ungreased 13- x 9-inch baking dish. Brush with egg.

Bake for 45 minutes or until golden brown. Before serving, pour some of the Cucumber Dill Sauce over the top of the loaf with remaining sauce served on the side.

Yield: 6 servings.

CUCUMBER-DILL SAUCE:
Parve

1   large cucumber, seeded
    and diced
¾   cup mayonnaise
3   tablespoons chopped
    onion

1   tablespoon chopped fresh
    dill or 1 teaspoon dried
    dill
½   cup water

Combine cucumber, mayonnaise, onion, and dill. Gradually add enough water to desired consistency; cover and chill. Serve in a small dish or in a fresh lemon basket.

Yield: 1½ cups.

Lemon Baskets

1 smooth-skinned lemon
with no blemishes

3-inch paring knife

Slice thin layer from stem end of lemon to create a level bottom for the basket. Do not cut through to the pulp of the lemon. To make the handle, place lemon horizontally on a cutting surface. Place the knife at the top of the lemon, slightly off center. Cut halfway through the lemon. Turn lemon upright and make a cut perpendicular to the first cut, removing a wedge of lemon. Repeat with opposite side of lemon, leaving a ¼-inch strip across top to form the basket handle.

Cut away the flesh under the handle and scoop out pulp. Fill basket with sauce or a tiny bouquet of herbs and flowers. Use fruits such as grapefruits, oranges or limes to decorate a large platter.

BRUSCHETTA

Parve

Bruschetta is a nice, light opener. Bread that is chewy makes the best bruschetta. For extra flavor, you can rub the slices with a garlic clove, then sprinkle with olive oil before toasting the bread.

10	plum tomatoes, seeded and chopped	2	tablespoons olive oil
10	fresh basil leaves, sliced into thin strips		Salt
			Freshly ground pepper
1	teaspoon fresh oregano or rosemary, minced	10	(1-inch) slices French bread, toasted or grilled
½	onion, minced		Garnish: fresh basil leaves

Combine tomatoes, basil, oregano or rosemary, onion, and oil in a small bowl. Season to taste with salt and pepper. Spoon mixture on top of toasted bread and garnish, if desired.

Yield: 10 servings.

Stunning Iced Vodka

For a spectacular way to serve chilled vodka, simply gather lemon slices, berries, flowers, or leaves to complement your color scheme. Fill a metal champagne bucket, large metal can, or plastic bucket with water. Place a vodka bottle in the center and tuck fruits, flowers, and leaves around the sides. Place in the freezer and freeze overnight until solid.

Hold frozen mold under hot running water to release. Place Iced Vodka Mold on a rimmed plate with an absorbent towel underneath to catch melting water.

MINI BLINI

Dairy

"When I was growing up, my parents hosted many cocktail parties. I remember sitting at the top of the stairs and the unbelievable aroma that would waft upstairs from the Mini Blini. The great thing about this recipe is that you are supposed to make them in advance and freeze. I bake them in small batches so there is always a hot and fresh tray coming out of the oven."

2	(8-ounce) packages cream cheese, softened	3	loaves sliced white bread, crusts removed
2	egg yolks	1	cup butter, melted
½	cup sugar		Cinnamon
			Sugar

Beat together cream cheese, egg yolks, and sugar in a large mixing bowl.

Roll bread slices as thinly as possible with a rolling pin. Spread with cream cheese mixture. Roll up and dip in melted butter. Sprinkle with cinnamon and sugar. Cover with plastic wrap and freeze.

Preheat oven to 400°.

Remove Mini Blini from freezer and cut each piece in half. Place on a baking sheet and bake 10 to 13 minutes.

Yield: 8 dozen.

BABY LAMB CHOPS

Meat

20 very small, lean lamb
     chops
½ cup olive oil

¼ cup fresh rosemary leaves
Garnish: paper frills

Trim all of the fat from the chops, exposing 2 to 3 inches of the bone.

Combine oil and rosemary in a large bowl; add chops. Cover and chill 3 to 4 hours, turning occasionally.

Preheat oven to broil with rack 3 to 5 inches from heat.

Remove chops from marinade, discarding marinade. Place chops on rack in a broiler pan and broil (with electric oven door partially open) 3 to 4 minutes on each side or to desired degree of doneness. Garnish chops with paper frills.

Yield: 4 servings.

LEMON TOPIARY

Create a beautiful tall lemon topiary. You can use lemons, limes, oranges, apples, or pomegranates.

Large decorative vase with round opening
20 lemons (all but four cut in half lengthwise)
1-2 ft. thin round wooden pole (green or spray painted green)
1-1½ sprays willow vine
½ sheet green moss
10-20 green hydrangea
2 dozen 12 inch (1 ft.) green sticks (can use wooden shish kabob skewers)
2 (8x8-inch) floral moss blocks
Green floral wire
Green floral tape

Fill the vase with moss block and tape in place. At the base, add hydrangea and vine to cover moss block completely. Wrap long pole with vine using wire to secure in place. Place pole in center of vase. Attach second moss block to top of pole. Completely surround the second moss block with vine and hydrangea forming flowers in a topiary (ball shape.) Cut all but four lemons in half. Place each of the lemons (both halves and wholes) on an individual stick. Place four whole lemons around the perimeter of the base of the topiary by carefully pushing the stick into the moss. Arrange the half lemons evenly around the upper portion of the topiary by carefully pushing each stick into the moss.

ROASTED VEGETABLE PIZZA PUFFS

Dairy

1 *sheet frozen puff pastry, thawed*
1 *large egg, lightly beaten*
1 *zucchini, halved lengthwise*
2-3 *small tomatoes (about 2-3 inches in diameter), thinly sliced*

4 *artichoke hearts, drained and cut into ½-inch cubes*
¾ *cup shredded mozzarella cheese*
  Chopped oregano
  Chopped basil
  Pepper

Preheat oven to broil with rack 6 inches from heat.

Place puff pastry on a lightly greased baking sheet. Brush with egg and refrigerate until ready to assemble.

Place zucchini on a baking sheet, skin side up. Broil (with electric oven door partially open) until skin blackens and zucchini is soft. Remove from heat and slice ¼-inch thick.

Preheat oven to bake at 400° with rack in center of oven.

Remove puff pastry from refrigerator. Cut circles from pastry using a 2-inch round cookie cutter and place on a lightly greased baking sheet.

Top each pastry circle with a slice of tomato, an artichoke cube, and 1 or 2 pieces of zucchini. Sprinkle with cheese, oregano, basil, and pepper.

Bake 8 to 10 minutes or until puffed and bubbly. Serve immediately.

Yield: about 1 dozen.

VEGETARIAN CHOPPED LIVER

Parve

For those of you concerned about cholesterol and fat content, this recipe is just for you. This dish will satisfy your craving for chopped liver without any health worries. Served with "lite" crackers or crudité, this meatless version is definitely not your father's chopped liver!

2 teaspoons olive oil	1 cup chopped walnuts
1 large onion, chopped	½ teaspoon salt
1 (15-ounce) can green peas, drained well	Dash pepper
1 (14½-ounce) can green beans, drained well	1 teaspoon browning-and-seasoning sauce
	2 hard-cooked eggs

Heat oil in a large nonstick skillet over medium-high heat until hot. Add onion and sauté until very golden brown; set aside. (Can be done ahead.)

Place peas and green beans in the container of a food processor fitted with a knife blade; process until very smooth. Spoon mixture into a large bowl.

Place walnuts in processor bowl and pulse until very smooth. Spoon about 90% of vegetable mixture into processor bowl with walnuts; pulse until blended. Stir walnut mixture into remaining vegetable mixture. Season to taste with salt and pepper. Stir in browning-and-seasoning sauce.

Place the sautéed onion in processor bowl; pulse 3 or 4 times. Stir onion into vegetable mixture.

Mash eggs with a fork and stir into vegetable mixture. Cover and refrigerate until serving. Recipe may be doubled.

Yield: 6 to 8 servings.

EGGPLANT CAVIAR

Parve

1	large eggplant, unpeeled	1	clove garlic, crushed
½	cup olive oil	½	teaspoon salt
½	large onion, minced	¼	teaspoon pepper
1	green pepper, seeded and chopped	2	tablespoons white wine
		1	tablespoon lemon juice

Preheat oven to 400°.

Bake eggplant (whole) for 1 hour. Peel and cut into pieces. Place eggplant in the container of a food processor fitted with a knife blade; process until coarsely chopped. (You can also chop by hand with a knife.) Set aside.

Heat oil in a large skillet over medium-high heat. Add onion, green pepper, and garlic; sauté until tender. Stir in eggplant, salt, pepper, wine, and lemon juice.

Bring mixture to a boil, reduce heat, and simmer 15 minutes or until thickened.

Cover and chill until serving. Serve on a bed of lettuce or with pita chips. This dish can also be served as a dip for crudité or tortilla chips.

Yield: 8 servings.

Make Your Own Pita Chips

Separate the pita pockets into 2 halves by cutting around the circumference with kitchen scissors. Brush one side lightly with olive oil seasoned with crushed garlic and dried rosemary. For a dairy meal, sprinkle with freshly grated Parmesan cheese, coarse salt, and cayenne pepper. Stack the layers and cut into wedges with a large, sharp knife. Place in a single layer on a baking sheet and bake at 250° for 15 to 20 minutes until golden brown.

BEST EVER GUACAMOLE

Parve

Guacamole is one of those foods associated with good friends and good times. Images come to mind of sitting together on a long, lazy day sharing confidences and retelling old stories. Whip up this guacamole recipe and enjoy the time together.

4	ripe Haas (black skin) avocados	1	teaspoon kosher salt
3	tablespoons fresh lemon or lime juice	1	teaspoon freshly ground pepper
½	cup finely diced red onion	8	dashes hot sauce or 2 jalapeños, seeded and minced
2	tablespoons chopped cilantro, optional	1	medium tomato, seeded and finely diced
1	clove garlic, minced		

Cut avocados in half and remove pit. Scoop flesh out into a bowl with a large spoon. Toss avocado with lemon juice and coarsely chop or mash with a fork.

Stir in onion, cilantro, garlic, salt, pepper, and hot sauce. Stir in tomatoes. Cover immediately with plastic wrap and chill until serving.

Yield: 4½ cups.

CHICKEN WRAP
Meat

2 tablespoons soy sauce
1 teaspoon ground cumin
1 teaspoon turmeric
½ teaspoon ground
    coriander
¼ teaspoon grated orange
    peel
⅛ teaspoon cayenne pepper
1 pound boneless, skinless
    chicken breasts
2 teaspoons sesame oil,
    divided
6 carrots, peeled and cut
    into thin strips
8 scallions, cut into thin
    strips
¼ cup loosely packed fresh
    cilantro, chopped
4 (6-inch) flour tortillas
    Tomato-Curry Sauce
    Mesclun or gourmet
    mixed salad greens
½ cup mango chutney or
    other dressing

Combine soy sauce, cumin, turmeric, coriander, orange peel, and cayenne pepper in a large bowl. Add chicken, tossing to coat. Cover and refrigerate 8 hours or overnight.

Remove chicken from marinade, discarding marinade.

Heat 1 teaspoon sesame oil in a large nonstick skillet over medium-high heat. Add chicken and sauté 10 minutes or until done. Remove from pan; cool slightly. Slice chicken diagonally into thin strips; keep warm.

Heat remaining 1 teaspoon sesame oil in skillet; add carrots and scallions and sauté about 10 minutes or until browned. Stir in cilantro.

Spread tortillas evenly with Tomato-Curry Sauce. Top each with chicken and vegetable mixture. Roll tortillas tightly and wrap with plastic wrap. Refrigerate until ready to serve. Allow tortilla wraps to come to room temperature before serving.

Toss salad greens with mango chutney and place on 8 serving plates. Cut wraps in half diagonally and place one half on each plate.

Yield: 8 servings.

TOMATO-CURRY SAUCE:
Parve

1 cup parve sour cream
½ cup tomato sauce
¾ teaspoon curry powder
¼ teaspoon sugar
⅛ teaspoon pepper

Combine all ingredients in a small bowl. Cover and chill until assembling wraps.

Yield: 1½ cups.

SWEET AND SOUR STUFFED PEPPERS

Meat

3 red bell peppers	½ cup cooked white or
3 green bell peppers	brown rice
1 pound lean ground beef	½ teaspoon salt
2 large eggs	⅛ teaspoon pepper
1 onion, minced	Tomato Sauce
1 carrot, peeled and grated	

Slice tops off of peppers and remove core and seeds. Place peppers in boiling water to cover; remove from heat and let peppers stand in the water 5 minutes. Drain and place in a 13- x 9-inch baking dish.

Preheat oven to 350°.

Combine beef, eggs, onion, carrot, rice, salt, and pepper in a small bowl. Stuff peppers with meat mixture and add a small amount of water to bottom of dish. Cover and bake 40 minutes.

Increase heat to 400°. Add Tomato Sauce to peppers and bake an additional 10 minutes.

Yield: 6 servings.

TOMATO SAUCE:

Parve

1¼ cups tomato purée	3 tablespoons lemon juice
½ cup water	3 tablespoons brown sugar
¼ cup raisins	Paprika

Combine tomato purée, water, raisins, lemon juice, sugar, and paprika in a large saucepan over medium heat. Bring mixture to a boil, reduce heat, and simmer 15 minutes.

Yield: 2 cups.

Wild Berry Soup,
page 47

SOUPS

VEGETABLE STOCK

Parve or Dairy

Fresh stock is a key ingredient in soups as well as many sauces. It is also more flavorful than water for cooking rice and risotto. It is easy to make and can be frozen for several months. Simply freeze smaller, measured amounts so you just thaw what you need.

2	leeks	1	parsnip, peeled and cut into 2-inch pieces
3	tablespoons butter or margarine	$12\frac{1}{3}$	cups cold water, divided
3	yellow onions, chopped	12	sprigs parsley
2	potatoes, peeled and quartered	6	cloves garlic, unpeeled
2	carrots, peeled and cut into 2-inch pieces	1	bay leaf
		1	teaspoon salt
2	stalks celery (no leaves), chopped	$\frac{1}{2}$	teaspoon dried thyme, crumbled
		$\frac{1}{2}$	teaspoon black peppercorns

Cut the roots from leeks and discard tough outer leaves. Cut each leek in half lengthwise. Rinse thoroughly with cold running water to remove grit. Chop leeks and set aside.

Heat butter in a large soup pot over medium heat. Add onions and sauté, stirring constantly, until golden brown.

Add leeks, potato, carrots, celery, parsnip, and ⅓ cup water. Bring mixture to a boil, reduce heat, and simmer, covered, for 5 minutes, stirring occasionally.

Stir in remaining 12 cups water, parsley, garlic, bay leaf, salt, thyme, and peppercorns.

Bring mixture to a boil, reduce heat, and simmer, uncovered, for 2 hours.

Strain the stock through a sieve or colander, discarding vegetables, and let cool. Cover and refrigerate the stock until chilled. Remove fat from top. Divide stock into heavy-duty plastic zip-top bags and freeze.

Yield: about 2 quarts.

If time does not allow you to prepare fresh stock, use bouillon, but boost its flavor with fresh vegetables. Combine the bouillon with water as directed on the package, then add any chopped vegetable you have in the house such as onions, carrots, or celery. Add parsley or a bay leaf for added flavor. Simmer, covered, for 10 to 15 minutes, adding more water if necessary. Strain the broth through a sieve or colander and it's ready to use.

CHICKEN STOCK

Meat

4	pounds chicken pieces such as back, bones, necks, drumsticks, and wings (not white)
3	quarts cold water
3	onions, quartered

2	large carrots, cut into 3-inch pieces
2	stalks celery, cut into quarters
1	tablespoon whole peppercorns
1	bouquet garni (see sidebar)

Wash the chicken pieces; place in a large pan and cover with cold water. Add the onions, carrots, celery, and peppercorns to the pot. Add bouquet garni.

Slowly bring mixture to a boil, reduce heat to low, and simmer 2 hours, occasionally skimming off residue from top of stock. Do not allow stock to boil rapidly or the particles will be churned and make the stock cloudy.

Strain the stock through a sieve or colander, discarding vegetables and bones, and let cool. Cover and refrigerate until chilled. Divide stock into heavy-duty plastic zip-top bags and freeze.

Yield: 2 quarts.

CRYSTAL CLEAR CHICKEN SOUP

Meat

1	(3½- 4-pound) whole chicken, cut into 8 pieces, with skin on
1	large onion
6-8	carrots, peeled and cut into strips
2	stalks celery, cut into large pieces

2	parsley roots
1	bunch parsley
1	green bell pepper, seeded and cut into large pieces
1	teaspoon salt
1	teaspoon black peppercorns

Place chicken, onion, carrots, celery, parsley roots, parsley, and green pepper into a large soup pot. Fill with cold water to cover. Add salt and peppercorns.

Bring mixture to a boil, skimming residue from top. Reduce heat, and simmer 1½ to 2 hours, uncovered. (Slow cooking in an uncovered pot will produce a clear broth.)

Remove chicken from soup. Pull meat from chicken and cut into small pieces. Transfer chicken back to soup, discarding bones.

Yield: 8 servings.

Bouquet Garni

A bouquet garni is a bundle of several fresh herbs tied together or wrapped in cheesecloth. Typical herbs include parsley, thyme, and bay leaves. We suggest 1 bunch of parsley, 5 sprigs of thyme, and 1 bay leaf.

PERFECT FRENCH ONION SOUP

Dairy

*D*on't be intimidated by the length of this recipe. The steps are laid out very carefully to allow you to follow them with extreme ease. When you have completed all of the directions, you will be rewarded with a French onion soup so authentic, if you close your eyes, you will be able to see the lights of Paris.

¼	cup unsalted butter	3	quarts parve chicken or beef bouillon
2	tablespoons olive oil	1½	cups dry white wine
6	cups yellow onions – sliced into rings	¼	teaspoon freshly ground pepper
4	cloves garlic, minced	¼	teaspoon salt
1	teaspoon sugar		French Bread Croutons (see sidebar)
⅓	cup brandy or cognac	2	cups (8 ounces) shredded mozzarella cheese
1	tablespoon Dijon mustard	1	cup (4 ounces) grated Parmesan cheese
½	teaspoon fresh thyme		
3	tablespoons all-purpose flour		

Heat the butter and oil in a large soup pot over high heat. Add onions and sauté for 10 minutes. Reduce heat to medium.

Add garlic and sugar; sauté 30 minutes, stirring occasionally, or until onions are lightly browned.

Stir in brandy and cook until hot. Carefully ignite brandy mixture with a long match. (This will burn off the alcohol, but leave the essence of the brandy.) When flames die, stir in mustard and thyme.

Add flour, whisking until smooth. Cook 1 minute, whisking constantly. Gradually add broth and white wine, whisking until blended. Stir in salt and pepper. Bring mixture to a boil, reduce heat, and simmer over medium heat, 1 hour, stirring occasionally. The soup can be made in advance up to this point and reheated.

Preheat oven to broil with rack 6 inches from heat.

Arrange 8 ovenproof bowls or crocks on a baking sheet. Using a ladle, fill bowls ¾ full. Place 1 French Bread Crouton on top.

Combine mozzarella and Parmesan cheese and sprinkle over each crouton. Broil 2 to 3 minutes or until bubbly. Serve immediately.

Yield: 8 servings.

FRENCH BREAD CROUTONS

Dairy

8 (1-inch) thick slices French bread

¼ cup butter, softened

¼ cup olive oil

2 cloves garlic, minced

Preheat oven to 350°.

Arrange bread slices in a single layer on a baking sheet. Spread with butter and drizzle evenly with olive oil. Sprinkle with minced garlic.

Bake for 15 minutes or until lightly brown.

Yield: 8 croutons.

CREAM OF TOMATO-BASIL SOUP

Dairy

2 tablespoons canola or
   vegetable oil
2 large cloves garlic, minced
2 cups lightly packed fresh
   basil, (about 8 sprigs)
   stems removed and
   leaves minced
2 (14.5-ounce) cans whole
   peeled tomatoes,
   undrained

2 cups vegetable stock
   (page 38) or parve
   chicken bouillon
   Salt
   Pepper
½ cup heavy cream
   Garnish: fresh basil
   leaves

Heat oil in a large soup pot over medium heat. Add garlic and basil; sauté 1 to 2 minutes, stirring constantly (do not overcook).

Stir in tomatoes with liquid and broth. Bring to a boil, reduce heat, and simmer for 45 minutes. Season to taste with salt and pepper. Remove from heat.

Transfer the soup in batches to the container of a blender; process until smooth. (You may also use an immersion blender and process directly in the soup pot.)

Return soup to pot and reheat. Remove from heat and stir in cream. Garnish bowls with fresh basil leaves, if desired.

Yield: 4 to 6 servings.

Turn your dairy soup into a visual treat using this restaurant trick. Spoon a circle of heavy cream on top of each serving of soup. Use a toothpick to drag or feather the cream using in and out strokes. Try other patterns, as well. Fill a squeeze bottle with cream and squeeze drops in a circle. Drag a toothpick through the circles to form hearts or paisley shapes.

A stylish way to garnish this soup is to place fresh basil leaves in the soup around the entire rim of the bowl to resemble a sunflower. You will need about 14 to 16 leaves per serving, depending on the size of your bowl.

SPLIT PEA–BARLEY SOUP

Meat

1 pound soup bones or
   flanken
2 quarts water
2 cups split peas
1 cup barley
1 onion, diced

3 carrots, sliced
2 stalks celery, sliced
2 potatoes, diced
2 tablespoons fresh dill
   Salt

Combine bones or flanken meat and water in a large soup pot. Bring to a boil.

Add split peas, barley, and onion. Bring mixture back to a boil, reduce heat, and simmer until split peas are tender.

Add carrots, celery, potatoes, and dill. Simmer until vegetables are cooked. Stir in additional water if soup becomes too thick.

Remove soup bones and sprinkle with salt.

This soup tastes even better the day after you make it. If soup thickens, add water to achieve desired consistency, then reheat.

Yield: 10 to 12 servings.

CARROT SOUP

Parve or Meat

3 tablespoons margarine
1 onion, sliced
1 pound carrots, peeled
   and cut into pieces
6 cups chicken stock
   (page 39) or vegetable
   stock (page 38)

2-3 bay leaves
⅓ cup rice, uncooked
1 teaspoon kosher salt
½ teaspoon pepper
1 cup non-dairy creamer
   Garnish: chopped fresh
   parsley

Heat margarine in a large soup pot over medium heat. Add onions and carrots; sauté 15 minutes, stirring occasionally.

Stir in stock, bay leaves, rice, salt, and pepper. Bring mixture to a boil, reduce heat, and simmer 30 minutes or until the rice is cooked and the carrots are tender. Remove bay leaves and discard.

Transfer the soup in batches to the container of a blender or food processor fitted with a knife blade; process until smooth. (You may also use an immersion blender and process directly in the soup pot.)

Return soup to pot and reheat. Stir in creamer. Garnish with chopped parsley or croutons.

Yield: 6 to 8 servings.

Create your own fun-shaped croutons using slices of bread and miniature cookie cutters. Cut shapes that are suitable for any occasion or holiday. Sauté in melted margarine or use butter for a dairy soup. When croutons are crisp and lightly browned, remove from heat. Sprinkle over each serving of soup.

MUSHROOM AND WILD RICE SOUP

Parve or Meat

"*While serving this soup at a dinner party, I actually lost one of my guests. He was later found in the kitchen scraping the bottom of the soup pot. So, by all means, make this delicious soup recipe — just keep a running head count of all your guests.*"

½ cup wild rice, uncooked	5 cups warm chicken stock (page 39) or bouillon
1¼ cups cold water	1 cup non-dairy creamer
4 tablespoons margarine	Freshly grated nutmeg
2 medium onions, chopped	Salt
3 cloves garlic, minced	Pepper
1 pound mushrooms, sliced	Garnish: chopped fresh parsley
⅓ cup all-purpose flour	

Rinse rice under cold running water. Combine rice and water in a medium saucepan over medium-high heat. Bring to a boil, reduce heat, and simmer, covered, 30 to 40 minutes, or until tender. Drain and set aside.

Heat margarine in a large, heavy saucepan over medium heat until melted. Add onions and sauté until translucent. Add garlic and mushrooms; sauté for 3 minutes.

Add flour, whisking until smooth. Cook 2 minutes, whisking constantly. Gradually add chicken stock; cook over medium heat for 10 minutes, whisking constantly, or until mixture is thickened and bubbly.

Stir in wild rice, milk or creamer, and nutmeg. Season to taste with salt and pepper. Cook over medium heat for 5 minutes. Adjust seasonings, if desired. To serve, sprinkle with chopped parsley.

Yield: 6 servings.

MINESTRONE SOUP

Parve

3 tablespoons olive oil	½ cup marinara sauce
1 large onion, chopped	½ cup chopped fresh parsley
2 cloves garlic, minced	1 teaspoon dried basil
4 large tomatoes, seeded and diced	1 teaspoon dried oregano
2 carrots, diced	1 teaspoon salt
2 stalks celery, diced	1 teaspoon freshly ground pepper
12 cups water	¼ cup dry white wine
1 cup tomato sauce	½ cup macaroni, cooked

Heat oil in a large soup pot over medium-high heat. Add onion and garlic; sauté 3 to 5 minutes. Stir in tomatoes, carrots, and celery; sauté 2 minutes.

Add water, tomato sauce, marinara sauce, parsley, basil, oregano, salt, and pepper. Bring mixture to a boil, reduce heat, and simmer 1 hour.

Stir in wine and macaroni. Cook 10 to 15 minutes.

Yield: 8 servings.

POTATO-LEEK SOUP

Parve or Dairy

As a variation, turn this hot soup recipe into a cold (dairy) Vichyssoise. Sauté the leeks in ½ cup butter. Substitute 5 cups parve chicken bouillon for the 8 cups chicken stock. After you have puréed the soup, cook over low heat and stir in 1 cup heavy whipping cream and 1 cup milk. Cook until just heated through. Pour soup into a large bowl. Cover and refrigerate until chilled. To serve, garnish with dill sprigs.

5-6 leeks	8 cups chicken stock (page 39) or bouillon
½ cup margarine	Salt
2 stalks celery, chopped	Pepper
1 large onion, chopped	
3-4 potatoes, peeled and cubed	

Cut the roots from leeks and discard tough outer leaves. Cut each leek in half lengthwise. Rinse thoroughly with cold running water to remove grit. Slice leeks crosswise into ¼-inch pieces starting with the white end and using enough of the green part to make 5 cups.

Melt margarine in a large soup pot over medium heat. Add leeks, celery, and onion; sauté until tender and lightly browned.

Add stock and potatoes. Bring mixture to a boil, reduce heat to low, and simmer, covered, for 30 to 40 minutes or until potatoes are tender. Season to taste with salt and pepper.

Transfer the soup in batches to the container of a blender or food processor; process until smooth. (You may also use an immersion blender and process directly in the soup pot.) Return soup to pot and reheat.

Yield: 8 servings.

SPINACH–SPLIT PEA SOUP

Parve or Meat

2 tablespoons oil
1 onion, chopped
2 stalks celery, chopped
6 cups chicken bouillon or
   stock (page 39), divided
¾ cup dried split peas
1 bay leaf
4-6 cups chopped zucchini

2 teaspoons salt
½ teaspoon dried basil
¼ teaspoon pepper
1 (10-ounce) package
   frozen leaf spinach,
   thawed and coarsely
   chopped
¼ cup chopped fresh parsley

Heat oil in a large soup pot over medium-high heat. Add onion and celery; sauté until tender.

Add 4 cups of stock, split peas, and bay leaf. Bring mixture to a boil, reduce heat, and simmer 40 minutes.

Add remaining 2 cups broth, zucchini, salt, basil, and pepper. Cook an additional 15 to 20 minutes. Discard bay leaf.

Transfer the soup in batches to the container of a blender; process until smooth. (You may also use an immersion blender and process directly in the soup pot.)

Return soup to soup pot. Stir in spinach and parsley; cook until thoroughly heated.

Yield: 6 servings.

Yellow and Orange Pepper Soup

Parve or Meat

⅓ cup olive oil

1 large onion, chopped

5 cups vegetable stock
(page 38), chicken stock
(page 39), or water

2 large yellow bell peppers,
seeded and chopped

2 large orange bell peppers,
seeded and chopped

2 potatoes, peeled and
chopped

Salt

Freshly ground pepper

6 tablespoons margarine,
softened

6 tablespoons olive oil

Heat olive oil in a large soup pot over medium-high heat. Add onion and sauté 10 minutes.

Add stock or water, peppers, and potatoes. Bring mixture to a boil, reduce heat to low, and simmer 30 minutes.

Strain soup, reserving liquid. Spoon vegetables into the container of a food processor fitted with a knife blade. Process until smooth.

Press mixture through a sieve or wire mesh colander, discard peels, and add to reserved liquid. Season to taste with salt and pepper.

Bring mixture to a boil; remove from heat. Gradually add margarine, 1 tablespoon at a time, stirring until well blended.

To serve, pour soup into bowls and add 1 tablespoon of olive oil to each bowl.

Yield: 6 servings.

WILD BERRY SOUP

Dairy

The unique pastel hue of this soup lends itself to a beautiful garnish. One suggestion is to serve it in half of a scooped out honeydew melon with a strawberry fan or berries floating in the middle.

4 cups assorted fresh berries such as strawberries, raspberries, blueberries, or blackberries	1 cup heavy whipping cream
4 cups plain yogurt	½ cup pineapple juice
	½ cup Orange-Ginger Sauce
	⅓ cup honey

Place berries in the container of a blender; process until smooth. Add yogurt, cream, juice, sauce, and honey; process until smooth.

Strain mixture through a sieve or wire mesh strainer, pressing berries with the back of a spoon. Cover and chill until ready to serve.

Yield: 4 to 6 servings.

ORANGE-GINGER SAUCE:

½ cup fresh orange juice	2 tablespoons honey
½ cup white Zinfandel or blush wine	2 slices peeled fresh ginger

Combine juice, wine, honey, and ginger in a small saucepan. Bring mixture to a boil, reduce heat, and simmer until mixture reduces by half. Remove sliced ginger. Cover and refrigerate until chilled.

Yield: ½ cup.

Strawberry Fans

Select firm, ripe strawberries with bright red color. Slice the leaves and stem from the berries. Stand each berry, hull side down, on your work surface. Make 4 even slices, cutting almost to the hull, but not all of the way through. Press the sides of the berries slightly, and fan out slices with your fingers. Place a sprig of fresh mint at the hull end.

ICED CUCUMBER SOUP

Dairy or Parve

2 tablespoons butter or margarine	¼ teaspoon pepper
3 leeks	¼ teaspoon dry mustard
2 cups diced cucumber, unpeeled	2 sprigs parsley
½ cup diced potato, uncooked	4 cups chicken or vegetable stock (pages 38 and 39)
¼ cup chopped spinach	1 cup heavy whipping cream or non-dairy creamer

Cut the roots from leeks and discard tough outer leaves. Cut each leek in half lengthwise. Rinse thoroughly with cold running water to remove grit. Slice leeks and set aside.

Heat butter or margarine in a large soup pot over medium-high heat. Add leeks and sauté until tender.

Add cucumber, potato, spinach, pepper, mustard, and parsley. Sauté 5 minutes.

Stir in the stock. Bring mixture to a boil, reduce heat, and simmer 20 minutes.

Transfer the soup in batches to the container of a blender and process until smooth. (You may also use an immersion blender and process directly in the soup pot.)

Return soup to pot and stir in cream. Correct the seasonings, if desired. Cover and refrigerate until well chilled. Recipe may be made a day or two ahead.

Yield: 6 servings.

For a stunning presentation, garnish this or almost any soup with diced scallions, radishes, and cucumbers. Sprinkle with shelled pumpkin seeds. If the soup is dairy, dollop with whipped heavy cream, then sprinkle with vegetables and seeds.

WILD MUSHROOM BISQUE

Dairy or Meat

½ cup butter or margarine
2 cups carrots, finely chopped in food processor
2 cups onion, finely chopped in food processor
1 cup celery, finely chopped in food processor
4 cups assorted wild mushrooms such as shiitake, portobello, cremini, etc.
6 cloves garlic, minced
1 tablespoon fresh thyme

1 tablespoon fresh oregano
1 tablespoon chopped fresh parsley
Freshly ground pepper
½ cup white wine
4 cups strong chicken (page 39) or vegetable stock (page 38), or bouillon
3 cups light cream or non-dairy creamer
¼ cup cornstarch
¼ cup water
Salt
1-2 ounces brandy (optional)

Heat margarine in a large skillet over medium-high heat. Add carrots, onions, celery, and mushrooms; sauté until tender, but not brown.

Stir in garlic, thyme, oregano, parsley, and pepper.

Add wine and cook for 2 minutes, stirring constantly.

Add stock and cream. Bring to a boil, reduce heat to medium-low, and simmer until reduced by one-third.

Combine cornstarch and water; stir into soup. Cook until slightly thickened. Season to taste with salt and pepper. Stir in brandy, if desired.

Yield: 10 servings.

Serve this soup in half of an acorn or pumpkin squash that has been roasted at 350° for about 40 minutes. Remove seeds but leave most of the flesh intact to retain the shape of the bowl and to remain strong enough to hold the soup.

CREAM OF ANY VEGETABLE SOUP

Dairy

" I got this recipe from my college roommate who had her jaw wired for 6 months and could only eat food with a straw. For variety, or out of boredom, she tried this recipe with every vegetable known to man. They were all delicious, but our favorites are broccoli, carrot, and butternut squash. Although this recipe requires many pots, we both agree that it is well worth it."

6 tablespoons butter, divided	1½ quarts vegetable stock
4 tablespoons all-purpose flour	(page 38) or bouillon
1 large onion, chopped	1 cup half-and-half
2 pounds broccoli, or 2 pounds carrots (peeled), or 2 pounds butternut squash flesh, cut into pieces	

To serve this recipe as a Tri-Color Vegetable Soup, (photo below), prepare 3 separate recipes of soup using broccoli, carrot, and butternut squash. Pour each into a teacup or jar. Slowly pour all three soups at the same time, starting at the outer rim of the bowl so each soup meets in the center. (You will need an assistant to pour 3 soups at the same time.) Pour heavy whipping cream or Crème Fraîche (page 136) into a squeeze bottle and cover the area where the soups meet. You can also prepare Two-Color Soup using the same technique with 2 different soups.

To prepare a roux: heat 4 tablespoons butter in a small pan over low heat; add flour, whisking until smooth. Cook 1 minute, whisking constantly; remove from heat.

Bring vegetable stock to a boil; keep warm.

Heat remaining 2 tablespoons butter in a large soup pot over medium-high heat. Add onion and sauté 3 to 5 minutes. Add vegetables and sauté 3 to 5 minutes.

Stir hot vegetable stock into vegetables. Bring mixture to a boil, reduce heat, and simmer.

Stir in roux; simmer 30 minutes, covered.

Transfer the soup in batches to the container of a blender; process until smooth. (You may also use an immersion blender and process directly in the soup pot.)

Return to soup pot and reheat. Stir in half-and-half and season to taste with salt and pepper.

Yield: 4 servings.

You can make this soup in a parve version. Substitute margarine for the butter. Non-dairy cream or soy milk can replace the half-and-half.

BEET AND TOMATO BISQUE

Meat

3 tablespoons olive oil, divided
1 onion, diced
1 clove garlic, minced
4 small beets (1 pound), peeled
1 pound carrots, peeled, halved, and sliced
1 (28-ounce) can plum tomatoes, drained

4½ cups chicken stock (page 39) or bouillon
2 teaspoons sugar
4 teaspoons salt, divided
1 teaspoon freshly ground pepper
5 tablespoons lemon juice, divided
2 tablespoons chopped fresh parsley (optional)

Heat 2 tablespoons oil in a large saucepan over medium-high heat. Add onion and garlic; sauté for 5 minutes or until tender.

Stir in beets, carrots, tomatoes, stock, and sugar. Bring mixture to a boil, reduce heat, and simmer 1 hour. Remove 1 beet and 2 carrots; set aside.

Transfer the bisque in batches to the container of a blender; process until smooth. (You may also use an immersion blender and process directly in the soup pot.) Stir in 3 tablespoons lemon juice, 3 teaspoons salt and 1 teaspoon pepper; set aside.

Cut the reserved beet and carrots into ¼-inch cubes and place in a small bowl. Add remaining 2 tablespoons lemon juice, remaining 1 tablespoon oil, and remaining 1 teaspoon salt. Season to taste with additional freshly ground pepper.

Spoon beet mixture evenly into 6 serving bowls. Pour bisque evenly over beet mixture. Sprinkle each bowl with 1 teaspoon chopped fresh parsley, if desired. The bisque may be served hot or cold.

Yield: 6 servings.

CREAMY POTATO SOUP

Parve

"This is a wonderful winter soup. It is a favorite among children and adults. In fact, my good friend's son celebrated his 12th birthday last month. When I asked him what he wanted for a gift, he said, 'a big pot of your potato soup!' How's that for an endorsement!"

3 tablespoons oil	1 teaspoon paprika
8 large Idaho potatoes, peeled and cubed	½ gallon water
	1 cup non-dairy creamer
6 carrots, peeled and thinly sliced	1 whole onion, peeled
	2 stalks celery
3 tablespoons all-purpose flour	2-3 bay leaves
	Garnish: finely chopped fresh parsley
1 teaspoon salt	

Heat oil in a large soup pot over medium heat. Add potatoes and sauté 3 to 5 minutes, stirring constantly.

Add carrots, stirring well. Stir in flour, salt, and paprika. Add water, creamer, onion, celery, and bay leaves.

Bring to a boil and immediately lower flame. Simmer, covered, for at least 1½ hours, stirring occasionally to prevent potatoes from sticking to bottom of pot. Remove onion, celery, and bay leaves.

Garnish bowls with fresh parsley and serve with warm, crusty bread.

Soup will be slightly chunky. Soup may be held in the refrigerator for over a week.

Yield: 24 servings.

SALADS

Endive Salad with
Tangerines, Beets & Olives,
page 55

ORIENTAL COLESLAW

Parve

1½ pounds cabbage, thinly sliced (about 12 cups)
4 stalks celery, thinly sliced
1 red onion, very thinly sliced
1 cup fresh cilantro, chopped
2 tablespoons peeled and chopped fresh ginger
1 tablespoon sugar
½ teaspoon crushed red pepper
¼ cup soy sauce
2 tablespoons white wine vinegar
2 tablespoons sesame oil
Salt
Pepper

Combine cabbage, celery, onion, and cilantro in a large bowl.

Whisk together ginger, sugar, pepper, soy sauce, vinegar, and sesame oil. Pour dressing over cabbage, tossing gently. Season with salt and pepper to taste. Cover and chill at least 1 hour, stirring occasionally.

Yield: 8 to 12 servings.

BOK CHOY SALAD

Parve

2 (3-ounce) packages ramen noodles, Oriental flavor
¾ cup sugar
¾ cup olive oil
⅓ cup white vinegar
2 teaspoons soy sauce
3 heads bok choy
2 bunches scallions, chopped
1 (7.25-ounce) jar sunflower kernels
3 cups sliced almonds

Remove seasoning packets from ramen and set noodles aside. Combine seasoning, sugar, oil, vinegar, and soy sauce in a cruet or jar. Cover tightly, and shake vigorously. (Dressing may be prepared in advance.)

Slice bok choy into bite size pieces, including the stems. Combine bok choy, scallions, sunflower kernels, and almonds in a large bowl. Toss gently with dressing. Add ramen noodles just before serving to keep them from getting soggy.

Yield: 8 to 12 servings.

Endive Salad with Tangerines, Beets, and Olives

Parve

This unique salad is truly a starburst of color. The nuts, fruit and vegetables combine for a textured dish that appeals to all of your senses.

1½ cups pecan halves	1 cup small niçoise or
Salt	Italian black olives,
3 small yellow beets	pitted
3 small red beets	⅔ cup olive oil
5 seedless tangerines or	4 heads Belgian endive
4 oranges, seeded	Garnish: cilantro or
	chervil sprigs

Preheat oven to 450°.

Place pecans on a baking sheet lined with foil. Sprinkle lightly with salt and bake 4 minutes or until lightly browned. Do not overcook or pecans will turn bitter. Cool and set aside.

Place yellow and red beets in separate saucepans with cold, salted water to cover. Bring to a boil, reduce heat, and simmer 45 minutes to 1 hour, or until tender. Remove skin, cut into small wedges, and place in separate bowls.

Squeeze juice from 1 tangerine (½ cup) and set aside. Peel and section remaining tangerines.

Combine pecans, tangerines, juice, olives, and olive oil in a large bowl. Add beets and toss gently.

Cut 1 inch from the bottom of each head of endive and discard. Cut 2 heads crosswise into thin slices. Separate remaining 2 heads into individual leaves.

To serve, arrange the endive leaves in a circular pattern on a large platter or individual serving plates. Spoon beet mixture using a slotted spoon and place in the center, reserving liquid. Add sliced endive to bowl of reserved liquid, tossing to coat. Arrange sliced endive on top of salad. Garnish with cilantro or chervil.

Yield: 4 to 6 servings.

Smoked Turkey Salad

Meat

¼ cup mayonnaise
¼ cup sugar
¼ cup olive oil
2 cloves garlic, minced
1 tablespoon chopped fresh chives
1 tablespoon chopped fresh parsley
½ teaspoon dry mustard
½ teaspoon lemon juice
1 head romaine lettuce, torn
½ pound smoked turkey, cut into thin strips
¼ cup shredded carrots

Whisk together mayonnaise, sugar, oil, garlic, chives, parsley, mustard, and lemon juice. Cover and chill until serving.

Combine lettuce, turkey, and carrots. Toss with dressing just before serving.

Yield: 4 servings.

Curried Couscous Salad

Parve

2 cups couscous
1 bunch scallions, chopped
1 red bell pepper, chopped
½ cup raisins
½ cup golden raisins
½ cup canned chickpeas, drained
¼ cup fresh lemon juice
2½ teaspoons curry powder
½ teaspoon allspice
½ teaspoon salt
½ teaspoon pepper
¾ cup olive oil

Prepare couscous according to package directions; cool and fluff with fork.

Combine scallions, bell pepper, raisins, and chickpeas in a large bowl. Stir in couscous.

Whisk together lemon juice, curry powder, allspice, salt, and pepper. Gradually add olive oil, whisking until well blended.

Stir dressing into couscous mixture. Cover and chill.

Yield: 8 to 10 servings.

Tomato-Basil Couscous Salad

Meat

2½ cups canned clear
    chicken broth
1 (10-ounce) package
    couscous
1 cup chopped scallions
1 cup seeded and diced
    plum tomatoes

⅓ cup fresh basil, thinly
    sliced
½ cup olive oil
¼ cup balsamic vinegar
¼ teaspoon crushed red
    pepper flakes
1 pint cherry tomatoes,
    halved

Bring soup to a boil in a large saucepan. Cook over medium-high heat until boiling. Stir in couscous. Cover, remove from heat, and let stand 5 minutes. Transfer to a large bowl and fluff with a fork; cool.

Stir in scallions, plum tomatoes, and basil.

Combine oil, vinegar, and pepper. Stir into couscous, tossing gently. Garnish with cherry tomatoes.

Yield: 10 to 12 servings.

Middle Eastern Bean Salad

Parve

2 (16-ounce) cans white
    lima beans or butter
    beans, rinsed and
    drained
12-15 cured black olives,
    drained, pitted, and
    chopped
½ cup minced red onion
½ cup diced red bell pepper
½ cup diced yellow bell
    pepper

½ cup chopped fresh parsley
¼ cup chopped fresh mint
¼ cup chopped fresh dill
½ cup extra virgin olive oil
¼ cup lemon juice
1 tablespoon red wine
    vinegar
1 teaspoon crushed red
    pepper flakes (optional)
Salt
Pepper

Combine beans, olives, onion, bell peppers, parsley, mint, and dill in a large bowl.

Combine oil, lemon juice, vinegar, and red pepper flakes. Add to bean mixture, tossing to coat. Season to taste with salt and pepper. Let stand several hours before serving.

Yield: 4 servings.

When a recipe calls for diced or chopped bell peppers, use small canapé cutters to cut fun, interesting shapes such as stars, hearts, or flowers.

Serve your salads in edible tortilla bowls.

Tortilla Salad Bowls

Vegetable oil

4 large flour tortillas

Find two glass or aluminum mixing bowls that fit one inside the other but are just about the same size. Invert them. Heat 1-inch of vegetable oil in a large frying pan until very hot but not smoky, about 360°. If you touch the handle of a wooden spoon to the oil and it bubbles, it is ready. Place one tortilla into the hot oil and fry for 20 to 30 seconds. Use tongs to turn over and fry on the other side for 20 to 30 seconds. Remove from oil and place over one of the inverted bowls. Place the other bowl over the tortilla to "sandwich" the tortilla and help it form a bowl shape. After 3 to 4 minutes remove top bowl, remove the tortilla and set aside until ready to use. Continue with the other tortillas. It takes a little practice to get the hang of it so have a few extra tortillas on hand for errors.

Fill the Tortilla Bowls with Grilled Chicken Salad or other favorite salad.

Grilled Chicken Salad

Meat

4 boneless, skinless chicken breasts	2 tablespoons light brown sugar
1½ cups barbecue sauce	2 tablespoons chopped fresh chives
1 (1-pound) bunch asparagus	1 teaspoon soy sauce
2 tablespoons margarine	2 cloves garlic, pressed
1 (8-ounce) package mushrooms, sliced	1 head Bibb lettuce
Salt	2 (11-ounce) cans mandarin oranges, drained
Pepper	⅓ cup pine nuts
½ cup oil	
⅓ cup balsamic vinegar	

Preheat grill to medium-high heat. Grill chicken 10 to 15 minutes, turning once and basting with barbecue sauce. Cool slightly and slice; set aside.

Cook asparagus in boiling water to cover 6 to 8 minutes or until slightly tender. (Do not overcook). Cut into 1-inch pieces and set aside.

Melt margarine in a skillet over medium-high heat. Add mushrooms and sauté until tender; drain. Season with salt and pepper to taste; set aside.

Combine oil, vinegar, sugar, chives, soy sauce, and garlic in a cruet or jar; cover tightly, and shake vigorously.

Combine lettuce, oranges, chicken, asparagus, mushrooms, and dressing, tossing gently. Sprinkle with pine nuts.

Yield: 4 servings.

SUMMER HERBED ORZO SALAD

Parve

6 ounces sugar snap peas, trimmed and cut into ¾-inch pieces
1 (16-ounce) box orzo
1½ cups seeded and diced tomatoes
¾ cup peeled, seeded, and cubed cucumber
½ cup chopped scallions
⅓ cup chopped fresh mint
¼ cup chopped fresh parsley
1 tablespoon minced garlic
1 teaspoon chopped lemon peel
Salt
Pepper
Lemon Vinaigrette
Bibb lettuce

Cook sugar snap peas in boiling water to cover for 1 minute. Remove peas with a strainer and rinse under cold water; set aside.

Add orzo to boiling pot of water. Boil 8 minutes or until tender. (Do not overcook or orzo will be too soft.) Drain; let cool.

Combine sugar snaps, orzo, tomatoes, cucumber, scallions, mint, parsley, garlic, and lemon peel in a large bowl. Pour half of Lemon Vinaigrette over vegetables, tossing to coat. Cover and refrigerate until 1 hour before serving. Toss salad with enough remaining dressing to coat. Season to taste with salt and pepper. To serve, place lettuce leaves on salad plates and spoon a mound of salad on leaves.

Yield: 8 servings.

LEMON VINAIGRETTE:

½ cup olive oil
¼ cup freshly squeezed lemon juice
2 teaspoons finely chopped lemon peel
2 teaspoons minced garlic
Salt
Freshly ground pepper

Combine oil, juice, peel, and garlic in a cruet or jar. Cover tightly, and shake vigorously. Season to taste with salt and pepper. Dressing may be prepared ahead.

Yield: 1 cup.

THREE LEAF SALAD

Parve

1 head red leaf lettuce	1 cup sun-dried tomato
1 head green leaf lettuce	pieces, packed in oil
1 head romaine lettuce	Garlic-Dijon Vinaigrette
	1½ cups croutons

Tear lettuces and combine with sun-dried tomatoes in a large serving bowl, tossing to combine. Toss with enough Garlic-Dijon Vinaigrette to coat. Sprinkle with croutons and toss to combine.

Yield: 6 to 8 servings.

GARLIC-DIJON VINAIGRETTE:

¼ cup Dijon mustard	¾ cup olive oil
2 tablespoon red wine	1 teaspoon celery seeds
vinegar	1 teaspoon dried parsley
10 cloves garlic, minced	

Whisk together mustard, vinegar, and garlic in a small bowl. Gradually add oil in a steady stream, whisking until well blended. Stir in celery seeds and parsley.

Yield: 1¼ cups.

Cleaning and Preparing Salad Leaves

Separate the leaves using your hands instead of a knife (except for tough heads like cabbage). By tearing instead of cutting, you avoid bruising and discoloring the leaves. When ready to use, wash the leaves in cold water and simply tear lettuce leaves into bite-size pieces with your fingers. Lettuce can be stored in a bowl of cold water, topped with ice cubes and left on the counter until ready to use. At that time, use a salad spinner to spin dry the lettuce to use in your recipe.

MANDARIN ORANGE SALAD

Parve

1 onion, quartered	1 head Bibb lettuce
1 cup vegetable oil	1 head red leaf lettuce
⅓ cup balsamic vinegar	1 cup crunchy sprouts
¼ cup sugar	(optional)
1 tablespoon honey Dijon	2 (11-ounce) cans
mustard	mandarin oranges,
½ teaspoon salt	drained
Garlic powder	⅓ cup sliced almonds
Pepper	

Combine onion, oil, vinegar, sugar, mustard, and salt in the container of a food processor fitted with knife blade. Process until mixture is well blended and onion is chopped. Season with garlic powder and pepper, to taste. Set dressing aside. Dressing can be prepared 1 to 2 days ahead.

Tear lettuces into bite size pieces and place in a large bowl. Toss in sprouts and oranges. Before serving, add dressing, tossing to coat. Sprinkle with almonds.

Yield: 6 to 8 servings.

GREEK SALAD

Dairy

1 head iceberg lettuce, torn
    into pieces
1 head chickory lettuce,
    torn into pieces
2 cucumbers, thinly sliced
2 large tomatoes, chopped
1 (5½-ounce) jar Greek
    olives or 1 (6-ounce)
    can black olives,
    drained and pitted
1 (2-ounce) can anchovies,
    drained (optional)

2 scallions, chopped
2 tablespoons capers,
    drained (optional)
8 ounces crumbled feta
    cheese
½ cup olive oil
3 tablespoons red wine
    vinegar
1 tablespoon dried oregano
    Salt
    Pepper

Combine lettuce, cucumbers, tomatoes, olives, anchovies, scallions, capers, and feta cheese. Combine oil, vinegar, and oregano in a small bowl. Season to taste with salt and pepper.

Pour dressing over salad, tossing to coat.

Yield: 6 to 8 servings.

BAKED BRIE AND RASPBERRY SALAD

Dairy

1 cup fresh or frozen
    raspberries
¾ cup sour cream
¼ cup raspberry vinegar
1 (17.3-ounce) package
    puff pastry, thawed

½ pound Brie cheese, rind
    removed and cut into
    6 pieces
1 head Bibb lettuce, torn
    into pieces
1 small head romaine
    lettuce, torn into pieces

Combine raspberries, sour cream, and vinegar in the container of a blender. Process until smooth; set aside.

Preheat oven to 400°.

Cut puff pastry into circles, large enough to wrap around a piece of Brie. Place a piece of Brie in the center of the pastry circle and bring edges together, pinching to seal. Place Brie, seam side down, on a lightly greased baking sheet. Repeat with remaining pieces of Brie and pastry.

Bake 20 to 25 minutes or until pastry is puffed and golden brown.

Combine lettuce and arrange on salad plates. Top each with pastry. Drizzle with raspberry dressing and garnish with fresh raspberries.

Yield: 6 servings.

Try this dressing variation:

RASPBERRY VINAIGRETTE

⅔ cup olive oil

¼ cup raspberry vinegar

½ teaspoon dry mustard

¼ teaspoon pepper

1 clove garlic, pressed

1 teaspoon chopped chives

Whisk together oil, vinegar, mustard, pepper, and garlic. Add chives just before serving.

Yield: ¾ cup.

STRAWBERRY–MANGO MESCLUN SALAD

Parve

"I serve this salad to almost everyone who passes through my doorway. All my guests, both men and women, beg to know the ingredients in this spectacular salad. My response is always the same, 'I'm not supposed to give out the recipe until the cookbook comes out, but...if you promise to buy a cookbook, I'll reveal that insider information.' I have already pre-sold 5 cases of cookbooks and going strong."

½ cup sugar
¾ cup canola or vegetable oil
⅓ cup balsamic vinegar
1 teaspoon salt
8 cups mesclun or gourmet mixed salad greens
2 cups sweetened dried cranberries (cranraisins)

8 ounces strawberries, quartered
1 large mango, peeled, pitted and cubed
½ cup chopped onion
1 cup slivered almonds

Combine sugar, oil, vinegar, and salt in a cruet or jar. Cover tightly, and shake vigorously.

Combine greens, cranberries, strawberries, mango, and onion in a large bowl, tossing well. To serve, toss with enough dressing to coat. Sprinkle with almonds.

Yield: 6 to 8 servings.

HEARTS OF PALM AND SPINACH

Parve

2 (10-ounce) bags fresh spinach
1 (15-ounce) can whole hearts of palm, drained
1 pint cherry or grape tomatoes
2 avocados, pitted, peeled, and diced
10 ounces sliced mushrooms
½ cup sliced almonds

½ cup sugar
1 teaspoon salt
½ teaspoon dry mustard powder
½ teaspoon paprika
¾ cup canola oil
½ cup white vinegar
½ cup ketchup
2 cloves garlic, chopped

Toss spinach, hearts of palm, tomatoes, avocados, mushrooms, and almonds together in a large serving bowl.

Combine sugar, salt, dry mustard, paprika, oil, vinegar, ketchup, and garlic in a cruet or jar. Cover tightly and shake vigorously.

To serve, toss with enough dressing to coat.

Yield: 8 to 10 servings.

FLOWER SALAD

Parve

7 cups assorted greens such as radicchio, endive, arugula, Bibb, watercress, and spinach
2 tablespoons fresh snipped dill
2 tablespoons fresh chopped basil

2 tablespoons fresh chopped chervil
Creamy Balsamic Vinaigrette
Edible flowers
Sunflower seeds

Combine greens, dill, basil, and chervil in a large bowl. Remove petals from one or two of the flowers and sprinkle over the greens. Add vinaigrette, tossing gently. Top with 4 to 5 blossoms of each type of edible flower. Sprinkle with sunflower seeds.

Yield: 6 servings.

CREAMY BALSAMIC VINAIGRETTE:

3 tablespoons Dijon mustard
1-2 tablespoons mayonnaise
2 tablespoons balsamic vinegar

1 teaspoon lemon juice
1 large clove garlic, pressed
¾ cup extra virgin olive oil
Salt
Pepper

Combine mustard, mayonnaise, vinegar, lemon juice, and garlic in a blender. Process until smooth. Turn blender on high; gradually add oil in a slow, steady stream until emulsified. (Ingredients can also be placed in bowl and processed with an immersion blender.) Season to taste with salt and pepper. Chill until serving.

Yield: 1 cup.

Edible Flowers

Edible flowers may be used in many beautiful and eye-catching ways. The flowers can be eaten in salads, or used as garnishes for any dish. Be careful when selecting flowers to eat. Like mushrooms, not all are edible. Flowers from florists have generally been treated with pesticides. Either rely on gourmet markets that sell packaged edible flowers or grow your own. Some of the more popular edible flowers are:

Dandelions - slightly bitter

Johnny Jump-ups - mild wintergreen flavor

Nasturtium - peppery flavor

Violets - subtle, delicate flavor

Marigolds - citrusy flavor

Roses - mild flavor

Borage - cucumber flavor

APPLE WALNUT SALAD WITH CRANBERRY VINAIGRETTE

Parve

1	Red Delicious apple	1	teaspoon Dijon mustard
1	Granny Smith apple	½	cup walnut oil
	Lemon juice	¼	cup canola oil
¼	cup fresh or frozen	¼	cup water
	cranberries, thawed		Salt
¼	cup balsamic vinegar		Pepper
1	tablespoon chopped red	10	cups mixed baby greens
	onion	½	cup chopped walnuts,
1	tablespoon plus 1 pinch		toasted
	sugar		

Core and slice the apples very thin. Place apple slices in a bowl of ice water with lemon juice to keep them from discoloring; set aside.

Place cranberries in the container of a food processor fitted with a knife blade; process until smooth. Add vinegar, onion, sugar, and mustard; process until well blended. With processor running, gradually add the oils and water in a steady stream until well blended. Transfer to a small bowl. Season to taste with salt and pepper. Dressing can be made a day ahead. Cover and refrigerate. To serve, bring to room temperature and whisk to blend. Do not slice the apples until ready to serve.

Combine the greens and apples in a large bowl. Toss with enough dressing to coat. Sprinkle with walnuts.

Yield: 6 servings.

GRILLED CHICKEN SALAD
WITH RASPBERRIES

Meat

*T*his is not only the most beautiful salad we're ever seen, it's also one of the most delicious. The mango and raspberries add splashes of color with a lovely tartness. One nice thing about this recipe is that you can prepare the dressing and chicken the day before, then toss it together just before serving.

3 boneless, skinless chicken breasts
1 cup tomato-basil salad dressing (bottled)

8 cups assorted greens such as Bibb, romaine, endive, or red leaf
1 pint fresh raspberries
1 mango, peeled, pitted, and diced

Combine chicken and bottled dressing in a bowl; cover and refrigerate 30 minutes.

Preheat grill to medium-hot heat. Remove chicken from tomato-basil dressing, discarding dressing.

Grill 7 to 8 minutes on each side or until done. Cut chicken into 1-inch cubes; set aside.

BALSAMIC DIJON HONEY WALNUT VINAIGRETTE:

½ cup balsamic vinegar
¼ cup Dijon mustard
1 tablespoon chopped fresh parsley
1 tablespoon honey
2 teaspoons cracked black pepper

½ teaspoon fresh minced garlic
¾ cup olive oil
¾ cup walnut oil
½ cup coarsely chopped walnuts

Whisk together vinegar, mustard, parsley, honey, pepper, and garlic in a medium bowl. Gradually add oils in a steady stream, whisking until blended. Stir in walnuts.

Combine greens and dressing in a large bowl, tossing to coat. Stir in chicken and sprinkle with raspberries and mango.

Yield: 6 side dish or 3 main dish servings.

New Potato Salad

Parve

"This recipe has been invited to almost as many barbecues as our family. It is a potato salad with a burst of flavor and NO mayonnaise."

8 large new potatoes, unpeeled	½ teaspoon dry mustard
1 cup olive oil	2 cloves garlic, minced
¼ cup tarragon vinegar	1 cup diced celery (optional)
1 tablespoon sugar	1 cup grated carrot (optional)
1 tablespoon Worcestershire sauce	½ cup diced onion
1 teaspoon salt	½ cup chopped fresh parsley

Cook potatoes in boiling water until just soft (pierce with a fork). Do not overcook. Drain and transfer to a large bowl to cool. Cut potatoes into medium size chunks; set aside.

Combine oil, vinegar, sugar, Worcestershire sauce, salt, dry mustard, and garlic, mixing well.

Add celery, carrot, onions, and parsley to potatoes, tossing lightly. Add sauce, tossing gently to coat. Do not overmix or potatoes will fall apart. Cover and refrigerate. Let salad come to room temperature before serving (chilled olive oil will solidify).

Yield: 6 to 8 servings.

Corn Salad

Parve

"At my last barbecue, I multiplied the recipe for a crowd of 50. Not one kernel was left."

2 (15-ounce) cans whole kernel yellow corn, drained	8 ounces snow peas, sliced diagonally into small pieces
1 (7-ounce) can white shoepeg corn, drained	3 tablespoons olive oil
1 small red onion, diced	Salt
1 red bell pepper, diced	Pepper

Combine yellow corn, white corn, onion, bell pepper, snow peas, and olive oil in a large bowl. Season to taste with salt and pepper.

Yield: 8 servings.

Serve this as a side dish in corn husks, trimmed and tied at one end with raffia ribbon.

APRICOT PASTA CHICKEN SALAD

Meat

*T*his gorgeous summer salad can be served hot or cold. The combination of colors and flavors is really eye catching and delicious. If you are going to prepare the recipe ahead, store the pasta separately.

1 (8-ounce) package fusilli (corkscrew) pasta	2 cloves garlic, minced
4-5 tablespoons olive oil	1 portobello mushroom, sliced
4 boneless, skinless chicken breasts	5 apricots, pitted and quartered
1 red bell pepper, cut into thin strips	3 tablespoons chopped fresh basil or 1 tablespoon dried
1 large zucchini, cut into thin strips	Apricot Dressing

Prepare pasta according to package directions; drain and set aside.

Heat oil in a large skillet over medium heat. Add breasts and sauté until browned on both sides.

Add pepper, zucchini, garlic, mushrooms, and apricots. Sauté until tender.

Remove chicken and cut into ¼-inch slices. Return chicken and add basil to skillet. Sauté 3 minutes. Toss with Apricot Dressing and serve.

Yield: 4 to 6 servings.

APRICOT DRESSING:

2 fresh apricots, pitted	¼ cup vegetable oil
1 tablespoon sugar	1 tablespoon chopped fresh basil or 1 teaspoon dried
2 tablespoons apple cider vinegar	

Combine apricots, sugar, and vinegar in a blender. Process until smooth. Turn blender on high; gradually add oil in a slow, steady stream until emulsified. (Ingredients can also be placed in bowl and processed with an immersion blender.) Stir in basil.

Yield: ¾ cup.

TERRA CHIP SALAD

Parve

⅓ cup oil
⅓ cup red wine vinegar
¼ cup sugar
3 tablespoons ketchup
2 tablespoons grated onion
1 head romaine lettuce
1 cup spinach leaves
½ red bell pepper, cut into thin strips
½ yellow bell pepper, cut into thin strips
1 avocado, peeled, pitted, and cubed
1 (6-ounce) package slivered almonds
1 (4-ounce) jar pine nuts
1 (6-ounce) package Terra chips, divided

Combine oil, vinegar, sugar, ketchup, and onion in a cruet or jar. Cover tightly and shake vigorously; set aside.

Tear and combine lettuce, spinach, bell peppers, and avocado in a large bowl. Sprinkle with almonds and pine nuts.

To serve, add dressing, tossing to coat. Crumble ¾ package chips and sprinkle on top. Arrange whole chips around edge of bowl as a garnish.

Yield: 6 to 8 servings.

Warm Mushroom Salad

Parve

The textures and various temperatures make this a very interesting salad. The dressing is delicious on any salad as well as a marinade for grilled vegetables.

2 tablespoons oil	2 heads Bibb lettuce, torn
1 (8-ounce) package button	into pieces
mushrooms, sliced	Fresh Dill Vinaigrette
1 pound shiitake	
mushrooms, sliced	

Heat oil in a large skillet over medium-high heat. Add mushrooms and sauté until tender.

Combine mushrooms and lettuce in a large bowl. To serve, add enough dressing to coat, tossing well.

Yield: 6 servings.

Fresh Dill Vinaigrette:

1 cup vegetable oil	½ teaspoon dry mustard
¼ cup white vinegar	powder
1 tablespoon fresh lemon	½ teaspoon pepper
juice	¼ teaspoon sugar
2-3 teaspoons chopped fresh	¼ teaspoon dried oregano
dill	2 cloves garlic, pressed
1¼ teaspoons salt	Pinch thyme

Combine all ingredients in a cruet or jar. Cover tightly and shake vigorously.

Yield: 1⅓ cups.

Spicy Beef Breadsticks

Meat

½ cup dark brown sugar

Chili powder

12 slices pastrami

12 thin breadsticks (such as Grissini)

Preheat oven to 350°.

Combine brown sugar and chili powder to taste on a large piece of wax paper. Dredge pastrami in seasoned brown sugar on both sides and spiral wrap around breadstick. Place on lightly greased baking sheet; bake 5 to 8 minutes until cooked. Serve 2 breadsticks with each plate of salad. Recipe is best made just before serving.

Yield: 12 breadsticks.

CAESAR SALAD

Dairy

4 cloves garlic	1 teaspoon Dijon mustard
¾ cup mayonnaise	4 anchovy fillets (optional)
½ cup grated Parmesan cheese, divided	Salt Freshly ground pepper
1 tablespoon fresh lemon juice	1-2 heads romaine lettuce, torn into pieces
1 teaspoon Worcestershire sauce	Garlic Croutons

Place garlic in the container of a food processor fitted with knife blade. Process until minced. Add mayonnaise, 2 tablespoons Parmesan cheese, lemon juice, Worcestershire sauce, mustard, and anchovies, if desired. Process until well blended. Season to taste with salt and pepper.

Place lettuce in a large bowl. Toss with enough dressing to coat. Add remaining Parmesan cheese and croutons, tossing gently to blend.

Yield: 8 servings.

GARLIC CROUTONS:

3 cups Italian or sourdough bread cubes, cut into ¾-inch squares	2 large cloves garlic, minced
1 tablespoon olive oil	½ teaspoon garlic powder
	½ teaspoon salt

Preheat oven to 325°.

Place bread cubes in a single layer in a large baking dish. Drizzle with olive oil and sprinkle with garlic, garlic powder, and salt. Toss to coat well.

Bake 20 to 25 minutes or until lightly toasted. Cool.

Yield: 3 cups.

Angel Hair Pasta Salad

Parve

8 ounces angel hair pasta	1 teaspoon salt
2 tablespoons oil	1 teaspoon white pepper
1 cup slivered almonds	1 small red cabbage,
¼ cup sesame seeds	shredded
⅓ cup olive oil	6 scallions, chopped
¼ cup sugar	1 (8-ounce) can water
¼ cup apple cider vinegar	chestnuts, drained

Cook pasta according to package directions; drain and set aside.

Heat oil in a small skillet over medium-low heat. Add almonds and sesame seeds. Sauté until slightly brown; set aside.

Combine oil, sugar, vinegar, salt, and white pepper in a cruet or jar. Cover tightly and shake vigorously; set aside.

Combine cabbage, scallions, water chestnuts, and pasta in a large bowl. Toss in nut mixture. Toss with dressing just before serving.

Yield: 4 to 6 servings.

Black and White Rice Salad

Parve

1 cup long grain white rice	1½ tablespoons fresh lemon
1 cup wild rice	juice
2 teaspoons dried thyme,	1 cup seedless red grapes,
divided	halved
2 teaspoons dried sage,	1 cup chopped walnuts or
divided	pecans
¼ cup olive or walnut oil	Salt
	Pepper

Combine 1 teaspoon thyme and 1 teaspoon sage with white rice and water and cook according to directions (page 209); cool.

Combine remaining 1 teaspoon thyme and remaining 1 teaspoon sage with wild rice and cook according to directions (page 209); cool.

Combine rices, oil, lemon juice, salt and pepper in a serving bowl. Stir in grapes and chopped nuts just before serving.

Yield: 8 to 10 servings.

CLASSIC FRENCH VINAIGRETTE

Parve

2	tablespoons rice wine vinegar	¾	cup olive oil
2	tablespoons sherry vinegar		Salt
1	tablespoon Dijon mustard		Pepper
1	tablespoon mayonnaise	1	clove garlic, crushed
		2	teaspoons chopped shallot (optional)

Whisk together vinegars, mustard, and mayonnaise in a small bowl. Gradually add oil in a steady stream, whisking until well blended. Season to taste with salt and pepper.

Add garlic and let stand a few hours; discard garlic. Add shallot, if desired. Whisk before serving.

Yield: 1 cup.

BALSAMIC VINAIGRETTE

Parve

2	tablespoons balsamic vinegar	1	shallot, minced
2	tablespoons white wine vinegar	⅔	cup olive oil
2	teaspoons Dijon mustard		Salt
			Pepper

Whisk together vinegars, mustard, and shallot in a small bowl. Gradually add oil in a steady stream, whisking until well blended. Season to taste with salt and pepper.

Yield: 1 cup.

Stuffed Turkey Breast,
page 75

POULTRY

CHICKEN MARSALA

3 boneless chicken breasts, with skin	1 pound mushrooms, thinly sliced
Salt	½ cup Marsala wine
Pepper	1 cup chicken stock
All-purpose flour	(page 39)
1½ tablespoons olive oil	1 tablespoon tomato paste
3½ tablespoons margarine, divided	2 tablespoons cornstarch
1 onion, thinly sliced into rings	¼ cup cold water
	Garnish: minced fresh parsley

Place chicken between 2 sheets of heavy-duty plastic wrap, and flatten to an even thickness using a meat mallet. Sprinkle chicken with salt and pepper. Dredge in flour, shaking off excess.

Heat olive oil and 1½ tablespoons margarine in a heavy skillet over medium-high heat. Add chicken and sauté, turning once, until browned on both sides. Transfer chicken to a plate and set aside.

Drain most, but not all, of the fat from the skillet. Heat skillet over medium-high heat. Add onion and mushrooms; sauté, stirring occasionally, until liquid evaporates.

Add Marsala and sauté until most of liquid evaporates.

Add stock, tomato paste, and reserved chicken, and bring mixture to a boil. Reduce heat, and simmer 15 minutes, turning once, until chicken is cooked through. Transfer chicken to a serving platter. Cover and keep warm.

Continue to simmer mushroom sauce until liquid is reduced to about ½ cup.

Combine cornstarch and cold water, stirring until smooth. Stir into mushroom mixture. Cook over medium heat, stirring constantly, until mixture boils. Boil 1 minute, stirring constantly. Remove from heat and stir in remaining 2 tablespoons margarine. Season with salt and pepper, to taste.

Spoon sauce over chicken and sprinkle with parsley.

Yield: 3 servings.

When this dish has been completed, return the chicken to the skillet. Cut 8 paper-thin slices of lemon and place over chicken. Cover skillet and let stand for 5 minutes. Transfer to a serving platter and sprinkle with chopped parsley.

Stuffed Turkey Breast

As you can see from the photo on this section's cover, this magnificent dish is sure to be the highlight of any dinner table. It is healthier than red meat and simple enough to prepare that it doesn't have to be served on special occasions. A boned turkey breast cooks quickly, makes a beautiful presentation, and is easy to carve. Ask your butcher to help you bone and butterfly it.

½ cup margarine	Freshly ground pepper
½ cup finely chopped celery	¼ cup chicken stock, if necessary
½ cup finely chopped onion	
3 cups fresh white bread crumbs (page 188)	1 (6- to 8- pound) turkey breast, boned and butterflied (must have skin intact)
1 teaspoon dried thyme	
1 teaspoon dried sage	
⅓ cup raisins	Vegetable oil
⅓ cup chopped walnuts	Paprika
½ cup chopped cremini mushrooms	White pepper
	Garlic powder
Salt	Onion powder

Preheat oven to 350°.

Heat margarine in a skillet over medium-high heat. Add celery and onion; sauté 5 minutes or until tender. Transfer to a large bowl.

Add bread crumbs, thyme, sage, raisins, walnuts, and mushrooms; mix well. Season with salt and pepper, to taste. Mixture should be moist, but not wet. Add chicken stock, if necessary.

Place turkey breast, skin side down, on a work surface. You should have two large flaps of meat connected in the center. Sprinkle with salt and pepper; set aside.

Spread the stuffing down the center and over one side of breast, then fold other flap over it. Tie the breast together in 5 or 6 places with heavy kitchen string to make a tight cylindrical roll. Rub with oil and sprinkle with paprika, white pepper, garlic powder, and onion powder. Insert meat thermometer in center of breast, if desired.

Bake for 2 hours, turning twice, or until done. (Temperature should read 170° with meat thermometer or you may cut into meat to make sure it is no longer pink in center.)

Preheat oven to broil with rack 10 inches away from heat.

Broil turkey breast 5 minutes or until skin is browned. Remove strings and cut into slices.

Yield: 8 servings.

Pine Nut Crusted Chicken with Garlic and White Wine

1⅓ cups white wine
4 cloves garlic, chopped
2½ teaspoons salt, divided
½ teaspoon dried savory
½ teaspoon dried rosemary
1 (3½ to 4-pound) chicken, cut into 8 pieces
½ cup dry bread crumbs
4 ounces pine nuts (about ⅔ cup), ground
½ teaspoon paprika

Combine wine, garlic, 2 teaspoons salt, savory, and rosemary in a small bowl. Place half of marinade in a heavy-duty, plastic zip-top bag. Cover and refrigerate remaining marinade until ready to bake chicken. Add chicken to the bag, tossing to coat. Refrigerate 8 hours or overnight.

Preheat oven to 350°.

Combine bread crumbs, pine nuts, paprika, and remaining ½ teaspoon salt.

Remove chicken from marinade, discarding this batch of marinade. Roll chicken in bread crumb mixture and place on a lightly greased baking pan. Drizzle with olive oil.

Bake chicken, covered, 45 minutes. Uncover and pour reserved marinade over chicken. Bake, uncovered, 1 hour or until chicken is done and golden brown.

Yield: 4 servings.

For an informal floral touch at your table, place several teacups filled with small flowers about the table or at each place setting.

Grilled Moroccan Chicken

½ cup extra virgin olive oil
¼ cup chopped scallions (white part only)
¼ cup chopped fresh parsley
¼ cup chopped fresh cilantro
1 tablespoon minced garlic
2 teaspoons paprika
2 teaspoons ground cumin
1 teaspoon salt
¼ teaspoon turmeric
¼ teaspoon cayenne pepper
4 boneless, skinless chicken breasts

Combine oil, scallions, parsley, cilantro, garlic, paprika, cumin, salt, turmeric, and cayenne pepper in the container of a blender or food processor. Process until smooth.

Rub the mixture on both sides of the chicken breasts and let stand 30 minutes.

Preheat grill to medium-hot heat.

Grill chicken breasts 5 to 7 minutes on each side or until done.

Yield: 4 servings.

Round out your menu by serving this dish with Middle Eastern Bean Salad (page 57) and Couscous with Roasted Peppers and Artichokes (page 200).

Enjoy a glass of a full-bodied, spicy red wine such as Zinfandel with this meal.

LEMON CHICKEN AND CAPERS

2 boneless, skinless chicken breasts
½ cup all-purpose flour
½ teaspoon salt
½ teaspoon pepper
2 tablespoons olive oil, divided

2 scallions, chopped
¾ cup chicken stock (page 39)
½ cup dry white wine
1½ tablespoons lemon juice
1 tablespoon capers, drained

Preheat oven to 350°.

Flatten the chicken cutlets. (See sidebar.)

Combine flour, salt, and pepper in a shallow bowl. Dredge chicken breasts in seasoned flour; set aside.

Heat 1 tablespoon oil in a skillet over medium-high heat. Add chicken and sauté 5 to 7 minutes on each side or until done. Transfer chicken to a baking dish; cover and keep warm.

Heat remaining 1 tablespoon oil in a skillet over medium-high heat. Add scallions and sauté until tender. Stir in stock, wine, lemon juice, and capers, scraping bottom of pan to loosen bits. Bring mixture to a boil, reduce heat, and simmer on low heat for 10 minutes. Pour sauce over chicken. Cover and bake 10 minutes.

Yield: 2 servings.

GRILLED CHICKEN BREASTS WITH PEANUT SAUCE

This simple, tasty dish can be part of a delicious menu when served with rice, mushrooms, and broccoli.

½ cup sesame oil
¼ cup soy sauce
¼ cup smooth peanut butter
3 tablespoons dry sherry
2 tablespoons minced garlic

1 teaspoon chili oil or crushed red pepper flakes
4 boneless, skinless chicken breasts

Combine oil, soy sauce, peanut butter, sherry, garlic, and crushed red pepper flakes in a small bowl, whisking until smooth.

Place chicken breasts in a plastic, zip-top bag and add peanut mixture, tossing to coat. Refrigerate 8 hours or overnight.

Preheat grill to medium-hot heat.

Remove chicken breasts from marinade, discarding marinade.

Grill chicken breasts 5 to 7 minutes on each side or until done.

Yield: 4 servings.

Boneless chicken breasts look more elegant and cook quickly when flattened to an even thickness. To avoid tearing the meat, place each breast between sheets of plastic wrap, and pound flat with a meat mallet. Avoid using a notched mallet – this type is generally used to tenderize tough cuts of meat. You can also use the bottom of a skillet or rolling pin.

Serve with a dry, white wine such as Pinot Grigio. Pinot Grigio is an aromatic Italian wine. Its French counterpart is called Pinot Gris.

PESTO STUFFED CHICKEN ROLLS

For an interesting presentation of this dish, cut each roll into diagonal slices and fan out on plate. Place vegetables, cut into disks, such as sliced and steamed zucchini and yellow squash, at the base of the "fan."

6 boneless, skinless chicken breasts	¼ cup pesto (see page 195)
¼ teaspoon salt	½ cup minced red bell pepper
¼ teaspoon freshly ground pepper	¾ cup crushed corn flakes
3 tablespoons margarine, softened	½ teaspoon paprika
	Vegetable cooking spray
	Garnish: fresh basil sprigs

Place chicken between 2 sheets of heavy-duty plastic wrap, and flatten to an even thickness using a meat mallet. Sprinkle with salt and pepper.

Combine margarine, pesto, and bell pepper, stirring until smooth. Spread 2 tablespoons across each chicken breast. Roll up lengthwise, securing with a toothpick.

Combine corn flakes and paprika in a shallow bowl. Dredge chicken in crumb mixture and place in a baking dish coated with cooking spray. Cover and refrigerate 6 to 8 hours.

Preheat oven to 350°. Remove chicken from refrigerator; bring to room temperature.

Bake, uncovered, for 35 minutes. Let stand 10 minutes. Remove toothpicks and slice into 1-inch pieces. Garnish with fresh basil.

Yield: 6 servings.

GRILLED DIJON CORNISH GAME HENS

For a simple and elegant way to present this recipe, arrange the hen halves around the rim of a round platter with the wings on the inside and the legs on the outside, spoke fashion. Place mesclun or gourmet salad greens in the center for added color.

2 (1-pound) Cornish game hens	1½ tablespoons olive oil
2 tablespoons Dijon mustard	1 tablespoon balsamic vinegar
	1 clove garlic, minced

Preheat oven to broil with rack 6 to 8 inches from heat.

For each hen, carefully cut along both sides of backbone and remove, using poultry or kitchen shears. Press hens flat.

Combine mustard, oil, vinegar, and garlic in a small bowl. Brush half of mustard mixture on both sides of meat. Place hens, skin side down, on a broiler pan.

Broil 10 minutes (with electric oven door partially open). Turn hens over and brush with remaining mustard mixture. Broil 5 to 10 minutes or until meat is no longer pink and skin is golden brown.

Yield: 2 servings.

HERBED BAKED CHICKEN

1 cup all-purpose flour
1 teaspoon salt
1 teaspoon pepper
4 teaspoons chopped fresh
 or dried tarragon,
 divided
4 teaspoons chopped fresh
 or dried chives, divided
4 teaspoons chopped fresh
 parsley, divided
2 (3-pound) chickens,
 quartered
½ cup margarine
½ cup dry sherry
¼ cup fresh lemon juice
 Paprika

Preheat oven to 375°.

Combine flour, salt, pepper, 2 teaspoons tarragon, 2 teaspoons chives, and 2 teaspoons parsley in a large, plastic zip-top bag. Add chicken, a few pieces at a time, tossing to coat. Place chicken, skin side up, in a large roasting pan.

Combine margarine, sherry, lemon juice and remaining herbs in a small saucepan. Cook over medium heat, stirring until well blended. Pour over chicken.

Bake chicken 1 hour, covered with foil. Uncover and sprinkle with paprika. Bake 20 minutes, uncovered, or until chicken is done and lightly browned. Add sherry or water to the pan, if necessary, to make sure there is enough sauce to serve.

Yield: 8 servings.

TURKEY ROAST

1 (3- to 4-pound) boneless
 turkey breast with skin,
 tied in a roll
1 cup firmly packed dark
 brown sugar
1 cup ketchup
¾ cup water
¼ cup oil
3 tablespoons balsamic
 vinegar
3 tablespoons soy sauce
1 small onion, diced

Preheat oven to 450°.

Place turkey breast in a roasting pan. Insert meat thermometer in center of meat, if desired.

Combine sugar, ketchup, water, oil, vinegar, soy sauce, and onion; pour over turkey.

Bake, covered, for 1 hour. Reduce oven temperature to 350° and bake, uncovered, for 30 to 40 minutes or until done. (Temperature should read 170° with meat thermometer or you may cut into meat to make sure it is no longer pink in center.)

Yield: 6 to 8 servings.

Herb-Dusted Plates

You can easily liven up any meal by decorating the plate with herbs and spices that complement the food.

Select spices such as chili powder, ground cumin, paprika, or pepper. Prepare finely chopped herbs such as basil, chives, mint, parsley, or rosemary. Use a mini-food processor to mince the herbs, if desired.

Lightly and evenly coat the rim of each plate with margarine. Sprinkle or sift the herbs and spices around the edge of the plate. Use a dry paper towel to clean off excess from inside of plate to give a finished appearance.

Sun-Dried Tomato and Scallion Stuffed Chicken Breast

8 whole, boneless chicken breasts, skin intact
8 teaspoons Dijon mustard
8 scallions, white part only
16 whole sun-dried tomatoes, packed in oil
Paprika
Salt
Freshly ground pepper

Preheat oven to 350°.

Place chicken breasts on a work surface, skin side down, with center of breasts running vertically. Spread 1 teaspoon of mustard on bone side of breast. Place 1 scallion and 2 sun-dried tomatoes in the center.

Roll the breast so the scallion is sticking out of both ends. Secure with toothpicks if necessary. Place each breast, seam side down, in a lightly greased shallow roasting pan. Repeat with remaining ingredients.

Sprinkle chicken with paprika, salt, and pepper.

Bake for 50 to 55 minutes, or until breasts are done and golden brown.

Yield: 8 servings.

FORTY CLOVE GARLIC CHICKEN

"*I was not married for more than a month when I invited my in-laws over for a special dinner. I knew my father-in-law loved roasted garlic, so when I came across this recipe, I knew it was the one for that special night.*

The original recipe did not state if the garlic should be peeled or unpeeled. Since my mom's garlic came minced in jars, proficiency with fresh vegetables did not come easily to me. I marched down to the grocery store and proceeded to purchase 40 heads of garlic. About 200 cloves into this culinary adventure, my husband and sous-chef asked if I was sure I had read the recipe correctly. I responded, 'Of course I'm sure — quit asking questions and keep peeling!' Needless to say, it was quite the spicy dish. After shoveling through the garlic cloves to get to the chicken, my darling father-in-law remarked what a great meal it was."

1 (3½- to 4-pound) chicken, quartered or cut into 8 pieces	40 cloves garlic, unpeeled
¼-½ teaspoon freshly ground pepper	3 tablespoons balsamic vinegar
¼-½ teaspoon paprika	Garnish: 3 to 4 sprigs fresh rosemary

Preheat oven to 375°.

Place chicken in bottom of a baking dish. Sprinkle with pepper and paprika.

Place garlic around and on top of chicken. Sprinkle chicken and garlic with vinegar.

Bake, uncovered and basting occasionally, for 1½ to 2 hours or until chicken is done. Place chicken on serving platter, reserving pan juices.

Remove several garlic cloves for garnish. Press remaining garlic in a sieve or colander using the back of a large spoon. Discard peels.

Add several teaspoons of the garlic purée to the juices in the pan, stirring well. Spoon sauce over chicken. Garnish the plate with the reserved garlic cloves and rosemary. Serve any extra garlic purée with toasted French bread.

Yield: 4 servings.

 Don't overwhelm simple, aromatic entrées with complicated side dishes. Your guests will be delighted with a side of Creamy Mashed Potatoes (page 192).

CARAMELIZED CHICKEN WITH ALMONDS

2 (3-pound) chickens, cut
   into 8 pieces
   Paprika
   Garlic powder
6 tablespoons margarine
3 onions, sliced into rings

2 cups firmly packed light
   brown sugar
3 tablespoons soy sauce
   Blanched almonds,
   toasted (optional)

Preheat oven to broil with rack 8 to 10 inches from heat.

Place chicken pieces, skin side up, in a broiling pan and sprinkle with paprika and garlic powder.

Broil 7 minutes (with electric oven door partially open) until golden brown. Transfer chicken to an ovenproof serving dish.

Preheat oven to bake at 350°.

Heat margarine in a saucepan over medium heat. Add onion and sauté 15 minutes or until translucent. Reduce heat to low; add brown sugar and soy sauce, stirring until sugar dissolves.

Spoon sauce over chicken. Cover with foil and bake 1 hour or until chicken is done. Sprinkle with toasted almonds.

Yield: 6 to 8 servings.

PEKING CHICKEN

2-3 tablespoons oil
1½ pounds boneless, skinless
   chicken breasts, thinly
   sliced
1 pound mushrooms, sliced
2 tablespoons soy sauce
1 tablespoon peeled and
   minced fresh ginger

   Hoisin sauce, divided
   Freshly ground pepper
1 tablespoon sesame oil
¼ cup chopped scallions
8 (10-inch) flour tortillas
1½ cups seedless cucumber,
   cut into thin strips

Heat oil in a large skillet over medium-high heat. Add chicken and mushrooms; sauté 1 to 2 minutes.

Add soy sauce, ginger, and 1 tablespoon hoisin sauce; sauté 5 to 7 minutes or until chicken is done. Season with pepper, to taste.

Stir in sesame oil and scallions. Remove from heat; set aside.

Spread tortillas with hoisin sauce. Top evenly with cucumbers and chicken mixture. (Do not overfill or tortillas will not wrap tightly.)

Wrap the tortillas starting from the bottom, folding in the sides as you wrap.

Yield: 6 to 8 servings.

Whole Roasted Chicken with Herbs and Wine

1 small onion, finely
    chopped
1 carrot, peeled and finely
    chopped
1 stalk celery, finely
    chopped
3 tablespoons olive oil,
    divided
6 cloves garlic
6 sprigs fresh rosemary

1 (4- to 5-pound) chicken
    Salt
    Pepper
    Paprika
    Garlic powder
1½ cups dry red wine
1 tablespoon margarine,
    softened
1 tablespoon all-purpose
    flour

Preheat oven to 400°.

Place onion, carrot, and celery in the bottom of a large roasting pan and drizzle with 2 tablespoons olive oil.

Dry chicken well with paper towels. Place garlic and rosemary in the cavity of the chicken. Place chicken, breast side down, on top of the vegetables and rub with remaining 1 tablespoon oil. Sprinkle with salt, pepper, paprika, and garlic powder.

Bake chicken and vegetables for 30 minutes. Turn chicken, breast side up, being careful not to tear skin. Bake for 1 hour, basting occasionally with pan juices.

Pour ¾ cup wine over the chicken. Increase temperature to 425°. Bake 15 minutes or until golden brown. Chicken will be done when juices run clear when pierced with fork. Transfer chicken to a serving platter. Cover and keep warm.

Strain liquid from roasting pan into a heavy saucepan. Add remaining ¾ cup wine and bring to a boil for 1 minute.

Combine margarine and flour; whisk into sauce. Bring mixture to a boil, reduce heat, and simmer 3 to 4 minutes or until thickened and bubbly. Serve sauce on the side.

Yield: 4 to 6 servings.

To add more flavor to a baked or roasted chicken dish, prepare a marinade rub called "Aglione."

Aglione
Parve

2 tablespoons olive oil

1 tablespoon chopped
    fresh rosemary

1 clove garlic, coarsely
    chopped

1 teaspoon kosher salt

Combine oil, fresh rosemary, garlic, and salt. Rub this mixture all over the chicken, both inside and out. Cover and refrigerate overnight.

When you are ready to prepare the recipe, remove large pieces of garlic and rosemary and proceed.

Yield: about ¼ cup.

Always cook with a wine you would like to drink- not cooking wine. Serve the same wine at the table that you used to prepare the dish.

CHICKEN IN BEER AND MUSTARD

¼ cup olive oil, divided
1 (3-pound) chicken, cut into 8 pieces
½ cup chopped onion
½ cup chopped celery
2 cloves garlic, minced
2 teaspoons chopped fresh rosemary
2 teaspoons all-purpose flour
½ cup beer
½ cup chicken stock (page 39)
¼ cup whole grain mustard
Salt
Freshly ground pepper
¼ cup chopped fresh parsley, divided
Garnish: fresh rosemary sprigs

Heat 2 tablespoons oil in a large skillet over medium-high heat. Add chicken and sauté until browned on all sides. (Be sure skillet is large enough to hold chicken in a single layer. If not, sauté the chicken in batches so it browns instead of steams.) Remove chicken and set aside.

Pour off used oil from skillet and heat remaining 2 tablespoons oil over medium heat. Add onion and celery; sauté until tender.

Whisk in garlic, rosemary, and flour. Cook 1 minute, stirring constantly. Gradually add beer and stock; cook over medium heat, whisking constantly, until mixture is thickened and bubbly.

Add chicken pieces and sprinkle with salt and pepper. Cover and simmer over low heat, turning once, for 40 minutes or until chicken is done. Remove chicken from skillet and set aside.

Stir mustard into skillet mixture. Season with salt and pepper, to taste. Return chicken to skillet and sprinkle with 2 tablespoons parsley. Baste chicken with sauce and reheat, if necessary.

Transfer chicken and sauce to a serving platter and sprinkle with remaining 2 tablespoons parsley. Garnish with fresh rosemary, if desired.

Yield: 4 servings.

CHICKEN STRUDEL

¾ cup extra virgin olive oil,
    divided

4-6 boneless, skinless chicken
    breasts

2 large portobello
    mushrooms, cut into
    strips

2 tablespoons chopped
    shallots

3 tablespoons chopped fresh
    basil, divided

1 tablespoon chopped fresh
    parsley

8 sheets phyllo dough,
    thawed

    Melted margarine

3 tablespoons white vinegar

4 cloves garlic, chopped

3 tablespoons seeded and
    chopped tomato

Heat 2 tablespoons oil in a large skillet over medium-high heat. Add chicken and sauté 5 minutes on each side. Remove from skillet and cut into thin strips.

Heat 2 tablespoons oil in the skillet over medium-high heat. Add mushrooms and sauté 5 minutes. Add shallots; sauté for 2 minutes. Add 1 tablespoon basil and sauté 1 minute. Remove from heat and drain excess liquid. Stir in chicken and set aside.

Preheat oven to 375°.

Place one phyllo sheet lengthwise on a flat work surface and brush with melted margarine. Repeat with remaining 7 sheets of phyllo. (Cover unused phyllo dough with plastic wrap, then a damp towel to prevent drying.)

Spoon chicken mixture lengthwise across pastry in a 4-inch strip leaving a 2-inch border on the sides and a 3-inch border on the bottom.

Carefully fold the sides over the filling. Fold the bottom over the filling and roll up, jelly roll fashion.

Place the strudel, seam side down, on a lightly greased baking sheet. Brush with melted margarine. Strudel may be prepared 6 hours ahead. Cover and refrigerate until ready to bake.

Bake strudel for 20 to 25 minutes or until golden brown.

Combine vinegar and garlic in a small saucepan over medium-high heat. Bring to a boil, reduce heat, and gradually whisk in remaining oil. Remove from heat and stir in tomato and remaining 2 tablespoons basil. Spoon sauce over strudel just before serving.

Yield: 10 to 12 servings.

PLUM CHICKEN

1 (16-ounce) can purple
    plums, undrained
¼ cup olive oil or
    margarine
3 tablespoons minced
    onion
3 cloves garlic, minced
¼ cup sugar
¼ cup lemon juice

2 tablespoons chili sauce
2 (3-pound) broiler
    chickens, cut into
    8 pieces
2 oranges
    Paprika
    Garnish: orange slices,
    reserved plums

Remove pits from plums and place in a medium bowl with liquid, reserving 4 or 5 for garnish. Mash plums with a fork; set aside.

Heat oil in a skillet over medium-high heat. Add onion and sauté until lightly browned. Add garlic, and sauté for 30 seconds. Reduce heat to low and stir in plums and liquid.

Add sugar, lemon juice, and chili sauce; cook over low heat for 30 minutes.

Preheat oven to 350°.

Place chicken in a large roasting pan. Squeeze the juice of two oranges over chicken. Sprinkle with paprika and rub into skin.

Pour plum sauce over chicken and bake 1¼ hours, basting often. Garnish with orange slices and reserved plums.

Yield: 6 to 8 servings.

Scallion Curls

Garnish with scallion curls. Trim off the roots and remove any tough outer leaves. With a sharp knife, make several cuts down the length of the scallion almost to root end. Rotate the scallion a quarter turn and make several more thin cuts. Place scallions in ice water until curled.

CHICKEN À L'ORANGE

2-3½ pounds chicken pieces or
    1 whole chicken, cut
    into pieces
    Vegetable cooking spray
    Salt
    Pepper
1 carrot, thickly sliced
1 stalk celery, thickly sliced
1 onion, quartered
1 large orange
½ cup dry white wine
¼ cup orange liqueur or
    orange juice

¼ cup honey
1 tablespoon light soy sauce
1 tablespoon dark soy sauce
¼ teaspoon ground ginger
3 tablespoons margarine
3 tablespoons all-purpose
    flour
2-2½ cups reserved chicken
    cooking liquid or broth
    Garnishes: orange slices,
    fresh herbs
    Saffron Rice (page 208)

Preheat oven to 375°.

Place chicken pieces in a large baking pan lightly coated with cooking spray. Sprinkle chicken with salt and pepper. Place carrot, celery, and onion in the pan with the chicken.

Bake, covered, for 35 to 40 minutes.

Grate 2 tablespoons rind from orange; set aside. Cut orange in half and squeeze juice into a small bowl. Add wine, orange liqueur, honey, soy sauces, and ginger.

Remove chicken from oven and pour orange juice mixture over chicken and vegetables. Bake 30 minutes. Place chicken on a platter; set aside. Remove fat from cooking liquid and pour into a 2 to 2½ cup-measuring cup; set aside.

Heat margarine in a large skillet over medium heat until melted; add flour, whisking until smooth. Cook 1 minute, whisking constantly. Gradually add reserved liquid or broth; cook over medium heat, whisking constantly, until mixture is thickened and bubbly. Strain sauce through a sieve or cheesecloth-lined colander, discarding solids.

Pour sauce into a large skillet and stir in grated orange rind. Add chicken pieces and cook over medium heat for 5 minutes until thoroughly heated. Garnish with orange slices and fresh herbs. Serve with Saffron Rice.

Yield: 4 servings.

HONEY-SOY CHICKEN WINGS

These wings are great for so many occasions—Super Bowl parties, cocktail parties, and barbecues. Just make sure there are lots of napkins around for this sticky finger food.

1 cup chopped scallions	2 tablespoons white vinegar
½ cup soy sauce	1 tablespoon Dijon mustard
½ cup hoisin sauce	⅛ teaspoon cayenne pepper
2 tablespoons sesame oil	4 cloves garlic, minced
3 tablespoons honey	20 whole chicken wings,
2 tablespoons peeled and	thoroughly cleaned
chopped fresh ginger	

Combine scallions, soy sauce, hoisin, sesame oil, honey, ginger, vinegar, mustard, cayenne pepper, and garlic in a large bowl. Add wings, tossing to coat. Cover and refrigerate up to 1 day.

Preheat oven to 375°.

Remove wings from marinade, discarding marinade. Arrange wings in a single layer on baking sheets.

Bake 15 minutes; turn, baste and bake 15 minutes.

Increase temperature to 450° and bake for 15 minutes or until crispy and browned.

Remake the marinade and pour into a saucepan. Bring mixture to a boil; boil 4 to 5 minutes or until slightly thickened. Pour into a serving bowl and use as a dipping sauce.

Yield: 3 to 4 servings.

Honey can be messy to measure. If your recipe calls for oil, measure that ingredient first and the honey will slide right off the measuring spoon.

Oven Fried Sesame Chicken

6 tablespoons sesame seeds
4 tablespoons all-purpose
     flour
½ teaspoon pepper
¼ cup low-sodium soy sauce

4 bone-in chicken breasts,
     skin removed
¼ cup margarine, melted or
     olive oil

Preheat oven to 400°.

Combine sesame seeds, flour, and pepper in a shallow bowl. Dip chicken in soy sauce; dredge in sesame seed mixture.

Arrange chicken, bone side down, in a large, shallow baking dish; drizzle with margarine.

Bake for 40 to 45 minutes or until chicken is done.

Yield: 4 servings.

Chicken and Broccoli Stir-Fry

¼ cup chicken broth
3 tablespoons soy sauce
2 tablespoons sherry
1 tablespoon cornstarch
4 boneless, skinless chicken
     breasts, cut into ½-inch
     wide strips
   Salt
   Pepper

2 tablespoons vegetable oil
2 cloves garlic, chopped
1 tablespoon peeled and
     chopped fresh ginger
2 cups broccoli florets
1 red bell pepper, thinly
     sliced
1 onion, thinly sliced
   Pinch red pepper flakes

Combine broth, soy sauce, sherry, and cornstarch in a small bowl, whisking until smooth; set aside.

Sprinkle chicken with salt and pepper; set aside.

Heat oil in a wok or large skillet over high heat. Add garlic and ginger; stir-fry 30 seconds. Add chicken; stir-fry 2 minutes.

Add broccoli, bell pepper, onion, and pepper flakes; stir-fry 5 minutes or until vegetables are crisp-tender and chicken is cooked through.

Add broth mixture and bring to a boil. Boil 1 minute, stirring constantly until thickened and bubbly.

Yield: 4 servings.

To prepare your entire meal in a healthful way, serve this dish with steamed bok choy seasoned with garlic, ginger, and scallions. Or, try Oriental Cole Slaw (page 54).

CHICKEN MARBELLA

1 cup pitted prunes
½ cup pitted green olives
½ cup capers with
   3 teaspoons liquid
¼ cup chopped fresh
   oregano
½ cup red wine vinegar
½ cup olive oil
1 head garlic, minced
   Kosher salt

Pepper
1 (3½- to 4-pound)
   chicken, cut into
   8 pieces
1 cup firmly packed dark
   brown sugar
1 cup white wine
½ cup chopped fresh Italian
   parsley

Combine prunes, olives, capers, liquid, oregano, vinegar, olive oil, and garlic in a large, shallow, ovenproof dish. Season with salt and pepper, to taste.

Add chicken, tossing to coat. Cover and refrigerate 8 hours or overnight.

Preheat oven to 350°.

Uncover chicken and sprinkle with brown sugar. Pour wine over chicken and bake 1 hour, covered.

Uncover chicken and bake 30 minutes or until golden browned. (Broil for 5 minutes if skin is not browned.)

Yield: 4 servings.

As an accompaniment, serve this dish with French Fried Orzo (page 208) and Sangría Punch (recipe follows).

Sangria Punch
Parve

1 (6-ounce) can peach
   nectar

1 (6-ounce) can apricot
   nectar

1 (750 ml) bottle red
   wine

½ cup rum or Triple Sec

1 cup sliced oranges

1 cup sliced apples

Combine nectars, wine, and rum in a large pitcher. Stir in oranges and apples. Salud!

Yield: 7 cups

Chicken and Vinegar

1 (3-pound) chicken, cut
  into 8 pieces
Salt
Pepper
All-purpose flour
¼ cup olive oil, divided
½ cup chopped shallots
2 medium carrots, peeled
  and finely chopped
1 tablespoon garlic

1½ cups low-sodium chicken
  broth or chicken stock
  (page 39)
⅓ cup sherry vinegar or red
  wine vinegar
1 teaspoon tomato paste
1 bay leaf
1 tomato, peeled, seeded,
  and chopped

Wash and pat chicken dry. Season with salt and pepper; dredge in flour, shaking off excess.

Heat 2 tablespoons oil in a large skillet over medium-high heat. Add chicken; sauté until browned on all sides. Remove from skillet and set aside. Drain oil from skillet.

Heat remaining 2 tablespoons oil in skillet over medium heat. Add shallots and carrots; sauté until tender. Add garlic and sauté until fragrant.

Stir in broth, vinegar, tomato paste, and bay leaf. Add chicken pieces except for breasts. Bring mixture to a boil, reduce heat, and simmer, covered, for 10 minutes. Add breasts and simmer, covered, 20 minutes. Remove chicken; cover and keep warm.

Add chopped tomato to skillet. Cook over medium-high heat until sauce thickens enough to coat chicken. Remove bay leaf and adjust seasonings. Stir chicken into sauce and serve.

Yield: 4 servings.

ROASTED DUCK WITH RASPBERRY SAUCE AND WILD RICE PANCAKES

"*My husband reminds me often that at our wedding, he ate the most incredible Roasted Duck and Raspberry Sauce. He has nudged me over the years to find a recipe and to make it. Like many people, I was afraid of making duck because of its bad reputation for being difficult to handle. When we got the solicitation for recipes for this cookbook, right around our anniversary I might add, I became inspired to reproduce this wedding meal. I went to work and became an expert on cooking duck. Below is the solution to the duck problem— a fabulous rendition of our wedding dinner.*

Included are easy steps that will help with the release of fat and help to give a deep, rich color and nice, crisp skin. The process is very simple, it just requires some advanced planning since you need to have ample time to defrost the duck if it has been frozen and then an extra day to leave it on the rack to circulate the air to drip off some of the fat. Just like a marriage, this recipe takes a little thought and time, but the rewards are great."

1 (4- to 5-pound) fresh duck or frozen and thawed	Salt
	Raspberry Marinade
	Raspberry Sauce
2 lemons, halved	Garnish: fresh raspberries

Rinse inside of duck and drain. Place duck in a large soup pot and fill with water to 2 inches above duck. Bring to a boil over high heat; boil 3 minutes. Drain. (Briefly poaching the duck will release some of the fat and makes it easier to clean.)

Remove any feathers and cut excess skin around neck with poultry shears. Place duck on a broiling rack in a disposable pan or broiling pan covered with foil. Refrigerate, uncovered, 1 day.

Preheat oven to 350°.

Remove duck from refrigerator and discard any fat that has dripped off duck into the pan.

Place lemons inside cavity and sprinkle duck with salt. Place duck on broiling rack. Pierce skin all over, taking care not to cut into the meat. (This will allow excess fat to run out from under skin during roasting.) Brush duck with Raspberry Marinade.

Bake, uncovered, for 1½ hours, basting every 15 to 20 minutes.

Increase temperature to 450° and bake 30 minutes. Remove duck and place on carving board. (Do not cover in order to retain crispness.)

ROASTED DUCK (continued)

Carefully cut along both sides of backbone using poultry or kitchen shears and remove backbone. Cut duck into quarters and arrange on a platter. Spoon Raspberry Sauce over the duck. Garnish with fresh raspberries.

Yield: 4 servings.

RASPBERRY MARINADE:

1 tablespoon olive oil
2 cloves garlic, minced
½ cup Cabernet Sauvignon
    or red wine
½ cup seedless raspberry jam
2 cups chicken stock
    (page 39) or bouillon
    Pepper

Heat oil in a small saucepan over medium heat. Add garlic and sauté 1 minute.

Add wine and bring to a boil for 10 minutes until reduced by half. Stir in preserves and chicken stock. Cook 15 minutes until mixture is reduced by one-third. Add pepper to taste.

Yield: 1½ cups.

RASPBERRY SAUCE:

2 tablespoons margarine
5 tablespoons sugar, divided
⅓ cup dry white wine
⅓ cup orange juice
2 tablespoons raspberry
    vinegar
1¼ cups frozen raspberries,
    thawed
1 cup beef stock or bouillon
½ cup chicken stock
    (page 39) or bouillon
½ cup seedless red raspberry
    preserves

Heat margarine in a saucepan over medium-high heat. Add 3 tablespoons sugar and cook for 5 minutes, stirring constantly, or until sugar turns a deep amber color.

Stir in wine, orange juice, and vinegar (mixture will bubble vigorously). Bring to a boil, stirring to dissolve caramelized sugar.

Add raspberries, beef stock, chicken stock, preserves and remaining 2 tablespoons sugar; bring to a boil. Reduce heat and simmer, stirring occasionally, for 25 minutes or until sauce thickens and is reduced to about 1 cup. Strain sauce through a sieve or wire mesh colander, pressing berries with the back of a spoon.

Yield: 1 cup.

Partner this gourmet dish with steamed green beans and Wild Rice Pancakes. Your family will think you spent a week at a culinary school. The pancakes may be made ahead of time and reheated.

WILD RICE PANCAKES
Parve

1½ cups all-purpose
    flour

4 teaspoons baking
    powder

2 teaspoons sugar

1 teaspoon salt

½ teaspoon pepper

2 cups non-dairy
    creamer

¼ cup margarine, melted

2 large eggs, lightly
    beaten

2 cups cooked wild rice
    (page 209)

Combine flour, baking powder, sugar, salt, and pepper in a large bowl.

Combine creamer, margarine, and eggs. Add to flour mixture, whisking until smooth. Stir in rice.

Pour about ¼ cup batter for each pancake onto a hot, lightly greased skillet. Cook pancakes until tops are covered with bubbles and edges are lightly browned; turn and cook other side.

Yield: 1½ dozen.

CRUNCHY CHICKEN CAESAR

1 tablespoon Dijon mustard	½ teaspoon pepper
1 tablespoon reduced-fat mayonnaise	½ cup crushed corn flakes
4 boneless, skinless chicken breasts	2 teaspoons olive oil
½ teaspoon salt	1 head romaine lettuce, torn into pieces
	Caesar Dressing

Preheat oven to 400°.

Combine mustard and mayonnaise in a small bowl; set aside.

Place chicken between 2 sheets of heavy-duty plastic wrap, and flatten to an even thickness using a meat mallet. Sprinkle with salt and pepper; brush with mustard mixture.

Cover chicken with corn flakes and place on a lightly greased baking sheet. Drizzle each piece of chicken with ½ teaspoon oil.

Bake for 5 to 10 minutes on each side or until chicken is done. Cut chicken into strips.

Combine chicken, lettuce, and dressing in a large bowl, tossing well.

Yield: 4 servings.

CAESAR DRESSING:

1 clove garlic	1 teaspoon steak sauce or Worcestershire sauce (see note on page 112)
1 lemon	
2 tablespoons olive oil	
⅓ cup chicken broth	½ teaspoon coarsely ground pepper
2 teaspoons Dijon mustard	

Mash garlic in a wooden salad bowl with a spoon. Cut lemon in half and squeeze juice into bowl, mixing with garlic.

Whisk in olive oil. Add broth, mustard, steak sauce, and pepper; whisk until well blended.

Yield: ½ cup.

An eye-catching way to present this dish is to toss the romaine with the dressing and place in the center of a large serving plate. Slice the chicken into 1-inch strips and place in the center of the greens. Sprinkle with croutons. Decorate the rim with halved or quartered yellow and red cherry tomatoes.

FIESTA CHICKEN

*T*his chicken dish can be the centerpiece to a Mexican theme dinner. With Best Ever Guacamole (page 34) and a batch of margaritas, you'll really feel like you're south of the border!

¾	pound boneless, skinless chicken breasts	1	tablespoon fresh lime juice
2	medium cloves garlic, pressed	1	teaspoon olive oil
½	teaspoon dried oregano		Salt
¼	cup fresh orange juice		Pepper
			Fiesta Salsa

Place chicken between 2 sheets of heavy-duty plastic wrap, and flatten to an even ¼-inch thickness using a meat mallet. Rub chicken with garlic. Crush oregano between fingers and rub into chicken.

Combine orange juice and lime juice in a large, shallow container. Add chicken; cover and marinate 20 minutes.

Remove chicken from marinade, discarding marinade. Pat dry with paper towels.

Heat oil in a large skillet over medium-high heat. Add chicken and sauté 4 to 6 minutes on each side or until browned.

Sprinkle chicken with salt and pepper and serve with Fiesta Salsa.

Yield: 4 servings.

FIESTA SALSA:

1½	teaspoons fresh lime juice	¼	cup canned water chestnuts, diced
1	teaspoon olive oil	1	tablespoon diced red onion
1	small peach or mango, diced		Pinch red pepper flakes
½	tomato, diced		
½	cup diced, ripe avocado		

Combine juice and oil in a medium bowl. Add peach, tomato, avocado, water chestnuts, onion, and pepper flakes. Mix well.

Yield: 2 cups.

MARGARITAS
Parve

Juice of 3 limes

Coarse salt

2 jiggers tequila

1 jigger Triple Sec or Cointreau

2 tablespoons sugar

2 cups crushed ice

Run lime wedge along rim of 4 martini glasses and dip in coarse salt.

Fill a cocktail shaker with juice, liquors, sugar and ice. Shake vigorously for 1 minute. Let stand 1 minute, shake, and pour into prepared glasses.

Yield: 4 servings.

GOLDEN ROASTED TURKEY

1	head garlic, peeled and crushed	3	tablespoons oil
3	tablespoons paprika	3	tablespoons orange juice
1	tablespoon coarse salt	3	tablespoons lemon juice
1	teaspoon dried basil or 4 fresh leaves	1	teaspoon vinegar
		½	cup white wine
1	teaspoon dried rosemary	1	(10- to 12-pound) turkey
1	teaspoon pepper	6-8	stalks celery
		½	lemon
			Perfect Turkey Gravy

Combine garlic, paprika, salt, basil, rosemary, pepper, oil, orange juice, lemon juice, vinegar, and wine in the container of a food processor fitted with knife blade. Process until well blended.

Stuff turkey with celery and lemon. Brush garlic mixture over turkey and inside cavity. Cover and marinate in the refrigerator 8 hours or overnight.

Preheat oven to 325°.

Place turkey, breast side down, in a large roasting pan. Let turkey stand and come to room temperature. Bake for 1½ hours, basting every 20 minutes, or until skin is golden on top.

Turn turkey, breast side up, being careful not to prick skin. Bake 1½ to 2 hours or until turkey is done. Turkey is done when juices run clear when pierced with fork.

Place turkey on serving platter, reserving liquid for gravy recipe.

Yield: 12 to 15 servings.

When setting your Thanksgiving or Sukkoth table, take advantage of nature's bounty with a palette of warm colors. Collect leaves from your yard and use them to complement your floral arrangements.

To duplicate the photo, place a piece of chicken wire into the opening of a large round vase to support the flowers and leaves. Arrange 1 to 2 dozen roses (thorns removed) by placing stems through the openings of the wire. Add fall berry branches, such as bittersweet berries, and colorful, autumn leaves around the mouth of the vase.

PERFECT TURKEY GRAVY:

Pan drippings from
  Golden Roasted Turkey
2 tablespoons oil
½ pound sliced mushrooms
4 tablespoons all-purpose
  flour

1 beef flavored bouillon cube
2 cups water
Salt
Pepper
Paprika
Garlic salt

Strain pan drippings from roasting pan, reserving ½ cup liquid and set aside.

Heat oil in a saucepan over medium-high heat. Add mushrooms and sauté 3 minutes.

Add flour and bouillon, whisking until smooth. Cook 2 minutes or until mixture is lightly browned. Gradually add reserved pan drippings and water; cook over medium heat, whisking constantly, until mixture is thickened and bubbly. Season with salt, pepper, paprika, and garlic salt, to taste.

Yield: 3¾ cup.

Turkey is considered cooked when it reaches an internal temperature of 180°. The general rule is to cook a whole defrosted turkey for 25 minutes per pound at 325°. If you don't have a meat thermometer, make a discreet cut between the thigh and the back, checking to see that all of the juices run clear.

PARVE CORN BREAD

2 cups yellow cornmeal
2 tablespoons sugar
1 tablespoon baking
  powder

1 teaspoon salt
1 large egg
1 cup water
¼ cup vegetable oil

Preheat oven to 425°.

Combine cornmeal, sugar, baking powder, and salt in a large bowl.

Beat egg, water, and oil. Stir into cornmeal mixture. Pour into a lightly greased 8- x 8-inch baking pan.

Bake for 20 to 25 minutes or until golden brown.

Yield: 8 to 12 servings.

CHICKEN QUEEN VICTORIA

This regal dish is worthy of its name. The golden pastry packets surround the chicken, hiding a treasure of ground veal and sautéed mushrooms. The Cherry Sauce adds a crowning touch.

2	tablespoons oil	8	boneless, skinless chicken breasts
8	ounces mushrooms, sliced		
¾	pound ground veal	1	(16-ounce) package puff pastry squares (4- x 4-inch), thawed
2	large eggs, lightly beaten		
½	teaspoon onion powder		
2	tablespoons seasoned dry bread crumbs		Cherry Sauce

Heat oil in a skillet over medium-high heat. Add mushrooms and sauté 7 to 10 minutes or until tender; drain.

Combine mushrooms with veal in a large bowl. Stir in eggs, onion powder, and bread crumbs; set aside.

Preheat oven to 450°.

Place chicken between 2 sheets of heavy-duty plastic wrap, and flatten to an even thickness using a meat mallet. Spoon 1 to 2 tablespoons of veal mixture across the middle of each breast and roll.

Place the chicken roll, seam side down, on a pastry square. If pastry squares are unavailable, cut puff pastry sheets large enough to cover chicken roll. Wrap the pastry around the chicken, folding and pinching the edges to form a rectangular packet. Repeat with remaining ingredients.

Place chicken packets, seam side down, on a lightly greased baking sheet.

Bake 10 minutes. Reduce heat to 325° and bake for 50 to 55 minutes until golden brown.

Spoon with Cherry Sauce immediately before serving.

Yield: 8 servings.

CHERRY SAUCE:

1 (17-ounce) can sweet,
  dark pitted cherries
  Cold water
2 tablespoons sugar

1 tablespoon cornstarch
  dissolved in 1 tablespoon
  water

Drain liquid from the cherries into a measuring cup and add enough water to make 1 cup. Reserve cherries.

Combine the cherry liquid, sugar, and dissolved cornstarch in a small saucepan over medium heat, whisking until smooth. Bring mixture to a boil; boil 1 minute or until thickened and bubbly. Stir in reserved cherries.

Yield: 2 cups.

TARRAGON ROASTED CHICKEN

1 (3½- to 4-pound) chicken
1 onion, quartered
1 lemon, quartered
4 sprigs fresh tarragon

1 tablespoon margarine,
  softened
Kosher salt
Freshly ground pepper

Preheat oven to 400°.

Wash chicken and pat dry very well. Place chicken, breast side down, on a rack in a large roasting pan. The rack keeps the chicken above the juices so skin will stay crisp. Place onion, lemon, and tarragon in cavity. Rub margarine over chicken and sprinkle with salt and pepper.

Bake for 30 minutes.

Turn chicken, breast side up, being careful not to prick skin or juice will run out. Bake 1 hour and 15 minutes or until done. Shield chicken with foil, if necessary, to prevent overcooking.

Yield: 4 servings.

WORLD'S FAIR CHICKEN

"*When we did our taste testing, we hesitated to even try this recipe because of its 'eclectic' list of ingredients. However, the contributor is an excellent cook, so we had it tested anyway. This dish ended up being one of the hits of the evening. The dish tasted great and looked beautiful with the various colors that garnish it.*"

1	(3½-4-pound) chicken, cut into 8 pieces	½	teaspoon ground cinnamon
2	tablespoons margarine, cut into small pieces	½	teaspoon curry powder
	Salt	½	teaspoon dried thyme
	Pepper	1	cup mandarin orange segments
1½	cups orange juice	3	bananas, sliced
½	cup raisins		Chopped fresh parsley
½	cup slivered almonds		

Preheat oven to 425°.

Place chicken in a large roasting pan. Dot with margarine; sprinkle with salt and pepper.

Bake for 30 minutes.

Combine orange juice, raisins, almonds, cinnamon, curry powder, and thyme in a small saucepan over medium-high heat. Bring mixture to a boil, reduce heat, and simmer 10 minutes. Pour over chicken.

Reduce heat to 350° and bake for 1 hour or until chicken is done.

Place chicken on serving platter and garnish with orange segments and bananas. Sprinkle with parsley.

Yield: 3 to 5 servings.

CRISPY-COATED GARLIC CHICKEN

2 (3½- to 4-pound) chickens, cut into 8 pieces	2 cups corn flake crumbs
	2 tablespoons garlic powder
	Salt
1 cup olive oil	Pepper
8 cloves garlic, minced	Paprika

Place chicken in a large, shallow container. Combine oil and garlic; pour over chicken, tossing to coat. Cover and marinate 8 hours or overnight.

Preheat oven to 350°. Line a large, shallow roasting pan with foil; grease well with a thin layer of olive oil.

Combine crumbs, garlic powder, salt, pepper, and paprika in a shallow bowl. Dredge chicken in crumb mixture and place in prepared pan.

Bake uncovered for 1½ hours or until done.

Yield: 6 to 8 servings.

CHICKEN CACCIATORE

¼ cup olive oil, divided	1 (26-ounce) jar marinara sauce or Homemade Tomato Sauce (page 162)
1 (3-pound) chicken, cut into 8 pieces	
1 large onion, sliced	1 tablespoon chopped fresh oregano
3 cloves garlic, minced	
1 red bell pepper, diced, optional	¼ cup fresh basil leaves, shredded
8 ounces mushrooms, sliced	Spaghetti
½ cup white wine	

Heat 3 tablespoons oil in a wok or large skillet over medium heat. Add chicken and sauté until brown on all sides. Remove chicken and drain liquid from skillet.

Heat remaining 1 tablespoon oil in skillet. Add onion, garlic, bell pepper, mushrooms, and wine; sauté until tender.

Stir in pasta sauce, oregano, and basil. Add chicken to skillet and bring to a boil. Reduce heat and simmer, covered, 30 minutes or until chicken is done. Serve over hot, cooked spaghetti.

Yield: 4 servings.

Add your own unique touch to Italian recipes by preparing fresh tomato sauce (page 162). **It is not difficult to make, and you can really spice up your cooking!**

APRICOT-GLAZED STUFFED SQUAB

2 teaspoons olive oil
½ cup diced carrots
¼ cup diced celery
¼ cup leeks or scallions, cut into thin strips
5 dried peaches, diced
5 dried nectarines, diced
¼ cup dried cranberries
2 sprigs fresh basil, chopped
2 sprigs fresh tarragon, chopped
2 sprigs fresh sage, chopped
¼ cup chopped pecans
2 cups cooked wild rice (page 209)
6-8 (1-pound) squabs or Cornish hens, breast plate deboned (ask butcher to do this for you)
Apricot glaze
Garnish: fresh chervil sprigs

Preheat oven to 375°.

Heat oil in a large skillet over medium-high heat. Add carrots, celery, and leeks; sauté 1 minute.

Stir in peaches, nectarines, cranberries, basil, tarragon, sage, pecans, and wild rice.

Stuff the fruit mixture into the squabs and place on a roasting pan.

Bake for 35 to 40 minutes. Brush with Apricot Glaze. Serve remaining sauce on the side.

Yield: 6 to 8 servings.

APRICOT GLAZE:

8 fresh apricots
1 teaspoon oil
1 clove garlic, minced
1 shallot, minced
1 teaspoon peeled and minced fresh ginger
¼ cup chicken stock (page 39) or bouillon
2 teaspoons balsamic vinegar
1 teaspoon molasses
1 (8-ounce) jar apricot preserves

Cut apricots in half; remove pits and skin. Set aside.

Heat oil in a saucepan over medium heat. Add garlic, shallot, and ginger; sauté until tender.

Add stock, vinegar, and molasses. Bring mixture to a boil, reduce heat, and simmer until reduced slightly.

Stir in preserves; cook 10 minutes. Add reserved apricot halves and cook 10 to 12 minutes.

Brush over squabs and serve extra as a sauce on the side.

Yield: 1 cup.

SAVORY SOUTHWESTERN CHICKEN

2 tablespoons rubbed sage
2 tablespoons dried thyme
1 teaspoon paprika
1 teaspoon coarsely ground pepper
1 teaspoon garlic powder
1 large onion, sliced into rings
6 plum tomatoes, cut into pieces
1½ cups frozen yellow corn kernels, thawed
1 (6-ounce) can small or medium pitted ripe black olives, drained
6 cloves garlic, coarsely chopped
½ cup plus 3 tablespoons olive oil, divided
1 (3½- to 4-pound) chicken, quartered or cut into 8 pieces

Preheat oven to 375°.

Combine sage, thyme, paprika, pepper, and garlic powder in a small bowl; set aside.

Combine onion, tomatoes, corn, olives, and garlic in a large bowl. Add ½ cup of oil, tossing to coat.

Set aside 1 tablespoon of spice mixture. Add remaining spice mixture to vegetables, tossing to coat.

Place chicken in a roasting pan and surround with seasoned vegetables.

Sprinkle chicken with reserved spice mixture and drizzle with remaining 3 tablespoons oil.

Bake, uncovered, for 1½ hours, basting twice, or until chicken is done and golden brown.

Yield: 4 servings.

Spinach-Stuffed Chicken Breasts in Vermouth Sauce

6 chicken breasts, bone-in
   with skin
2 tablespoons unsalted
   margarine
3 tablespoons corn oil,
   divided
1 onion, finely chopped
2 cloves garlic, minced
2 (10-ounce) packages
   frozen chopped spinach,
   thawed and squeezed
   dry

2 tablespoons chopped fresh
   tarragon or 1 teaspoon
   dried
2 large eggs, lightly beaten
¾ cup dry bread crumbs
½ teaspoon kosher salt
   Black pepper
½ cup vermouth
1½ cups chicken stock
   (page 39)
1½ tablespoons cornstarch
1 tablespoon water

Remove bone from chicken breast, leaving skin intact (or ask butcher to do it for you) and set aside.

Heat margarine and 1 tablespoon oil in a large skillet over medium-high heat. Add onion and sauté until tender. Add garlic, spinach, and tarragon; sauté 2 minutes. Remove from heat and stir in eggs and bread crumbs. Season with salt and pepper.

Loosen skin from meat to form a pocket, being careful not to tear skin. Place 2 to 3 tablespoons spinach stuffing under the skin of each breast. Tuck ends of skin under to form a bundle. Cover and refrigerate 30 minutes.

Preheat oven to 375°.

Heat remaining 2 tablespoons oil in a skillet over medium-high heat. Add chicken, skin side down, and sauté until skin is crisp and golden. Transfer chicken, skin side up, to a lightly greased baking dish. Set skillet aside, reserving pan drippings.

Bake chicken, covered, for 15 to 20 minutes.

Preheat oven to broil with rack 6 to 8 inches from heat.

Uncover chicken and broil 3 to 4 minutes or until golden brown. Remove from oven and keep warm.

Add vermouth to skillet with pan drippings. Bring to a boil, scraping up the browned bits with a spatula until reduced by half.

Stir in stock and boil 5 minutes. Combine cornstarch and water, stirring until smooth. Stir into vermouth mixture. Bring to a boil; boil 1 minute or until thickened and bubbly. Season with salt and pepper, to taste.

To serve, spoon sauce around chicken.

Yield: 6 servings.

Braised Short Ribs,
page 128

MEATS

HONEY AND HERB VEAL ROAST

1 cup beer or ginger ale	1½ teaspoons crushed dried
1 cup honey	rosemary
½ cup Dijon mustard	1 teaspoon salt
¼ cup vegetable oil	1 teaspoon garlic powder
2 tablespoons onion powder	¼ teaspoon black pepper
	3 pounds boneless veal roast

Combine beer, honey, mustard, oil, onion powder, rosemary, salt, garlic powder, and pepper in a large plastic zip-top bag. Add veal, tossing gently to coat. Refrigerate for 3 hours, tossing occasionally.

Preheat oven to 350°.

Remove veal from marinade, reserving marinade, and place in a large roasting pan.

Bake 1½ to 2 hours, basting occasionally, or until desired degree of doneness.

Place reserved marinade in a saucepan over medium-high heat. Bring mixture to a boil; boil for 5 minutes. Serve over roast.

Yield: 8 servings.

PEPPER STEAK

2 pounds minute steak,	½ teaspoon peeled and
trimmed, or pepper steak	minced fresh ginger
sliced into thin strips	2 cloves garlic, chopped
½ cup soy sauce	2 onions, thinly sliced into
¼ cup sugar	rings
¼ cup vegetable oil	2 green bell peppers, cut
	into thin strips

Place steak in a shallow container.

Combine soy sauce and sugar; pour over meat. Let stand 30 minutes.

Heat oil in a large skillet over medium-high heat. Add ginger and garlic; sauté 1 minute. Remove garlic. Add sliced onions and bell peppers; sauté 4 to 6 minutes.

Add meat and marinade. Reduce heat to low and sauté 8 minutes or until done. Serve over hot cooked rice.

Yield: 4 servings.

Cutting meat into thin strips is easier if you partially freeze the meat before slicing.

Brisket with Vegetables and Dried Fruit

2 tablespoons olive oil
4 onions, sliced
3 cloves garlic, chopped
4-6 pounds beef brisket
1½ cups red wine
2 tablespoons dry onion
   soup mix
2 tablespoons tomato paste
2 tablespoons brown sugar
¼ cup water
2 carrots, peeled and cut
   into 1½-inch pieces
2 parsnips, peeled and cut
   into 1½-inch pieces
½ cup dried apricots
½ cup dried pitted prunes
¼ cup chopped fresh parsley

Preheat oven to 500°.

Heat oil in a skillet over medium-high heat. Add onions and garlic; sauté 15 minutes or until lightly browned.

Spoon onions into bottom of a large roasting pan; add brisket, fat side up. Pour wine over meat, cover, and bake 30 minutes.

Combine soup mix, tomato paste, brown sugar, and water in a small bowl; pour over meat. Arrange carrots, parsnips, apricots, and prunes around meat.

Reduce oven temperature to 325°.

Bake 2½ to 3 hours, covered, or until brisket is very tender.

Remove from oven and let stand 20 minutes. Remove brisket from pan and slice thinly across the grain. Arrange meat slices on a platter; spoon fruit and vegetables around brisket.

Skim fat from pan drippings and spoon over meat; sprinkle with parsley.

Brisket may be prepared 2 days ahead. Cover and refrigerate unsliced brisket. To serve, slice thinly and place in roasting pan. Remove solid fat from sauce and spoon over slices. Cover and bake at 325° for 30 minutes or until meal is thoroughly heated.

Yield: 8 servings.

Beef with Pea Pods

¼ cup light soy sauce
1 tablespoon dry sherry
1 tablespoon cornstarch
1 teaspoon sugar
1 pound trimmed minute
   steak or tenderloin, cut
   into thin strips
¼ teaspoon seasoned salt
¼ cup vegetable oil
¼ cup sliced onion
   Pinch ground ginger
¼ pound fresh snow peas

Combine soy sauce, sherry, cornstarch, and sugar, stirring until well blended.

Place steak in a shallow container; pour soy mixture over meat, turning to coat well. Cover and refrigerate 1 hour.

Heat oil in a nonstick skillet over medium-high heat. Add onion and salt; sauté 3 minutes or until tender.

Add steak; sauté 3 to 5 minutes or until cooked through. Stir in ginger and pea pods; sauté 3 minutes until pea pods are tender. Serve over hot, cooked rice.

Yield: 4 servings.

Beef Shish Kabobs

1 cup oil
½ cup soy sauce
¼ teaspoon ground ginger
6 cloves garlic
½ teaspoon salt
½ teaspoon pepper
2 pounds beef tenderloin,
   cut into 2-inch cubes
3 large onions, cut into
   cubes
1 pound cherry tomatoes
8 ounces button
   mushrooms
1 red bell pepper, cubed
1 green bell pepper, cubed

Combine oil, soy sauce, ginger, garlic, salt, and pepper in a large, plastic zip-top bag. Add meat, onions, tomatoes, mushrooms, and bell peppers. Squeeze out excess air and seal. Refrigerate 2 hours, turning occasionally.

Soak wooden skewers in water 15 to 20 minutes to prevent burning.

Preheat grill to medium heat.

Remove meat and vegetables from marinade, discarding marinade. Thread on skewers, alternating meat and vegetables.

Grill kabobs 4 minutes per side, or until desired degree of doneness.

Yield: 4 to 6 servings.

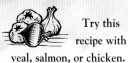 **Try this recipe with veal, salmon, or chicken.**

VEAL MEDALLIONS
WITH TWO MUSTARD SAUCE

⅔ cup beef stock or bouillon
⅓ cup dry red wine
2 tablespoons tomato purée
2½ pounds veal cutlets
    All-purpose flour
3 tablespoons olive oil
3 tablespoons white wine
¼ cup non-dairy creamer
3 tablespoons coarse
    ground mustard
2 tablespoons Dijon
    mustard

Combine stock, wine, and tomato purée in a saucepan over medium-high heat. Bring mixture to a boil; boil for 20 minutes or until reduced by half.

Place veal cutlets between 2 sheets of heavy-duty plastic wrap, and flatten to an even thickness using a meat mallet. Pound slightly with a meat tenderizer or pierce with tines of a fork. Dredge cutlets in flour, shaking off excess.

Heat oil in a large skillet over medium-high heat. Add cutlets and cook 2 to 3 minutes on each side or until brown. Cook veal in batches, if necessary, to avoid overcrowding in pan. Transfer veal to serving platter; keep warm.

Add wine to pan, stirring to scrape up browned bits from bottom of pan. Stir in non-dairy creamer, and coarse and Dijon mustards. Cook over medium-high heat 3 minutes. Stir in wine reduction. To serve, spoon sauce over veal.

Yield: 6 servings.

Serve with steamed haricot verts or green beans and Potato Kugel Muffins (page 196).

MARINATED LONDON BROIL

Try this delicious marinade with spare ribs, as well.

Serve with Cajun Sweet Potato Fries (page 194) and your favorite cole slaw.

2½ pounds London broil	1 teaspoon dried thyme or sage
½ cup peanut oil	1 teaspoon paprika
½ cup soy sauce	¼ teaspoon cayenne pepper
2 tablespoons vinegar	½ cup honey

Score the meat on both sides by making shallow, diagonal cuts ¼-inch deep at 1-inch intervals forming a diamond pattern. Place meat in a shallow dish or zip-top bag.

Combine oil, soy sauce, vinegar, thyme, paprika, cayenne pepper, and honey. Pour marinade over meat, tossing to coat. Cover or seal; refrigerate 6 hours or overnight.

Preheat grill to medium-hot.

Remove meat from marinade, reserving marinade. Grill, basting occasionally, for 10 minutes on each side for medium-rare or until desired degree of doneness.

Transfer steak to carving board; let stand 5 minutes. Cut across the grain into thin strips. Arrange on a platter and serve.

Yield: 8 to 10 servings.

STUFFED STEAK

2 tablespoons margarine	2 (1-inch thick) rib steaks
2 cloves garlic, minced	½ cup red wine
½ cup chopped onion	1 tablespoon soy sauce
¼ cup chopped celery	1 tablespoon prepared horseradish
¼ cup chopped mushrooms	
½ cup dry bread crumbs	

Heat margarine in a skillet over medium-high heat. Add garlic, onion, celery, and mushrooms; sauté 2 to 3 minutes. Remove from heat and stir in bread crumbs.

Trim excess fat from each steak and cut a slit in the side to form a deep pocket; be careful not to cut all the way through. Stuff steaks evenly with mushroom mixture. Pinch edges closed and secure with a toothpick.

Combine wine, soy sauce, and horseradish; spoon over steaks. Cover and refrigerate until ready to cook.

Preheat a large, heavy skillet over medium-high heat. Let steaks come to room temperature. Cook steaks 8 to 10 minutes on each side, basting constantly, or until desired degree of doneness. Steaks may also be grilled.

Yield: 2 servings.

GRILLED LONDON BROIL
WITH ROSEMARY

2½ pounds London broil
½ cup olive oil
½ cup low-sodium soy sauce
¼ cup honey
3 tablespoons chopped fresh
  rosemary or 1 tablespoon
  dried rosemary

1½ tablespoons coarsely
  ground pepper
1 teaspoon salt
6 cloves garlic, minced

Score the meat on both sides by making shallow, diagonal cuts ¼-inch deep at 1-inch intervals forming a diamond pattern. Place meat in a shallow dish or zip-top bag. Combine oil, soy sauce, honey, rosemary, pepper, salt, and garlic. Pour marinade over meat, tossing to coat. Cover or seal; refrigerate several hours or overnight.

Remove meat from refrigerator and let come to room temperature for 30 minutes.

Preheat grill to medium-hot or oven to broil.

Remove meat from marinade, reserving marinade. Grill or broil, basting occasionally, for 10 minutes on each side for medium-rare or until desired degree of doneness.

Transfer steak to carving board; let stand 5 minutes. Cut across the grain into thin strips. Arrange on a platter and serve.

Yield: 8 to 10 servings.

MARINATED LAMB CHOPS

18	baby lamb chops	¼	cup white vinegar
1	cup water	¼	cup Worcestershire sauce*
½	cup firmly packed dark brown sugar	1	teaspoon salt
		1	teaspoon celery salt
½	cup ketchup	1	teaspoon chili powder

Place lamb chops in a large shallow container; set aside.

Combine water, brown sugar, ketchup, vinegar, Worcestershire, salt, celery salt, and chili powder in a medium saucepan over medium-high heat. Bring mixture to a boil, reduce heat, and simmer until sugar dissolves.

Pour marinade over lamb chops. Cover and refrigerate 8 hours or overnight.

Preheat oven to broil with rack 6 to 8 inches from heat.

Remove chops from marinade, discarding marinade, and place in a broiling pan.

Broil chops (with electric oven door partially open) for 10 minutes per side or until desired degree of doneness.

Yield: 5 servings.

Note: all Worcestershire sauce contains anchovies. If the kosher certification mark stands alone, then the percentage of anchovies is less than 1.6% of the whole product. Many rabbinical authorities say that this is okay to use with meat.

If the kosher certification on the label has a fish notation next to it, the level exceeds the 1.6% and you should refrain from using it in meat dishes.

Ordinary cloth napkins can be turned into beautiful table decorations in an instant. Try wrapping each napkin with a strand of small-leaf ivy. Or, try herb napkin rings. Start by pleating the napkin and tying a raffia knot around the middle leaving 3 inches of raffia on either side. Fan out the pleats. Gather a selection of fresh herbs; put a few stems of flat leaf parsley at the back to support the bunch. Use the raffia to secure the herbs to the raffia napkin ring.

SWEETBREADS

1 pound sweetbreads
1 tablespoon vinegar
2 teaspoons salt
3 tablespoons olive oil
1 onion, diced
1 stalk celery, diced

⅓ pound mushrooms, sliced
2 tablespoons all-purpose
   flour
1 cup green peas
¾ teaspoon pepper

Serve this delicacy on an herb dusted plate (page 79) or in puff pastry shells.

Wash sweetbreads and place in a large saucepan with cold water to cover. Stir in vinegar and salt; bring to a boil over medium-high heat.

Reduce heat to low and simmer, covered tightly, for 20 minutes. Drain, reserving 1 cup liquid.

Place sweetbreads in cold water for 30 minutes. Drain and remove membrane. Cut out veins and connective tissue; cut into large cubes.

Heat oil in a large skillet over medium-high heat. Add onion and sauté 10 minutes. Add celery and mushrooms; sauté 10 minutes.

Sprinkle mushroom mixture with flour, stirring constantly. Add reserved 1 cup liquid, stirring until well blended.

Bring to a boil; add sweetbreads, peas, and pepper. Reduce heat to low and simmer, covered, for 10 minutes. Correct seasonings, if desired.

Yield: 4 servings.

SWEET & SOUR PINE NUT MEATBALLS

1 pound lean ground beef
2 tablespoons matzoh meal
1 tablespoon pine nuts
2 tablespoons water
¼ cup oil, divided
   Salt
   Pepper
3 onions, chopped

1 (17-ounce) can sweet,
   dark pitted cherries,
   undrained
½ cup dried apricots,
   quartered
½ cup sweet red wine
2 tablespoons sugar
3 tablespoons lemon juice

Combine beef, matzoh meal, nuts, water, 2 tablespoons oil, salt, and pepper, mixing well; shape into 1½-inch meatballs.

Heat remaining 2 tablespoons oil in a large saucepan over medium-high heat; add onions and sauté 5 minutes or until translucent. Add meatballs and sauté until browned.

Combine cherries, apricots, wine, sugar, and lemon juice. Add to meatballs, stirring gently until blended.

Bring to a boil, reduce heat to low, and simmer for 2 hours.

Yield: 6 to 8 servings.

SILVER TIP ROAST BEEF

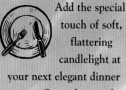

*T*he dry heat of an oven works well as a cooking method for large roasts. It allows the beef to develop a tasty, brown color while remaining moist and flavorful within. Splurge on the best roast you can find- you'll be rewarded with a very special meal.

2	onions, peeled and sliced		Pepper
1	(6- to 7-pound) silver tip roast beef	2	tablespoons teriyaki sauce
4	cloves garlic, halved Salt	2	tablespoons red wine Paprika

Place onions in a large roasting pan; place roast on a rack in the pan.

Rub roast with garlic halves. Cut garlic into slices and tuck under strings of roast; sprinkle with salt and pepper and brush with teriyaki sauce and wine.

Sprinkle with paprika and let stand 30 minutes.

Preheat oven to 400°.

Bake roast, uncovered, for 30 minutes. Lower heat to 350°. Bake for 1½ hours, basting occasionally, or until desired degree of doneness. Do not cook longer than 3 hours, or meat will toughen.

Let meat stand 15 to 20 minutes before carving. The juices will return to the center of the meat making it moister and easier to carve.

Yield: 8 servings.

Add the special touch of soft, flattering candlelight at your next elegant dinner party. Set a cluster of crystal candlesticks on a mirror and place it in the center of the table. The flicker and reflection of the lit candles will create a dazzling effect.

A silver tip roast loses about half of its weight during cooking, so a 10-pound roast cooks down to approximately six pounds that serves ten generous 8- to 10-ounce portions.

Serve with Cabernet Sauvignon.

Stuffed Breast of Veal with Sherry Wine Sauce

2   tablespoons olive oil,
      divided
1   bunch scallions, sliced
2   tablespoons minced fresh
      rosemary
3   cloves garlic, minced
8   ounces shiitake
      mushrooms, stems
      removed and sliced
1   (10-ounce) package
      frozen chopped spinach,
      thawed and squeezed
      dry
1½ cups sherry, port or
      Beaujolais, divided
1   cup fresh bread crumbs
      (page 188)
    Salt
    Freshly ground pepper
1   (3- to 4-pound) boneless
      veal breast
1   cup beef stock or bouillon

Preheat oven to 350°.

Heat 1 tablespoon oil in a large skillet over medium heat. Add scallions and rosemary; sauté 5 minutes. Add garlic, mushrooms, and spinach; sauté 6 minutes or until mushrooms are tender. Stir in 2 tablespoons of wine and bread crumbs. Season with salt.

Untie veal, reserving string. To "butterfly" the veal breast, turn veal on its side and slice down the center, cutting almost but not completely through. (You can ask your butcher to do it for you.) Open breast out flat; pound veal to an even thickness with a meat mallet.

Sprinkle breast with salt and pepper. Spoon stuffing mixture evenly over breast; reroll and tie with string at 2-inch intervals.

Brush meat with remaining olive oil. Place in a roasting pan; pour stock and remaining sherry over veal.

Bake 1 hour, basting occasionally. Remove from oven and let stand, covered loosely with foil, for 20 minutes. Transfer to a serving platter, remove string, and cut into 12 slices. Serve with pan juices.

Yield: 12 servings.

VEAL CHOPS IN
BALSAMIC SUNFLOWER SEED SAUCE

"The first time I ate this dish was when my boyfriend– now my husband– was trying to impress me with his cooking skills. He believes this dinner contributed to our getting married. As I imagine the veal chops' beautiful golden color and incredible aroma, my mouth waters. Maybe he's right, it is just that good."

¼	cup balsamic vinegar	2	(1-inch thick) veal chops
2	tablespoons salad oil	1	cup chicken stock
1	tablespoon finely chopped		(page 39) or broth
	garlic	2	tablespoons shelled
1	tablespoon finely chopped		sunflower seeds
	fresh cilantro	1	tablespoon margarine

Combine vinegar, oil, garlic, and cilantro in a plastic, zip-top bag; add veal. Seal and refrigerate at least 5 hours or overnight, turning occasionally.

Preheat oven to 375°.

Remove veal chops from marinade, reserving marinade. Place in a baking dish and loosely cover with foil.

Bake 20 to 30 minutes (meat thermometer will register 160° for medium) or until desired degree of doneness. Place veal on platter; keep warm.

Heat reserved marinade and stock in a small saucepan over high heat. Bring to a boil; cook until mixture reduces by one-fourth.

Add sunflower seeds and margarine, stirring until well blended. Remove from heat and let stand until just warm. Serve sauce over veal chops.

Yield: 2 servings.

Serve with Crusty Garlic and Rosemary Potatoes (page 194) and Vegetable Ribbons (page 186). Use 1 leaf of Bibb lettuce as a bowl for fresh blanched green peas.

A white wine such as a Chardonnay or Sauvignon Blanc partners well with the flavors of this veal dish.

BRAISED LAMB SHANKS WITH
ROSEMARY AND GARLIC

*T*ired of serving chicken? Want to impress guests? These flavorful, moist, and tender lamb shanks will not only dress your Shabbat table, but will definitely leave your guests begging for more — or at least the recipe!

1	bunch leeks		Salt
3	tablespoons olive oil		Freshly ground pepper
3-3½	pounds lamb shanks	¾	cup dry white wine
	(4 total)	½	cup sweetened dried
4-5	cloves garlic, sliced		cranberries (optional)
8-10	baby carrots		Garnish: rosemary sprigs
2	teaspoons chopped fresh		
	rosemary		

Cut the roots from leeks and discard tough outer leaves. Cut each leek in half lengthwise. Rinse thoroughly with cold running water to remove grit. Slice leeks crosswise into ½-inch pieces; set aside.

Heat oil in a Dutch oven or large, deep frying pan over medium-high heat. Add shanks and cook 10 to 12 minutes or until brown on all sides. Transfer meat to a plate.

Reduce heat to medium-low; add garlic and sauté 30 to 40 seconds. Add leeks and sauté 6 to 8 minutes or until translucent. Add the carrots.

Return shanks to pan; add rosemary, salt, pepper, and wine. Add cranberries if desired. Increase heat to medium-high and bring mixture to a boil. Reduce heat to low, cover, and simmer 2 to 2½ hours or until shanks are very tender when pierced with a knife. Turn once during cooking, adding water as necessary to maintain original amount of liquid.

Season shanks with salt and pepper. Garnish with rosemary sprigs and serve immediately with couscous, if desired. May be made a day ahead or frozen.

Yield: 4 servings.

Corned Beef with Three Glazes

1 (4- to 6-pound) corned
  beef
1 teaspoon pickling spice
1 orange, sliced
1 stalk celery, sliced
1 carrot, peeled and sliced
1 onion, peeled

1 bay leaf
5-6 black peppercorns
3 cloves garlic, peeled
  Tangy Mustard Glaze,
  Sweet and Sour Glaze,
  or Cranberry-
  Horseradish Glaze

Place the meat in a large pot of cold water. Make sure there is enough water to cover the meat by at least 2 inches. Bring to a boil and then discard the water. Repeat 3 times.

Cover with cold water again. Add pickling spice, celery, carrot, onion, bay leaf, peppercorns, and garlic. Bring to a boil. Turn the heat down so the cooking liquid is at a low simmer and cook covered, for about 3 hours or until fork tender.

Preheat oven to 350°. Drain the water, reserving ½ cup liquid to prepare glaze if necessary. Place the corned beef in a deep 13- x 9-inch roasting pan. Pour the glaze over the meat and bake, covered, for 35 to 40 minutes. Recipe may be made ahead. Using a very sharp knife, slice meat when cool; reheat slices.

Tangy Mustard Glaze:

⅔ cup firmly packed dark
  brown sugar

½ cup reserved cooking
  liquid from corned beef
2 tablespoons Dijon mustard

Combine sugar, liquid, and mustard in a small bowl, mixing well.
Yield: 1¼ cups.

Sweet and Sour Glaze:

1 cup firmly packed light
  brown sugar
⅓ cup ketchup
3 tablespoons apple cider
  vinegar

2 tablespoons margarine,
  melted
1 tablespoon mustard

Combine sugar, ketchup, vinegar, margarine, and mustard in a saucepan over medium heat. Bring to a boil, stirring constantly, until sugar dissolves and mixture is smooth.
Yield: 1⅔ cups.

Serve with
Tri-Color
Vegetable
Soufflé (page 198).

CORNED BEEF (continued)

CRANBERRY–HORSERADISH GLAZE:

¼ cup red prepared
    horseradish

¼ cup jellied cranberry sauce
2 tablespoons apricot jam

Combine horseradish, cranberry sauce, and jam in a small bowl, whisking until smooth.

Yield: ½ cup.

CHILI

1 tablespoon vegetable oil
1 pound lean ground beef
1 large onion, chopped
1 large clove garlic, minced
½ cup chopped green pepper
4 tablespoons hot chili powder
1 teaspoon salt
½ teaspoon sugar
¼ teaspoon ground cumin

Pinch crushed red pepper flakes
1 (28-ounce) can whole tomatoes
1 (15-ounce) can tomato sauce
1 (15-ounce) can kidney beans, rinsed and drained

Heat oil in a large skillet over medium-high heat. Brown beef, stirring until it crumbles; drain fat.

Add onion, garlic, green pepper, chili powder, salt, sugar, cumin, pepper flakes, tomatoes, tomato sauce, and beans. Bring mixture to a boil, reduce heat, and simmer for 45 minutes. Serve over Spanish rice or in a bowl topped with shredded lettuce, corn chips, and olives. This recipe freezes very well.

Yield: 4 to 6 servings.

OSSO BUCO

*O**sso Buco is an Italian stew. The veal shanks are braised to a melting tenderness in a rich, aromatic sauce. It is a great dish for a busy cook as the long, unattended cooking time allows a moment to relax or prepare the rest of the meal.***

1	cup unbleached all-purpose flour Freshly ground pepper	1	(28-ounce) can plum tomatoes, undrained and diced
3	pounds veal shanks, 1¼-inch thick and tied with twine		Salt Pepper
½	cup olive oil	2	cups dry wine
2	yellow onions, coarsely chopped or sliced	2	cups beef stock or bouillon
6	large cloves garlic, chopped	¾	cup chopped fresh flat leaf parsley
½	teaspoon dried basil	2	teaspoons freshly grated lemon peel
½	teaspoon dried oregano		

Combine flour and pepper in a shallow bowl. Dredge veal shanks in flour; set aside.

Heat oil in a large ovenproof skillet or Dutch oven over medium-high heat. Add veal and sear for 8 minutes or until brown on all sides. Drain veal on paper towels.

Add onions, garlic, basil, and oregano to the skillet and cook, stirring occasionally, for 10 minutes. Stir in tomatoes, salt, and pepper; cook 10 minutes. Skim off excess fat.

Stir in wine and bring mixture to a boil. Reduce heat and simmer, uncovered, for 15 minutes.

Preheat oven to 350°.

Return veal to skillet and add beef stock. Cover and bake 1½ hours. Bake, uncovered, for 30 minutes.

Combine parsley and lemon peel; sprinkle on veal.

Yield: 4 servings.

Serve with Wild Mushroom Risotto (page 205), a classic Italian accompaniment to this dish.

Choose a full-flavored white wine like Meursalt or a red selection such as Pinot Noir.

FRENCH ROAST

1 (4- to 5-pound) French roast
3 onions, chopped
3 cloves garlic, chopped
1 cup firmly packed dark brown sugar
1 cup ketchup
1 cup water
¾ cup balsamic vinegar
2 teaspoons soy sauce
2 teaspoons apricot preserves

Place roast in a large container; set aside.

Combine onions, garlic, brown sugar, ketchup, water, vinegar, soy sauce, and preserves in a saucepan over medium-high heat. Bring mixture to a boil, reduce heat, and simmer until sugar dissolves.

Pour marinade over roast. Cover and refrigerate 8 hours or overnight, turning occasionally.

Preheat oven to 350°.

Transfer the roast and marinade to a roasting pan. Bake, covered, for 2 hours. Place the roast on a serving platter; pour marinade over roast or serve on the side.

Yield: 8 to 10 servings.

VEAL AND POTATO CASSEROLE

2 tablespoons oil
1 large onion, thinly sliced
2 pounds veal steak, cubed
  Salt
  Pepper
  Garlic powder
1½-2 pounds potatoes, peeled and cut into thin slices
1¼ cup chicken stock (page 39) or bouillon

Preheat oven to 325°.

Heat 2 tablespoons oil in a skillet over medium heat. Add onions and sauté until golden brown. Remove onions and set aside.

Add veal to skillet. Sprinkle with salt, pepper, and garlic powder. Sauté until no longer pink; remove from heat.

Place one-third of potatoes in a lightly greased 2-quart round baking dish. Layer with half of veal and half of onions. Repeat layers with one-third potatoes, half of veal, and half of onions. Arrange remaining potatoes in concentric circles on top.

Pour stock over casserole, cover, and bake 2½ hours.

Increase temperature to 450°. Uncover and bake 20 minutes, or until potatoes are golden brown.

Yield: 4 to 6 servings.

VEGETABLES AND FLOWERS IN A BIRD'S NEST

This wonderful centerpiece is casual enough for an outdoor barbecue,
yet beautiful enough to decorate a Shabbat or holiday table.

You will need:

1 (12-inch) shallow bowl

*Moss block (available at floral
or arts and crafts supply stores)*

*Various green foliage including
leaves and berries*

*Flowers such as roses, baby
orchids, hydrangea*

4 red potatoes

3 small eggplants

3 green apples

4-5 long carrots

4-5 red bell peppers

4-5 green chili peppers

3-4 bunches radishes

Grape vine

Floral wire

*2 dozen thin, green floral sticks
or wooden skewers*

Fill bowl with moss block and
add flowers and leaves. Place
individual vegetables on a stick
and add to the arrangement.
Place the grape vine around
the base to cover the bowl,
securing with floral wire.

Ragin' Cajun Barbeque Ribs

4 teaspoons sugar
1½ teaspoons salt
1½ teaspoons paprika
1½ teaspoons chili powder
¾ teaspoon freshly ground
    pepper
¾ teaspoon dried sage
½ teaspoon dried thyme
¼ teaspoon cayenne pepper
3½ pounds beef spareribs or
    breast flanken cut into
    1¼-inch thickness

1 cup canned tomato purée
3 tablespoons light molasses
2 tablespoons apple cider
    vinegar
1 teaspoon hot pepper
    sauce
¾ teaspoon liquid smoke
    (optional)
¼ teaspoon ground
    cinnamon

Combine sugar, salt, paprika, chili powder, pepper, sage, thyme, and cayenne pepper in a small bowl.

Rub spice mixture into spareribs. Cover and refrigerate at least 1 hour, no longer than 8.

Combine purée, molasses, vinegar, pepper sauce, liquid smoke, and cinnamon in a medium bowl; set aside.

Preheat oven to 350°. Place a flat rack in a large roasting pan; pour water to a depth of 1 to 2 inches.

Place ribs on rack. (Be sure water does not touch the meat.) Cover pan loosely with foil.

Bake 1 hour and 15 minutes. Remove foil and carefully pour water out of pan.

Brush ribs with one-fourth of the sauce. Bake 1 hour, basting occasionally, or until meat is very tender.

Cut into individual portions and serve.

Yield: 4 servings.

 This dish is perfect for an early evening summer celebration. Add some fun by filling a small kiddie pool with ice. Place cans and bottles of beer and soda in the ice. Toss in a rubber duckie or two for a whimsical touch.

Nut-Crusted Lamb Chops

½ cup slivered almonds
½ cup pine nuts
½ cup pistachios
½ cup walnuts
½ cup Italian-style dry
   bread crumbs
   Salt
   Pepper

1 cup all-purpose flour
2 large eggs
1 teaspoon non-dairy
   creamer
8 (1- to 1½-inch thick)
   bone-in lamb chops
2 tablespoons olive oil

Preheat oven to 425°.

Combine almonds, pine nuts, pistachios, and walnuts in the container of a food processor fitted with a knife blade. Process until finely chopped.

Combine nuts and bread crumbs in a medium bowl. Season to taste with salt and pepper.

Place flour in a medium bowl.

Whisk eggs and non-dairy creamer together in a small bowl.

Dredge chops in flour, shaking off excess. Dip in egg mixture, and dredge in nut mixture, coating well.

Heat oil in a large, heavy skillet over medium heat. Add the chops, a few at a time, and sauté until golden brown. Repeat with remaining chops, adding more oil to the pan, if necessary. Transfer chops to a lightly greased baking dish.

Bake lamb chops 12 minutes for medium rare or to desired degree of doneness. Transfer to plates and serve immediately.

Yield: 8 servings.

PESTO STUFFED VEAL BREAST

*P*repare this recipe for an elegant meal. The pesto adds a special touch that makes for a lovely presentation. If you make the recipe ahead, you will find that the veal slices easier and cleaner when it is cold.

2 cups fresh basil leaves	Olive oil
½ cup fresh parsley	Salt
1 (2-ounce) jar pine nuts (⅓ cup)	Pepper
4-6 cloves garlic	1 teaspoon margarine
¾ cup olive oil	1 tablespoon chopped shallots
1 (7- to 8-pound) boneless veal breast	1 cup dry white wine
	1 cup beef stock or bouillon

Serve with a slightly chilled Beaujolais.

Preheat oven to broil with rack 6 inches from heat.

Combine basil, parsley, nuts, garlic, and olive oil in the container of a food processor fitted with a knife blade. Process until a soft paste is formed; set aside.

Flatten and tenderize the veal with a meat pounder. Spread pesto sauce over veal; roll up lengthwise and tie with string every 2 inches. Brush with oil and sprinkle with salt and pepper. Place veal in a large roasting pan.

Broil veal (with electric oven door partially open) until brown on all sides. Remove veal from oven.

Preheat oven to 325°.

Heat margarine in a small skillet over medium-high heat. Add shallots and sauté until tender. Add wine and stock; bring mixture to a boil. Reduce heat and simmer, uncovered, for 15 minutes or until reduced by one-third.

Pour shallot mixture over veal and cover with foil. Bake for 3 hours or until meat thermometer registers 160° (medium) to 170° (well done).

Let veal stand for 15 minutes; carve into serving slices.

Yield: 8 to 12 servings.

CROWN ROAST OF LAMB WITH BÉARNAISE SAUCE

"Growing up, this was always a specialty in my home for the feast on Purim night. My mom said the crown was in honor of Queen Esther. Queen Esther was the heroine of the Purim story, but with this stunning dish, my mom was the heroine at the dinner table."

2	(3½-pound) racks of lamb	Tarragon
	Olive oil	Garlic salt
	Pepper	Béarnaise Sauce

Trim and scrape fat from bone ends of lamb with a sharp knife (called Frenching) and tie the racks together to form a circle (or ask your butcher to do it for you).

Preheat oven to 325°.

Rub lamb with oil and sprinkle with pepper, tarragon, and garlic salt. Place on a flat rack in a roasting pan. Crumple foil into a ball and place in the center of the crown, completely filling the middle.

Bake 12 to 15 minutes per pound for medium-rare (meat thermometer will register 150°) or 30 to 35 minutes per pound for well done (170°). Baste occasionally and shield tips of bones with foil to prevent excessive browning.

Remove foil and place lamb on a serving platter. Place paper frills on exposed bones. You can fill the center of the crown with rice, colorful vegetables, or meatballs, but it is easier to carve unfilled. Cut lamb into serving portions and serve with Béarnaise Sauce.

Yield: 6 to 8 servings.

BÉARNAISE SAUCE:

1	cup margarine	½	teaspoon dry mustard
¼	cup tarragon vinegar	¼	teaspoon salt
4	egg yolks	2	sprigs fresh tarragon or
2	tablespoons lemon juice		1½ tablespoons dried
1	tablespoon dry red wine	1	shallot

Combine margarine and vinegar in a small saucepan over medium heat. Bring mixture to just below a boil.

Place cards are a wonderful addition to any dinner table. They can make your guests' transition into the dining room smoother as well as being a good conversation piece. Place small picture frames at each chair with an old photo of each guest. For an added touch, visit your local library or log on to the internet and pull up the front page of the New York Times for each guest's date of birth. Try small pots of herbs labeled with each name, small bouquets of dried flowers, bicycle nameplates, or miniature bottles of liquor for fun. Use your imagination- the possibilities are endless.

Combine yolks, juice, wine, mustard, salt, tarragon, and shallot in the container of a blender. Process 30 seconds until well blended, stopping once to scrape down sides. Turn blender on high; gradually add margarine mixture in a slow, steady stream. Serve immediately.

Yield: 1½ cups.

SWEET AND SOUR BRISKET

This brisket will bring rave reviews. It requires very little preparation time and is packed with fabulous flavor.

1 (12-ounce) bottle beer	1 head garlic, peeled and
1 cup whole berry	pressed
cranberry sauce	Kosher salt
½ cup ketchup	Pepper
¼ cup all-purpose flour	Paprika
1 (4- to 5-pound) brisket	2 tablespoons olive oil
	6 large onions, sliced

Preheat oven to 400°.

Combine beer, cranberry sauce, ketchup, and flour in a medium bowl; set aside.

Rub brisket with garlic, salt, pepper, and a generous amount of paprika.

Heat oil in a large, heavy pot or Dutch oven over high heat. Add brisket and sear 8 to 10 minutes on each side or until brown. Remove meat from pot.

Add onions to pot; sauté 8 minutes or until tender and brown. Stir frequently to scrape up browned bits from the bottom of the pot.

Place onions in the bottom of a large roasting pan and top with brisket. Pour the beer mixture over the meat.

Bake, covered, for 3 hours. Cool for 30 minutes; slice across the grain.

Recipe may be made ahead. Slice the meat when cool; reheat over low heat.

Yield: 6 to 8 servings.

BRAISED SHORT RIBS

2 tablespoons vegetable oil
4 pounds short ribs or
  flanken, thickly cut
  Kosher salt
  Freshly ground pepper
2 quarts beef stock or
  bouillon
1 teaspoon tomato paste
2 red potatoes, peeled and
  cut into 1-inch pieces

1 turnip, peeled and cut
  into 1-inch pieces
1 parsnip, peeled and cut
  into 1-inch pieces
1 carrot, peeled and cut
  into 1-inch pieces
1 stalk celery, cut into
  1-inch pieces
3 black peppercorns
3 sprigs fresh thyme
1 bay leaf

Heat oil in a large Dutch oven or soup pot over medium-high heat. Add meat and sear 3 to 4 minutes per side, or until golden brown. Sprinkle with salt and pepper. Remove meat and set aside.

Add stock, tomato paste, potatoes, turnip, parsnip, carrot, celery, peppercorns, thyme, and bay leaf to pan drippings, mixing well.

Bring mixture to a boil over medium-high heat. Add meat (liquid should cover all parts of meat). Reduce heat and simmer, covered, for 1½ hours or until tender.

Remove meat from liquid, reserving liquid, and place on carving board. Let meat cool for 30 minutes; cut meat away from bone and trim any excess fat. Cut into pieces to serve.

Skim fat off reserved liquid; strain and reheat, if necessary. Serve as gravy on the side.

Yield: 4 to 6 servings.

To serve with vegetables as shown in photograph (see page 105), bring reserved broth to boil. Peel and cut 2 potatoes, 1 turnip, 1 parsnip, 1 carrot, and 1 stalk of celery into 1-inch pieces. Boil vegetables 10 to 15 minutes, or until tender. Strain liquid and serve as gravy.

Serve with Merlot.

Chilean Sea Bass with
Sun-Dried Tomato
Vinaigrette, page 131

FISH

Garlic-Crusted Whitefish

Dairy

1¼ cups fresh bread crumbs (page 188)
1 tablespoon vegetable oil
4 cloves garlic, peeled
1 (8-ounce) package cream cheese, softened
1 tablespoon chopped fresh parsley
1 tablespoon butter, melted
4 (6-ounce) whitefish fillets
Salt and pepper

Preheat oven to 350°.

Spread bread crumbs evenly on a baking sheet. Bake 15 minutes, stirring twice; let cool.

Heat oil in a saucepan over low heat. Add garlic and sauté for 10 minutes or until tender (do not overcook).

Transfer garlic to a small bowl and mash. Stir in cream cheese; set aside.

Increase oven temperature to 400°.

Combine bread crumbs with parsley and butter in a shallow dish.

Sprinkle fillets with salt and pepper and press one side of fish into crumb mixture. Place fish, crumb side down, on a greased baking sheet. Spread cream cheese mixture evenly over tops of fish. Top evenly with remaining bread crumbs.

Bake 14 to 16 minutes or until fish flakes when tested with a fork.

Yield: 4 servings.

Salmon Teriyaki

Parve

1 pound salmon fillet
2 tablespoons sugar
2 tablespoons low-sodium soy sauce
2 tablespoons white wine or sake
1 clove garlic, pressed
1 teaspoon ground ginger

Place salmon in a shallow glass dish.

Combine sugar, soy sauce, wine, garlic, and ginger; pour over fish. Cover and refrigerate at least 1 hour.

Preheat oven to broil with rack 6 to 8 inches from heat.

Remove salmon from marinade, reserving marinade. Place on a broiling pan.

Broil 10 minutes per inch of thickness, basting with marinade halfway through cooking time, or until fish flakes when tested with a fork.

Yield: 4 servings.

Place a fresh parsley leaf on the bottom of a small teacup. Pack with hot cooked white rice. Turn cup over on a plate, unmold, and serve with the salmon.

Chilean Sea Bass with Sun-Dried Tomato Vinaigrette

Parve

4 cups water
4 cups white wine
1 orange, halved
1 lemon, halved
1 lime, halved
6 cardamom seeds, cracked
   with the back of a knife
3 slices peeled fresh ginger
2 sticks fresh lemon grass

1 bunch fresh cilantro
6 (5- to 6-ounce) sea bass
   fillets
   Sun-Dried Tomato
   Vinaigrette
   Garnish: 2 tablespoons
   sun-dried tomatoes
   packed in oil, cut into
   thin strips

Combine water and wine in a large poaching pan or deep roasting pan. Add the orange, lemon, lime, cardamom seeds, ginger, lemon grass, and cilantro. Bring to a boil; submerge sea bass and reduce heat. Poach at a gentle simmer for 8 to 12 minutes or until fish flakes when tested with a fork.

Transfer fish to a serving plate or platter; serve with Sun-Dried Tomato Vinaigrette. Garnish with sun-dried tomatoes.

Yield: 6 servings.

Sun-Dried Tomato Vinaigrette:

1 cup olive oil
¼ cup white vinegar
1 tablespoon chopped fresh
   cilantro
1 teaspoon chopped shallots

1 teaspoon chopped fresh
   parsley
½ teaspoon capers, drained
   Pinch dried oregano

Combine the oil and vinegar in the container of a blender; process until emulsified or well blended. Pour into a cruet or jar. Add the cilantro, shallots, parsley, capers, and oregano. Cover tightly and shake vigorously.

Yield: 1½ cups.

Confetti Plate Decoration

Cut yellow peppers, red peppers, and chives into tiny, confetti-sized pieces. Toss on the serving plate or platter to surround the food in a burst of color.

Lemon grass, an important spice in Thai-flavored dishes like this one, has long, thin, greenish leaves and a base like a scallion. It gives off a sour lemon fragrance and taste. Lemon grass is also known as citronella and sereh in Asian markets. Commonly found fresh or dried, it is also available in jars.

FILLET OF SOLE ROULADES

Dairy

24 fresh asparagus spears,
    trimmed
    Lemon juice
1   tablespoon Dijon mustard
6   sole fillets
1   teaspoon dried oregano
    Salt
    Pepper
¼   cup butter

2   cloves garlic, minced
1   tablespoon chopped
    scallion
1   cup Marsala
1   tablespoon tomato paste
2   large egg yolks
½   cup heavy whipping cream
¼   cup shredded mozzarella
    cheese

Preheat oven to 350°.

Blanch asparagus in boiling water 1 minute; drain. Plunge into ice water to stop the cooking process; drain. Sprinkle with lemon juice.

Spread mustard across each fillet and sprinkle with oregano, salt, and pepper.

Arrange 4 asparagus spears across the width of each fillet. Roll the fillets, starting at the short end of the fish, and secure with a toothpick. (Asparagus will protrude from both sides.)

Arrange rolls, seam side down, in a single layer in a buttered baking dish.

Heat butter in a small saucepan over low heat. Add garlic and scallion; cook until tender.

Stir in Marsala and tomato paste. Increase heat to medium and cook for 5 minutes until slightly reduced.

Pour the sauce over the rolls. Bake for 10 minutes or until fish flakes when tested with a fork. Remove fish from oven.

Preheat oven to broil with rack 6 inches from heat.

Pour cooking liquid into a saucepan over medium heat. Combine egg yolks and cream in a small bowl. Add one-fourth of the hot cooking liquid to the egg mixture. Stir warm egg mixture into saucepan. Cook, stirring constantly, until mixture thickens slightly. Pour sauce over fish.

Sprinkle with cheese and broil (with electric oven door partially open) for 2 minutes or until cheese melts.

Yield: 6 servings.

**Serve with
Roasted
Garlic
Mashed Potatoes
(page 193).**

TUNA STEAKS WITH MELON SALSA

Parve

2 (5- to 6-ounce) tuna steaks (½-inch thick)	Salt
	Pepper
2 tablespoons olive oil	Melon Salsa

Preheat grill to medium-hot heat.

Brush tuna with olive oil and sprinkle with salt and pepper. Grill 3 minutes on each side or until just pink inside.

Transfer tuna to serving plates and top with Melon Salsa.

Yield: 2 servings.

MELON SALSA:

¾ cup coarsely chopped cantaloupe	2 teaspoons olive oil
¼ cup chopped red onion	1 teaspoon fresh lime juice
2 tablespoons fresh cilantro, chopped	Dash hot sauce
	Salt
	Pepper

Combine cantaloupe, onion, cilantro, olive oil, lime juice, and hot sauce. Season to taste with salt and pepper.

Yield: 1 cup.

FILLET OF SOLE FRANCAIS

Parve

¼ cup all-purpose flour	2-3 tablespoons olive oil
2-3 large eggs, lightly beaten	1 cup hot water
¼ cup seasoned dry bread crumbs	1 parve chicken bouillon cube
2 pounds sole fillets	¼ cup fresh lemon juice
2-3 tablespoons margarine	1 teaspoon anchovy paste, optional

Preheat oven to 350°.

Place flour, eggs, and bread crumbs in three shallow bowls. Dredge fish in flour, shaking off excess. Dip in eggs and dredge in bread crumbs to evenly coat both sides.

Heat margarine and olive oil in a skillet over medium-high heat. Add fillets and sauté just until lightly browned. Place fish in a lightly greased 13- x 9-inch baking dish.

Combine water, bouillon cube, lemon juice, and anchovy paste, if desired; pour over fish.

Cover and bake for 20 minutes.

Yield: 4 to 6 servings.

A lovely way to present this dish is on a bed of sautéed greens. Blanch 8 ounces of fresh spinach and ½ head of Swiss chard in boiling water for 30 seconds. Drain, squeezing out moisture. Sauté greens in ¼ cup olive oil with 3 chopped cloves of garlic. Spread greens on plate and top with fish.

We suggest a Chardonnay or Muscadet to accompany this delicate dish.

Pan–Fried Sole
with Tomatoes and Pine Nuts

Parve

¼ cup pine nuts
½ cup all-purpose flour
Salt
Pepper
1 (1- to 2-pound) whole sole (or fillets) or small flounder
2-3 tablespoons olive oil

1 cup seeded and diced tomato
¼ cup chopped fresh parsley
2 tablespoons white wine
2 tablespoons fresh lemon juice
Garnish: parsley sprigs

Preheat oven to 350°.

Place pine nuts on a baking sheet. Bake for 5 to 7 minutes or until lightly toasted; cool.

Combine flour, salt, and pepper in a shallow dish. Dredge sole in flour mixture, shaking off excess.

Heat oil in a large skillet over medium heat. Add sole and cook 3 to 4 minutes or until golden brown. Carefully turn the fish and cook 5 minutes or until fish flakes when tested with a fork.

Transfer fish to a serving platter; cover and keep warm.

Add tomato, parsley, wine, and lemon juice to skillet. Cook over medium-high heat for 2 to 3 minutes or until the sauce is thickened and bubbly. Pour the sauce on the sole. Sprinkle with toasted pine nuts and garnish with parsley.

Yield: 4 to 6 servings.

Serve this dish with Wild Rice (page 209) and asparagus sautéed in a little peanut oil and rice vinegar.

Riesling is a fruity, almost spicy, wine that pairs well with this fish. It is also a good choice for Chinese or other exotic and spicy foods.

HONEY–BATTERED LEMON SOLE AND VIDALIA ONIONS

Parve

3 large eggs, lightly beaten
3 tablespoons honey
¼ teaspoon salt
3 tablespoons all-purpose flour
Canola oil

1 pound lemon sole fillets, patted dry
2 Vidalia or other sweet onions, cut into ¼-inch slices (do not separate into rings)

Combine eggs, honey, and salt in a medium bowl. Stir in flour until well blended, adding more flour, if necessary, to make a thick batter; set aside.

Pour oil to a depth of 1 inch in an electric skillet or large, heavy skillet. Heat oil 350° to 375° (do not let oil begin to smoke or fish will scorch).

Dip fillets in batter, coating both sides. Fry fillets in the hot oil for 3 minutes on each side or until golden brown. Do not fry too many pieces at one time as it lowers the temperature of the oil and the fish will steam. Drain fish on paper towels.

Dip onion slices in batter; fry on each side for 3 minutes or until golden brown. Drain.

Yield: 3 to 4 servings.

Serve with Oriental Cole Slaw (page 54) and Corn Salad in Husk Pockets (page 66).

GRAY SOLE IN PARCHMENT

Dairy

"*This recipe has been enjoyed by my company– even reluctant fish eaters. There will be a lot of liquid in the parchment after baking. You can remove the fish from the parchment with a slotted spatula or serve it in the parchment for an interesting presentation.*"

¼	cup olive oil	¾	cup crème fraîche
8	ounces shiitake mushrooms, sliced ½-inch thick	1	tablespoon mustard
			Salt
			Pepper
1	pound tomatoes, peeled, seeded, and chopped (sidebar page 153)	6	gray sole fillets (about 1½ pounds)
			Parchment paper

Heat oil in a large skillet over medium-high heat. Add mushrooms and sauté until tender. Add tomatoes and sauté until most liquid evaporates; let cool.

Stir in crème fraîche, mustard, salt, and pepper; set aside.

Preheat oven to 500°.

Cut six 11- x 15-inch pieces of parchment, fold in half lengthwise and place on a work surface. Open parchment and place the fish along the center fold. Top fish evenly with mushroom mixture; fold over parchment allowing plenty of room for expansion. Seal packages securely by folding edges toward the fold and place on a baking sheet.

Bake 10 minutes or until packages puff. To serve in parchment, cut an "X" in the top and carefully open packages as steam escapes.

Yield: 6 servings.

Crème Fraîche

Crème fraîche is a French specialty consisting of matured thickened cream with a tangy flavor and a velvety rich texture. It is wonderful spooned over desserts and is an easy addition to soups and sauces because it can be boiled without curdling. It is used very often to garnish the top of a soup bowl. It is not easy to find with kosher certification and is very expensive. Fortunately, it can easily be made at home.

Combine 1 cup heavy whipping cream and 2 tablespoons buttermilk in a glass container. Cover and let stand at room temperature (about 70°) for 8 to 24 hours. It will become very thick. Stir, cover, and refrigerate up to 10 days.

Pan-Fried Flounder with Almond Butter

Dairy

½ cup all-purpose flour
3 large eggs, lightly beaten
2 tablespoons grated
   Parmesan cheese
1 tablespoon chopped fresh
   parsley
½ teaspoon salt
¼ teaspoon pepper

3 tablespoons olive oil
2 pounds flounder fillets
½ cup butter
¼ cup sliced almonds
3 tablespoons lemon juice
2 tablespoons dry white
   wine

Place flour in a pie plate or shallow dish; set aside.

Combine eggs, cheese, parsley, salt, and pepper in a pie plate or shallow dish; set aside.

Heat oil in a large skillet over medium heat. (When the oil is hot enough, you will see ripples in the oil when the pan is tilted.)

Dredge fish in flour; shake off excess. Dip fish into egg mixture; drain off excess. Cook fish for 3 to 5 minutes on each side or until golden brown and fish flakes when tested with a fork. You may have to cook the fish in batches, using additional oil if necessary, to prevent overcrowding.

Transfer fish to a serving platter; cover loosely and keep warm. Wipe skillet clean.

Heat butter in skillet over medium heat. When butter foams, stir in almonds and cook until they are lightly browned. Remove from heat and stir in lemon juice and wine. Spoon sauce over fish and serve immediately.

Yield: 4 to 6 servings.

Lemon Wraps

Cut cheesecloth into 8-inch circles. Cut a small lemon in half and place it, cut side down, in the center of the cheesecloth. Draw up the edges of the circle to form a pouch. Tie the neck of the lemon wrap with string. Trim loose ends. Tuck sprigs of fresh herbs into the neck of the lemon wrap.

SESAME ENCRUSTED SALMON WITH SPINACH-WATERCRESS SAUCE

Dairy

*T*hese tasty fillets are surrounded in a delicate crust of sesame seeds and partnered with a creamy spinach-watercress sauce. Gorgeous and delicious.

1 cup dry white wine	¼ cup butter, chilled and
1 shallot, chopped	cut into pieces
1 cup heavy whipping cream	½ teaspoon salt
½ cup packed spinach	½ teaspoon pepper
leaves, stems removed	¼ cup sesame seeds
½ cup packed watercress,	6 (7-ounce) skinless salmon
trimmed	fillets
1 tablespoon chopped fresh	¼ cup vegetable oil, divided
dill	

Combine wine and shallot in a heavy saucepan over medium-high heat. Bring to a boil; boil 7 minutes until reduced to ¼ cup.

Add cream; reduce heat and simmer 12 minutes until reduced to ¾ cup.

Transfer hot mixture to the container of a blender or food processor. Add spinach, watercress, and dill; process until smooth. Add butter and blend until butter melts and sauce is smooth. Stir in salt and pepper.

Pour sauce into saucepan; cover and keep warm.

Place sesame seeds in a shallow container. Sprinkle salmon with salt and pepper; dredge in sesame seeds until lightly coated on all sides.

Heat 2 tablespoons oil in each of two large skillets over medium-low heat. Add three salmon fillets to each skillet; cook 3 minutes on each side or until opaque in center and fish flakes when tested with a fork.

Transfer salmon to serving plates and serve with sauce.

Yield: 6 servings.

To keep the seeds adhered to the salmon, coat the fillets lightly with vegetable oil or lightly beaten egg whites.

Sautéed Tuna with Caramelized Onions

Parve

3 tablespoons oil	Salt and pepper
2 large onions, sliced	1½ tablespoons balsamic
2 medium size tuna steaks	vinegar
2 teaspoons paprika,	2 tablespoons chopped fresh
divided	parsley

Heat oil in a large skillet over medium heat; add onions and sauté 10 minutes or until tender and golden brown. Move onions to the side of the skillet.

Place tuna steaks in the center of skillet; sprinkle with half of paprika, salt, and pepper. Cook tuna 5 minutes; turn and sprinkle with remaining paprika, salt, and pepper.

Cook 5 minutes or until tuna is no longer red in the center. If necessary, sprinkle pan with a little water to help cook tuna. (If onions begin to burn, transfer to a plate until tuna finishes cooking.) Remove skillet from heat.

Sprinkle vinegar on onions only. To serve, place tuna on plates and surround with onions. Sprinkle with chopped parsley.

Yield: 2 servings.

Mexican Sea Bass

Parve

2-3 pounds sea bass fillets	1 onion, sliced
3 tablespoons fresh lemon	1 red bell pepper, sliced
juice	½ cup pitted black or green
Salt and pepper	olives
2 tablespoons olive oil	½ cup capers, drained
4 tomatoes, peeled, seeded,	¼ teaspoon dried oregano
and chopped	

Preheat oven to 350°. Place sea bass in a single layer in a 13- x 9-inch baking dish. Sprinkle sea bass with lemon juice, salt, and pepper.

Bake, covered, for 25 minutes or until fish flakes when tested with a fork.

Heat oil in a medium saucepan over medium-high heat. Add tomatoes, onion, bell pepper, olives, and capers; sauté until onions are translucent and tomatoes and bell pepper are tender. Stir in oregano and season to taste with salt and pepper.

Pour sauce over fish. Bake, covered, for 30 minutes.

Yield: 4 to 6 servings.

Flavored Oils

Flavored oils and vinegar are exciting additions to garnish a plate with color and flavor. "Paint" the plate with wild zigzags for a stunning effect.

Balsamic Reduction

1 cup balsamic vinegar

Place vinegar in a saucepan over medium-high heat. Bring to a boil, reduce heat, and simmer for 10 to 15 minutes until reduced to ⅓ cup; cool. Pour into a squeeze bottle. Dot or drizzle on plates to garnish.

Basil Oil

¾ cup basil leaves

¼ cup spinach or watercress

1 cup olive oil

Blanch basil and spinach in boiling, salted water. Plunge into ice water to stop the cooking process; drain, squeezing out excess water.

Place basil and spinach in the container of a blender with enough oil to cover. Process until smooth. Add the remaining oil; process for 2 to 3 minutes. Cover and place in refrigerator to allow solids to settle to the bottom. Pour clear oil in a squeeze bottle, discarding solids. Dot or drizzle on plates to garnish.

Yield: 1 cup.

PAN-SEARED SALMON WITH GINGER-SHIITAKE CREAM SAUCE

Dairy

This dish can turn anyone into a regular at the fish market. The sauce is incredibly delicious and can also be used over pan-seared tuna.

2 tablespoons peanut oil	Ginger-Shiitake Cream
4 (6-ounce) salmon steaks	Sauce
Coarsely ground black	Garnish: lime wedges
pepper	

Preheat oven to 200°.

Sprinkle one side of salmon with black pepper.

Heat oil in a large skillet over high heat; add salmon, skin side down, and sear for 3 minutes. Turn salmon, and cook 4 minutes or until desired degree of doneness.

Transfer salmon to a baking sheet with sides; place in oven to keep warm until ready to serve.

Spoon sauce on plates and arrange salmon on top of sauce. Garnish with lime wedges.

Yield: 4 servings.

GINGER-SHIITAKE CREAM SAUCE:

3 tablespoons unsalted	8 ounces fresh shiitake,
butter	oyster, or cremini
⅓ cup thinly sliced scallions	mushrooms
2 tablespoons peeled and	⅓ cup soy sauce
finely chopped fresh	1½ cups heavy whipping
ginger	cream
4 cloves garlic, chopped	3 tablespoons fresh lime juice

Heat butter in a large skillet over medium-high heat. Add scallions, ginger, and garlic; sauté 30 seconds.

Stir in mushrooms and soy sauce; cook 30 seconds.

Stir in cream. Bring to a boil, reduce heat, and simmer 3 minutes or until sauce lightly coats the back of a spoon. Stir in lime juice.

Yield: 2½ cups.

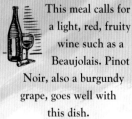

This meal calls for a light, red, fruity wine such as a Beaujolais. Pinot Noir, also a burgundy grape, goes well with this dish.

Oven Poached Sole
with Tarragon Sauce

Dairy

1½	*pounds small sole fillets*	3	*tablespoons butter*
	Salt	1½	*tablespoons all-purpose*
	White pepper		*flour*
1	*teaspoon dried tarragon*	2	*egg yolks*
½	*cup water*	½	*cup heavy whipping cream*
½	*cup dry white wine*		*Garnishes: chopped fresh*
¼	*pound sliced mushrooms*		*parsley, lemon wedges*

Preheat oven to 350°.

Sprinkle sole with salt and pepper. Fold each piece in half and place in a single layer in a buttered baking dish; sprinkle with tarragon. Combine water and wine; pour over fish.

Cover and bake for 20 to 25 minutes or until opaque in the center and fish flakes when tested with a fork. Remove fish from oven and carefully pour off liquid into a 2-cup measuring cup. Keep fish warm.

Heat butter in a skillet over medium-high heat; add mushrooms and sauté until lightly browned. Add flour, stirring until well blended. Cook 1 minute, stirring constantly. Gradually add 1 cup of the reserved fish liquid; cook over medium heat, stirring constantly, until mixture is thickened and bubbly.

Beat egg yolks and cream in a small bowl. Gradually stir one-fourth of the hot mushroom mixture into the egg mixture; add to remaining hot mixture, stirring constantly. Cook over low heat until thickened (do not boil). Season to taste with salt.

Preheat oven to broil with rack 6 inches from heat.

Transfer sole to an oven-safe serving dish; pour sauce over fish. Broil 2 to 3 minutes.

Garnish with fresh parsley and lemon wedges.

Yield: 4 servings.

RED SNAPPER
WITH MATCHSTICK VEGETABLES
Dairy

2 tablespoons butter
6 (4-ounce) red snapper
   fillets
¼ teaspoon salt
   Freshly ground white
   pepper
2 shallots, minced
12 sprigs of lemon thyme or
   thyme

¾ cup diagonally sliced
   snow pea pods
½ cup yellow squash cut
   into thin strips
¼ cup carrots cut into thin
   strips
¼ cup red bell pepper cut
   into thin strips
6 tablespoons dry white wine
6 thin slices lemon

Preheat oven to 400°.

Cut six 12- x 19-inch pieces of heavy-duty foil; fold in half lengthwise, creasing firmly. Trim each piece to form a large heart shape when unfolded. Unfold and place foil pieces on baking sheet with 1 teaspoon butter in each.

Place fillets, skin side down, on top of butter; sprinkle with salt and pepper. Top evenly with shallots and place 2 sprigs of lemon thyme on each fillet.

Add vegetables around fish. Drizzle 1 tablespoon wine over each fillet and top each with a slice of lemon.

Fold edges of foil packets together (allow room for expansion), pleating and crimping to seal; twist end tightly.

Bake for 15 to 20 minutes or until bags are puffed and fish flakes when tested with a fork. Cut each bag open with scissors and serve on plates.

Yield: 6 servings.

Serve with
Chardonnay or
Sauvignon Blanc.

PAN–SEARED YELLOWFIN TUNA STEAKS

Parve

Yellowfin tuna is an easy-to-cook, versatile fish. At the fish market, ask for ahi tuna steaks, which are tuna caught off the waters near Hawaii and prized for their high quality. This recipe calls for searing the tuna to seal in moisture and enhance flavor. Cook the fish to rare or medium for a tender and succulent dish.

½ cup teriyaki sauce
1 tablespoon fresh lemon
     juice
1 teaspoon minced garlic
½ teaspoon ground ginger
½ teaspoon olive oil

1 tablespoon whole black
     peppercorns
4 (6- to 8-ounce) tuna
     steaks
   Olive oil

Prepare the lemon teriyaki sauce: combine teriyaki sauce, lemon juice, garlic, ginger, and olive oil in the container of a blender; process until well blended. Set aside.

Place peppercorns in a zip-top bag and roll with a rolling pin to coarsely crack; set aside.

Heat a cast iron or other heavy skillet over high heat.

Brush tuna steaks with oil and lightly coat with cracked peppercorns. (Do not coat too heavily, or the pepper flavor will overwhelm the tuna.)

Sear each side of tuna 3 minutes for rare, or 5 minutes for medium. For rare, the center will remain pinkish-red and the outside will be browned. Serve with the prepared sauce.

Yield: 4 servings.

CHILI-CRUSTED TUNA STEAK WITH TORTILLA SALAD AND ORANGE VINAIGRETTE

Parve

"When our daughter lived and taught on a Navajo reservation at the four corners of Arizona, Colorado, New Mexico, and Utah, we developed a taste for Southwestern cooking. (We had to, or starve!) Here is one of our favorite dishes."

1	cup vegetable oil	½	teaspoon freshly ground pepper
3	(6-inch) tortillas, cut into very thin strips	4	teaspoons olive oil
1¼	tablespoons ground cumin	6	tuna steaks
1	tablespoon ancho chili powder	2	cups mixed gourmet greens such as mesclun and frisée
½	teaspoon salt		Orange Vinaigrette

Heat vegetable oil in a saucepan over medium-high heat. (The oil will be hot enough when a "test" strip of tortilla sizzles.) Fry a few strips at a time for 15 seconds. Drain on paper towels and set aside.

Combine cumin, ancho chili powder, salt, and pepper and press into one side of tuna.

Heat olive oil in a skillet over medium-high heat until nearly smokey. Add tuna, spice side down, and sauté 1 minute. Reduce heat to medium; turn and sauté tuna for 3 minutes for rare, 4 minutes for medium rare or to desired degree of doneness.

Toss greens with enough Orange Vinaigrette to lightly coat; place on serving plates.

Place tuna steak on top of greens and garnish with reserved tortilla strips.

Yield: 6 servings.

ORANGE VINAIGRETTE:

1 cup orange juice	1 teaspoon ancho chili
2 tablespoons fresh lime	powder
juice	½ cup olive oil
1 tablespoon red wine	Salt
vinegar	Pepper
1 teaspoon Dijon mustard	

Pour orange juice into a saucepan over medium-high heat. Bring to a boil, reduce heat, and simmer until reduced to a syrup (about ¼ cup).

Combine orange juice, lime juice, vinegar, mustard, and chili powder in the container of a blender. Process for 30 seconds. Turn blender on high; gradually add oil in a slow, steady stream until mixture emulsifies. Season to taste with salt and pepper. Dressing may be made ahead and refrigerated.

Yield: 1 cup.

POACHED SALMON WITH MUSTARD-DILL SAUCE

Parve or Dairy

Poaching fish is a quick and basic technique where the fish is immersed, skin side up, in a shallow pan of seasoned water. The liquid is brought to a boil, then reduced to a low simmer before the fish is added. The fish is simmered for about 8 to 10 minutes, depending on thickness. The fish is carefully removed with a slotted spatula, with skin and poaching liquid discarded. Most cooks use a poaching liquid called Court Bouillon.

COURT BOUILLON

Parve

7 cups cold water
1 cup plus
2 tablespoons red wine vinegar
3 cloves garlic
2 bay leaves
1 bouquet garni of fresh thyme, dill, and parsley (sidebar page 39)
1 onion, chopped
½ small leek, chopped (white and pale green parts only)
1 carrot, chopped
1 celery, chopped
1½ teaspoons white peppercorns
1 teaspoon fine sea salt

Place all ingredients in a large saucepan over medium-high heat; bring to a boil. Boil for 20 minutes; strain and discard solids. Cover and refrigerate up to 3 days or freeze for several months.

Yield: 2 quarts.

"*A friend of mine swears by her amazing poached salmon recipe. Apparently it is made in her dishwasher — dishes and detergent optional. We are not that adventurous in our house and prefer this easy, yet elegant rendition of poached salmon. It is wonderful on a hot summer day and makes a beautiful first course or main dish. The salmon can be served warm, room temperature, or cold. Also, we never measure ingredients!*"

1 (5- to 6-pound) salmon fillet	½ cup thinly sliced scallions (green part only)
White Zinfandel wine	Fresh dill
Water	Fresh parsley
Margarine or butter, cut into pieces	Fresh tarragon (optional)
	Freshly ground pepper
1 lemon, halved	Mustard-Dill Sauce
	Garnish: fresh dill sprigs

Preheat oven to 350°.

Check fillet for small bones and remove with tweezers, if necessary. Place fish in tray of a fish poacher.*

Pour wine to a depth of ¼ inch; dot fish with margarine or butter. Squeeze lemon juice over fish and sprinkle with scallions. Finely chop dill, parsley, and tarragon with kitchen scissors, snipping herbs evenly over fish. Sprinkle with pepper.

Cover with lid and bake for 25 minutes or until fish flakes when tested with a fork. Remove from oven; cool. Transfer to serving platter; cover with plastic wrap and refrigerate until chilled. Serve with Mustard-Dill Sauce and garnish with sprigs of fresh dill.

Yield: 8 to 10 servings.

*If you do not have a poacher, create one with an 18-inch piece of heavy-duty foil placed in the bottom of a deep roasting pan. Place whole fillet in the center of the foil and turn up edges around fish to hold ingredients around fish. If your fillet is too large, cut it in half and make two "poaching packets." Add wine, butter, lemon juice, scallions, herbs, and pepper as directed. To cover, seal foil edges tightly leaving room for steam to expand packet. Pour a small amount of water into the bottom of the roasting pan, under the foil poaching packet. Proceed with recipe.

MUSTARD-DILL SAUCE:

1¾ tablespoons sugar	⅓ cup Dijon mustard
1½ tablespoons white wine vinegar	1 tablespoon chopped fresh dill
½ cup olive oil	1 tablespoon white pepper

Whisk together sugar and vinegar in a small bowl until sugar dissolves. Gradually add olive oil, whisking until well blended. Stir in mustard, dill, and pepper. Cover and refrigerate.

Yield: 1 cup.

TERRA COTTA ROSES

1 small terra cotta pot– can be spray painted any color

1 dozen roses– use a color to complement the pot (pictured are Sari Roses)

1 moss block

2-3 hydrangea

4-5 pieces lemon leaf vine

Gold wired ribbon or raffia ribbon

Remove all leaves and thorns from the roses and wrap them together at the top with a rubber band. Fill the terra cotta pot with moss block. Cover the moss block with hydrangea and vine. Place roses in the center of the pot. Tie towards the top with a ribbon to cover the rubber band.

GRILLED GROUPER WITH ROASTED PECAN SAUCE

Dairy

1 tablespoon white pepper	1 teaspoon chili powder
½ tablespoon freshly ground pepper	½ teaspoon garlic powder
1 teaspoon salt	4 (6-ounce) grouper fillets, patted dry

Preheat grill to medium-hot heat.

Combine peppers, salt, chili powder, and garlic powder, coating fillets well.

Arrange fillets on a greased grill rack.

Grill 4 minutes on each side or until fish flakes when tested with a fork. (Grouper can also be broiled, if desired.)

Arrange grouper on a serving platter and drizzle with warm Roasted Pecan Sauce. Serve immediately.

ROASTED PECAN SAUCE:

2 cups chopped pecans	1 teaspoon hot sauce
¾ cup unsalted butter	2 cloves garlic, minced
⅓ cup minced onion	

Preheat oven to 350°.

Spread pecans in a single layer on a baking sheet. Bake for 4 minutes, shaking the pan once or twice, or until golden brown. Watch carefully since nuts burn very quickly.

Heat butter in a saucepan over medium heat. Stir in pecans, onion, hot sauce, and garlic; cook until thoroughly heated. Keep warm over low heat until serving.

Yield: 3 cups.

The menu is complete with the addition of a baked tomato stuffed with creamed spinach. Select firm, ripe tomatoes. Blanch in boiling water for 30 seconds; immediately run under cold water to remove skins. Cut each in half, removing seeds. Prepare creamed spinach according to package directions. Fill tomatoes evenly with spinach.

PASTA

*Pasta with Uncooked
Tomato & Olive Sauce,
page 151*

ZITI WITH PORTOBELLO MUSHROOMS AND GOAT CHEESE SAUCE

Dairy

12 ounces portobello mushrooms	1 tablespoon minced garlic
¼ cup butter, divided	3 scallions, sliced into disks
¼ cup olive oil, divided	16 ounces ziti
1 medium onion, chopped	6 quarts water
1 teaspoon salt, divided	1 tablespoon salt
½ teaspoon sugar	Goat Cheese Sauce
2 shallots, minced	Garnish: fresh chives

Remove stems from mushrooms. Cut caps in half and slice crosswise into ¼-inch slices; set aside.

Heat 2 tablespoons butter and 2 tablespoons oil in a large skillet over medium heat. Add onion, ½ teaspoon salt, and sugar; sauté 20 minutes. Add shallots; sauté 5 minutes or until tender. Add garlic and scallions; sauté 2 minutes. Remove from pan and set aside.

Heat remaining 2 tablespoons butter and 2 tablespoons oil in the skillet. Add mushrooms and remaining ½ teaspoon salt. Sauté 8 to 10 minutes, stirring occasionally, or until tender.

Stir in reserved onion mixture. Cook over low heat until pasta and sauce are prepared.

Cook ziti in 6 quarts boiling water and 1 tablespoon salt according to package directions until al dente; drain. Rinse pasta in cool water; drain.

Toss ziti with the mushroom mixture and place in a large serving dish. Top with Goat Cheese Sauce and garnish with chives.

Yield: 6 to 8 servings.

GOAT CHEESE SAUCE:
Dairy

2 cups heavy whipping cream	1½ tablespoons minced fresh chives
6 ounces fresh mild goat cheese, crumbled	Salt
	Freshly ground pepper

Pour cream into a medium saucepan over medium heat. Bring to a boil, reduce heat, and simmer 15 minutes or until reduced by one-third. Remove from heat.

Add goat cheese, stirring until smooth. Stir in chives. Season to taste with salt and pepper.

Yield: 2 cups.

Always cook pasta in a large pot of boiling water. Remove some of the water before the pasta is drained to thin sauces if they are too thick.

This recipe can also be made as manicotti. Prepare 12 manicotti according to package directions. Stuff with mushroom mixture and top with Goat Cheese Sauce. Garnish with whole chives.

Pasta with Uncooked Tomato and Olive Sauce

Dairy

3   medium vine-ripened
    tomatoes, seeded and
    chopped
1   yellow bell pepper, finely
    chopped
2   cloves garlic, minced
1   cup (4 ounces) shredded
    mozzarella cheese
½   cup niçoise or other
    brine-cured black olives,
    pitted and halved

3   tablespoons extra virgin
    olive oil
1   tablespoon balsamic
    vinegar, or to taste
    Salt and pepper
8   ounces cavatappi, rotini,
    or other spiral-shaped
    pasta
¾   cup finely chopped mixed
    fresh herbs such as basil,
    parsley and mint

Combine tomatoes, bell pepper, garlic, mozzarella, olives, oil, and vinegar in a large bowl. Season with salt and pepper to taste. Let stand 30 minutes.

Cook pasta according to package directions to al dente; drain. Toss pasta with sauce and fresh herbs.

Yield: 4 servings.

This dish can be served with a red or white wine. Try a Beaujolais or a Chardonnay, depending on your mood.

Mushroom Fettuccine

Parve

6   ounces sun-dried tomatoes
    (not packed in oil)
1   (12-ounce) package
    fettuccine
⅓   cup extra virgin olive oil

4   ounces shiitake
    mushrooms
4   ounces oyster mushrooms
3   cloves garlic, minced
    Salt and pepper

Place tomatoes in a small bowl with boiling water to cover. Let soften for 5 minutes. Drain, mince and set aside.

Cook the pasta according to package directions until al dente. Drain and place in a serving bowl.

Heat oil in a skillet over medium-high heat. Add the mushrooms, garlic, and reserved tomatoes; sauté 3 to 5 minutes. Remove from heat and toss with the fettuccine. Season with salt and pepper to taste.

Yield: 6 servings.

This dish can be prepared in advance and rewarmed. Add Parmesan cheese for dairy meals.

PENNE WITH ASPARAGUS

Parve

⅓ cup olive oil
1 can anchovy fillets, drained
5 quarts water

1 (16-ounce) package penne pasta
3 pounds asparagus, trimmed and cut into ¾-inch pieces

Heat oil in a large skillet over medium heat. Add anchovies and cook, mashing with a spatula, until blended. Set aside and keep warm.

Bring 5 quarts of water to a boil in a large soup pot over high heat. Add pasta; bring back to a boil and add asparagus. Cook pasta and asparagus 7 minutes or until al dente. Drain pasta and asparagus and toss with anchovy mixture. Serve immediately.

Yield: 6 to 8 servings.

ANGEL HAIR PASTA WITH SMOKED SALMON AND DILL

Dairy

8 ounces angel hair pasta or fettuccine
6 tablespoons unsalted butter
¼ cup chopped scallions
2½ tablespoons all-purpose flour
1 cup heavy whipping cream

1 cup milk
¼ cup fresh dill, snipped
1½ tablespoons capers, drained
4 ounces thinly sliced smoked salmon, cut into thin strips
Salt
Pepper

Cook the pasta according to package directions; drain and place in a large serving bowl.

Melt butter in a large skillet over medium heat. Add scallions and sauté 2 minutes. Stir in flour and cook 1 minute, stirring constantly.

Combine cream and milk; gradually whisk into flour mixture. Cook 5 minutes, stirring constantly, until thickened and bubbly. Stir in dill and capers.

Combine sauce, salmon, and pasta, tossing gently. Season with salt and pepper, to taste. Recipe may be doubled.

Yield: 2 servings.

Dill can easily be removed from its stem by snipping with a pair of small scissors.

Serve this dish with diced smoked salmon or salmon caviar in the center with fresh dill sprigs. Delicious served with a sparkling wine or champagne.

PENNE À LA VODKA

Dairy

"*I love to order this dish in restaurants, but have had a hard time trying to find a recipe in a cookbook that tastes as good...until now. If you are a Penne à la Vodka fan, you will love this tangy, creamy recipe. You may never need to go out to eat again.*"

1 (16-ounce) package penne pasta
5 tablespoons butter
1 small onion, minced
2 large cloves garlic, minced
½ teaspoon crushed red pepper flakes
½ cup vodka
1 (28-ounce) can plum tomatoes, crushed and undrained
1 cup heavy whipping cream
1 teaspoon salt
1 cup grated Parmesan cheese
Pepper

Cook the pasta according to package directions until al dente; drain and place in a large serving bowl.

Heat the butter in a saucepan over medium heat. Add the onion, garlic, and crushed red pepper flakes; sauté 3 minutes.

Stir in vodka; simmer 5 minutes.

Add tomatoes; simmer for 15 minutes, stirring occasionally, or until liquid evaporates.

Stir in cream and salt. Simmer for 10 minutes, stirring frequently.

Add Parmesan cheese, mixing well. Season with pepper to taste.

Pour sauce over pasta, tossing to coat. Serve immediately.

Yield: 6 to 8 servings.

Garnish this pasta with a sprinkle of diced fresh tomato fillet and chopped parsley in the center of the dish. To make a tomato fillet, cut an "X" in the blossom end. Blanch tomato in boiling water for 10 seconds and immediately plunge in ice water to stop the cooking process. Run tomato under cold running water and the skin will slip right off. Cut in half and scoop out the seeds. You are left with the fillet.

Chardonnay will add a nice, light touch to this meal.

LASAGNA PRIMAVERA

Dairy

3 quarts water
1 (8-ounce) package
  lasagna noodles
3 carrots, cut into ¼-inch
  slices
1 cup broccoli flowerets
1 cup (¼-inch thick) sliced
  zucchini
1 cup (¼-inch thick) sliced
  yellow squash
2 (10-ounce) packages
  frozen chopped spinach,
  thawed and squeezed dry

1 (8-ounce) container
  ricotta cheese
1 (26-ounce) jar marinara
  sauce with mushrooms
  or 3 cups Homemade
  Tomato Sauce (page 162)
6 cups shredded
  mozzarella cheese
½ cup grated Parmesan
  cheese

Bring 3 quarts of water to a boil in a 6-quart soup pot over high heat. Add lasagna noodles and cook 5 minutes. Add carrots and cook 2 minutes. Add broccoli, zucchini, and yellow squash and cook 2 minutes or until pasta is tender; drain well. Place noodles and vegetables in separate bowls; set aside.

Combine spinach and ricotta cheese; set aside.

Preheat oven to 400°.

Spread 1 cup marinara sauce on the bottom of a 13- x 9-inch baking dish. Layer with half of the noodles, half of each of the vegetables, half of the spinach mixture, and 3 cups of the mozzarella.

Pour 1 cup sauce over layers. Repeat layers with remaining noodles, vegetables, spinach mixture, and 1½ cups mozzarella. Top with remaining 1 cup sauce and sprinkle with Parmesan cheese and remaining 1½ cups mozzarella cheese.

Bake, uncovered, for 30 minutes or until thoroughly heated. Lasagna may be assembled, covered and refrigerated up to 2 days ahead. Remove from refrigerator 1 hour before baking. If cold, bake 1 hour.

Yield: 8 servings.

Pasta Place Cards

When setting a buffet table featuring pasta, you can write the name of each entrée on an uncooked lasagna noodle with a black marker and place it in front of the serving platter. This is also a great idea for individual place cards at your table.

SUN-DRIED TOMATO PENNE PASTA

Parve

The only thing missing from your table right now is warm Italian bread, a big Caesar salad (page 70), and this pasta.

1   (16-ounce) package
    penne noodles
10-12 sun-dried tomatoes
    (not packed in oil)
2   tablespoons olive oil
3-4 cloves garlic, chopped
    Lemon pepper

Garlic powder
1   (26-ounce) jar chunky
    marinara sauce or
    3 cups Homemade
    Tomato Sauce (page 162)
    Chopped fresh basil,
    divided

Cook the pasta according to package directions; drain and place in a large serving bowl.

Soak tomatoes in hot water for 10 minutes. Drain and cut into small pieces. Soak tomato pieces in olive oil for 5 to 10 minutes.

Heat the marinara sauce in a saucepan over medium-low heat. Add chopped garlic and season with lemon pepper and garlic powder to taste. Stir in a small amount of the chopped fresh basil. Stir in tomatoes and oil.

Pour the marinara sauce in the center of the pasta and sprinkle with chopped fresh basil.

Yield: 6 to 8 servings.

HOMEMADE SUN-DRIED TOMATOES

You can sun-dry tomatoes from your garden right at home in your kitchen. Plum tomatoes, also known as Roma tomatoes, work best because they contain less water and fewer seeds than other varieties.

4 pounds ripe plum tomatoes

3 tablespoons kosher salt

3 tablespoons sugar

Preheat oven to 150°.

Remove stems and slice tomatoes in half lengthwise. Place halves, cut side up, on cookie sheets or in a glass baking dish. Do not use aluminum foil; the acid in the tomatoes will react with the metal.

Combine salt and sugar; sprinkle each tomato half with about ½ teaspoon.

Bake slowly for 10 hours; cool. Refrigerate for later use.

Yield: 6 cups.

ROAST PEPPER PASTA

Parve

6   red or yellow bell peppers
1   (16-ounce) package
      penne pasta
½   cup extra virgin olive oil
3   onions, thinly sliced
¼   teaspoon white pepper

1   tablespoon minced garlic
1   tablespoon paprika
3   large tomatoes, seeded
      and diced
    Garnish: chopped fresh
      parsley

Preheat oven to broil with rack 5 inches away from heat.

Place peppers on an aluminum foil-lined baking sheet. Broil (with electric oven door partially open) about 5 minutes on each side or until peppers look blistered and blackened.

Place peppers in a paper bag; seal, and let stand 10 minutes to loosen skins. Peel peppers, discarding seeds; cut into thin strips.

Cook pasta according to package directions; drain and place in a large serving bowl.

Heat oil in a large skillet over medium-high heat. Add onions and white pepper; sauté until onion is tender and golden brown. Reduce heat; add garlic and sauté 1 minute.

Add paprika and cook 1 minute. Stir in tomatoes and reserved peppers; cook 1 minute. Remove from heat and toss with pasta. Garnish with chopped fresh parsley.

Yield: 6 to 8 servings.

Make this pasta as a creamy dairy dish. Add a few dashes of hot pepper sauce to 1½ cups sour cream. Toss with the pasta and peppers.

Serve with a flavorful red wine such as a French Côtes du Rhône or an Italian Montepulciano d'Abruzzo.

BROCCOLI–LASAGNA ROLL-UPS

Dairy

12 lasagna noodles
1 tablespoon vegetable oil
1 (10-ounce) package
   frozen chopped broccoli,
   thawed and squeezed
   dry
2 tablespoons minced
   scallions
1 (15-ounce) container
   ricotta cheese

⅓ cup grated Parmesan
   cheese
1 large egg, lightly beaten
½ teaspoon salt
1 (14-ounce) jar spaghetti
   sauce or 1½ cups
   Homemade Tomato
   Sauce (page 162)
½ cup water
1 cup shredded mozzarella
   cheese

Cook the lasagna noodles according to package directions; drain and set aside.

Heat oil in a large saucepan over medium heat. Sauté broccoli and scallions, stirring frequently, for 5 minutes or until tender. Remove from heat. Stir in ricotta cheese, Parmesan cheese, egg, and salt.

Preheat oven to 375°.

Combine sauce and ½ cup water. Spoon about three-fourths of the sauce into the bottom of an 11- x 7-inch baking dish.

Lay noodles out in a single layer on waxed paper. Spread cheese mixture evenly on each noodle. Roll up jelly roll style and place, seam side down, in the sauce.

Top rolls with mozzarella cheese and remaining sauce. Cover loosely with foil.

Bake 30 minutes or until hot and bubbly.

Yield: 6 servings.

Serve with a light
Italian red wine
such as a Barbera
or Dolcetto d'Alba.

BAKED PASTA WITH EGGPLANT

Dairy

2 eggplants, unpeeled and cut into ½-inch slices
6 tablespoons olive oil, divided
1 (12-ounce) package pasta such as farfalle, rigatoni, penne or spiral
Salt
Freshly ground pepper
½ cup chopped onion
4 cloves garlic, minced

½ teaspoon hot pepper flakes
1 (28-ounce) can plum tomatoes, coarsely chopped, not drained
2 tablespoons chopped flat leaf parsley
8 ounces fresh mozzarella, cut into small pieces
½ cup grated Parmesan cheese
½ cup dried bread crumbs

Preheat oven to broil with rack 6 inches from heat.

Brush eggplant slices lightly with oil and place on a broiling pan. Broil on both sides until nicely browned. Set aside.

Cook the pasta according to package directions; drain. Toss the pasta with 1 tablespoon oil, salt, and pepper; set aside.

Heat 2 tablespoons oil in a skillet over medium-high heat. Add garlic, onion, and pepper flakes; sauté until tender.

Add tomatoes and liquid. Bring to a boil, reduce heat, and simmer 15 minutes or until slightly thickened. Stir in parsley and season with salt and pepper to taste.

Preheat oven to 375°.

Place half of the pasta mixture in the bottom of a greased 11- x 7-inch baking dish. Layer with half of eggplant slices and half of the tomato sauce. Sprinkle with mozzarella.

Top with remaining eggplant, pasta, and sauce. Sprinkle with Parmesan cheese, bread crumbs, and remaining olive oil.

Bake for 30 minutes or until browned and bubbly.

Yield: 6 servings.

Vegetable Risotto

Dairy

6 cups vegetable broth, divided
5 tablespoons unsalted butter, divided
1 small onion, minced
2 cups Arborio rice
1 cup dry white wine or vermouth

2 cups diced cooked vegetables such as zucchini, carrots, broccoli, mushrooms, asparagus, or peas
1 cup grated Parmesan cheese, divided
Salt
Pepper

Heat broth in a large saucepan over low heat; keep warm.

Heat 4 tablespoons butter in a large saucepan over medium heat. Add onion and sauté 2 to 3 minutes or until tender. Stir in rice; cook 1 minute or until rice turns translucent.

Add wine and cook, stirring constantly, until the liquid almost evaporates. Ladle enough hot broth to cover the rice; cook over medium heat until almost all of the broth is absorbed.

Continue adding some of the broth, stirring constantly, for 15 minutes or until rice is al dente.

Add about ½ cup broth and vegetables. Cook 5 to 7 minutes. Season with salt and pepper to taste.

Add remaining 1 tablespoon butter and ⅓ cup of the Parmesan cheese, mixing well. The rice should be creamy while the grains remain separate. Reserve any extra broth for other uses.

Serve immediately with the remaining Parmesan cheese on the side.

Yield: 4 servings.

Farfalle with Pesto and Tomatoes

Dairy

2 cups packed fresh basil
   leaves (about 5 bunches)
¼ cup pine nuts
3 large cloves garlic,
   chopped
½ teaspoon salt
⅛ teaspoon freshly ground
   pepper
½ cup olive oil

½ cup grated Parmesan
   cheese, divided
12 ounces farfalle (bow tie)
   pasta
1½ cups heavy whipping
   cream
2 cups seeded, chopped
   plum tomatoes, divided
Garnish: fresh basil

Place basil, nuts, garlic, salt, and pepper in a food processor bowl fitted with knife blade. Process until basil is finely chopped, stopping once to scrape down sides. With processor running, gradually add oil in a steady stream. Process until smooth. Transfer to a small mixing bowl.

Combine basil mixture with ¼ cup Parmesan cheese. Pesto can be made a day in advance. Pour a small amount of olive oil to cover the top of the pesto to prevent browning. Cover and chill. Pour off layer of oil before using.

Cook the pasta according to package directions; drain and place in a large serving bowl.

Heat cream in a large skillet over medium heat until boiling. Reduce heat and simmer until thickened. Stir in reserved pesto, half of tomatoes, and remaining ¼ cup Parmesan cheese. Cook 3 to 4 minutes.

Toss sauce with hot pasta and remaining tomatoes. Garnish with sprigs of fresh basil.

Yield: 4 to 6 servings.

Rotini with Artichokes and Sun-Dried Tomatoes

Parve

1 (16-ounce) package
  rotini pasta
2 (6-ounce) jars marinated
  artichoke hearts,
  drained and quartered
1 (6-ounce) can pitted
  black olives, drained
  and quartered

4 ounces marinated sun-
  dried tomatoes, drained
  and chopped
10 fresh basil leaves, very
  thinly shredded
1 large red bell pepper,
  diced
  Italian dressing

Cook the pasta according to package directions until al dente; drain and place in a large serving bowl.

Combine artichoke hearts, olives, tomatoes, basil, and bell pepper. Toss in dressing to taste. Toss with pasta, adding more dressing, if so desired.

Yield: 8 servings.

Variation: Toss this recipe with olive oil and balsamic vinegar for a low calorie treat. Crumble feta or blue cheese over pasta for a delicious dairy dish.

Penne with Tuna

Parve

2 cups canned Italian plum
  tomatoes, crushed or put
  through food mill
⅓ cup olive oil
3 cloves garlic, minced
  Salt
  Freshly ground pepper
1 (7-ounce) can tuna
  packed in olive oil,
  drained

¼ cup fresh basil, cut into
  thin strips
2 tablespoons chopped fresh
  flat leaf parsley
¼ cup coarsely chopped
  pitted kalamata or
  Italian olives
1 (16-ounce) package
  penne or rigatoni pasta

Crush tomatoes with a spoon or force through a food mill; set aside.

Heat oil in a large skillet over medium heat; add garlic and sauté 30 seconds. Add tomatoes and cook, uncovered, for 10 minutes or until slightly thickened. Season with salt and pepper, to taste. Add tuna, basil, parsley, and olives. Set aside and keep warm.

Cook the pasta according to package directions to al dente. Drain and transfer to a large serving bowl. Add sauce, tossing carefully to avoid breaking up chunks of tuna.

Yield: 8 servings.

HOMEMADE TOMATO SAUCE

Parve

Homemade sauce adds so much flavor to recipes and it's really quite simple to prepare.

2 pounds ripe tomatoes, peeled, seeded, and chopped*
¼ cup extra virgin olive oil
2 large cloves garlic, minced
1 small onion, minced
1 small carrot, minced (optional)
1 small stalk celery, minced (optional)
1 teaspoon kosher salt
Freshly ground pepper
Sugar (optional)
3 tablespoons fresh basil leaves, shredded

Place fresh tomatoes in a saucepan over medium heat. Cook for 20 minutes or until soft and thickened.

Heat oil in a 3- to 4-quart saucepan over medium-low heat. Add garlic, onion, carrot, and celery. Sauté until golden brown. Add tomatoes, salt and pepper to taste. Bring mixture to a boil, reduce heat, and simmer 10 minutes or until thickened. Correct seasonings and add a pinch or two of sugar if desired. Stir in fresh basil.

Yield: 3 to 4 cups.

*Note: 1 (28-ounce) can plum tomatoes, undrained, may be substituted for fresh tomatoes. Chop tomatoes and strain to remove seeds. Use tomatoes with the strained liquid and proceed with recipe.

Feta-Stuffed Eggplant Rolls,
page 164

BRUNCH & DAIRY

FETA-STUFFED EGGPLANT ROLLS WITH SALSA VERDE

Dairy

1 (1-pound) firm eggplant
Olive oil
Salt
½ cup crumbled feta cheese
   (about 3 ounces)
⅓ cup whole milk ricotta
¼ cup finely chopped mint
   leaves

3 roasted bell peppers
   or 2 (7-ounce) jars
   roasted peppers, rinsed
   and drained
1 bunch arugula or
   spinach, coarse stems
   discarded
   Salsa Verde
   Salt and pepper

Preheat oven to broil with rack 5 inches from heat.

Cut eggplant lengthwise into ¼-inch slices and arrange 6 center slices in a single layer on a greased baking sheet. (Reserve remaining slices of eggplant for other uses.)

Brush eggplant with oil and sprinkle with salt.

Broil 5 minutes or until golden brown. Carefully turn eggplant with a metal spatula and broil 4 minutes or until golden brown. Transfer to a large platter in a single layer; cool.

Place peppers on a foil-lined baking sheet. Broil (with electric oven door partially open) about 5 minutes on each side or until peppers look blistered and blackened.

Place peppers in a paper bag; seal and let stand 10 minutes to loosen skins. Peel peppers, discarding seeds; cut into pieces approximately the same size as eggplant slices. Set aside.

Combine feta, ricotta, and mint. Season with salt and pepper, to taste.

To assemble, top eggplant slices with one layer of pepper pieces. Spoon 1 tablespoon of the cheese mixture at the bottom (narrow end) of the eggplant. Press 4 or 5 arugula or spinach leaves into cheese mixture so leaves stick out on either side. Roll up each slice of eggplant, starting at the end with the cheese, and place, seam side down, on a serving platter. Serve rolls drizzled with Salsa Verde.

Yield: 6 servings.

Salsa Verde:

1 cup packed fresh flat leaf
   parsley leaves
1 clove garlic
⅓ cup extra virgin olive oil

1 tablespoon red wine
   vinegar
½ teaspoon anchovy paste

Combine parsley, garlic, oil, vinegar, and anchovy paste in the container of a blender. Process until smooth. Salsa may be made one day ahead; cover and chill until ready to serve. Let salsa come to room temperature before serving.

Yield: 1 cup.

Salmon-Tuna Twists

Parve

1 (3-ounce) can tuna,
   drained
1 (3-ounce) can salmon,
   drained
¼-½ cup mayonnaise
1 small onion, minced
1 clove garlic, minced

2 tablespoons lemon juice
1½ teaspoons prepared white
   horseradish, drained
   Pepper
1 (17.3-ounce) package
   frozen puff pastry,
   thawed

Preheat oven to 400°.

Combine tuna, salmon, mayonnaise, onion, garlic, lemon juice, horseradish, and pepper in the container of a food processor fitted with knife blade. Process until smooth.

Roll pastry on a lightly floured surface. Spread tuna mixture over dough. (Any extra tuna mixture can be saved as a dip or spread with crackers.)

Cut into 2½ x 1½-inch rectangles. Fold top left corner of rectangle into center; fold bottom right corner of rectangle into center. Place on baking sheets.

Bake for 20 minutes or until lightly browned. (Dough may puff open a little.)

Yield: 3 dozen.

GRILLED VEGETABLE SANDWICHES

Dairy

"These sandwiches are the hit of every brunch I host. Although it looks difficult, this recipe is actually very simple to prepare and takes only 10 minutes to assemble. You can grill the vegetables a day or two ahead. Cover the grilled vegetables and refrigerate until assembling. Be sure to purchase fresh bread the day you serve the sandwiches."

½	cup olive oil	1	loaf crusty French or Italian bread
8	large cloves garlic, minced		Honey mustard
2	red bell peppers, halved and seeded		Sliced fresh mozzarella cheese*
2	yellow squash	8	fresh basil leaves
2	zucchini	6-8	sun-dried tomatoes, drained
2	large portobello mushroom caps		

Combine the oil and garlic in a small bowl; set aside.

Preheat oven to broil with rack 5 inches away from heat.

Place peppers, skin side up, on a foil-lined baking sheet. Brush with garlic oil mixture.

Broil (with electric oven door partially open) about 5 minutes or until peppers look blistered and blackened.

Place peppers in a paper bag; seal, and let stand 10 minutes to loosen skins. Peel peppers and slice. Set aside.

Slice squash and zucchini lengthwise into ¼-inch strips; place on a baking sheet and brush with garlic oil mixture. Broil 4 to 6 minutes, turning once, or until softened and lightly browned. Set aside.

Brush mushroom caps with garlic oil mixture and place on a baking sheet. Broil for 5 to 8 minutes or until tender. Slice into ¼-inch thick pieces; set aside.

Slice bread lengthwise; spread honey mustard on bottom half. Layer red pepper slices, squash, zucchini, mushroom slices, cheese, basil, and tomatoes over honey mustard. Cover with top half of bread and cut into 1½-inch slices.

Yield: 10 to 12 servings.

Note: Not typical kosher mozzarella, this is very white in color and available at kosher supermarkets.

If you prefer to make a grilled vegetable platter, brush radicchio and endive leaves with garlic oil mixture and top with grilled vegetables.

QUICK FOCACCIA TOPPED WITH VEGETABLES

Parve

The beauty of this recipe is that you can use dough purchased from your local pizza store or supermarket. It's a great shortcut for a terrific brunch food.

⅓ cup extra virgin olive oil
1 pound uncooked pizza dough
2 teaspoons kosher salt, divided
1 bunch arugula, coarsely chopped
6 shiitake mushroom caps, very thinly sliced
1 yellow squash, halved and thinly sliced
1 zucchini, halved and thinly sliced
4 pitted ripe olives, thinly sliced (optional)
1 clove garlic, minced
2 teaspoons freshly ground pepper

Preheat oven to 450°.

Brush 1 tablespoon olive oil onto a baking sheet. Press pizza dough into a ½-inch thick rectangle. Sprinkle with 1 teaspoon salt.

Layer arugula, mushrooms, squash, zucchini, and olives over and to the edges of the dough and sprinkle with garlic. Drizzle with remaining oil and sprinkle with remaining salt and pepper.

Bake for 20 minutes until the bottom is golden brown. Cut into 1½-inch squares.

Yield: 30 squares.

CHEESE NOODLE KUGEL
Dairy

*W*hen we solicited recipes for this cookbook, we received many versions of Cheese Noodle Kugel. It seems like every Jewish family has its own special way of preparing this dish. Many dirty dishes and calories later, we selected two of our testers' favorites.

8 ounces medium noodles	6 ounces cream cheese, softened
3 large eggs, separated	
1 cup sour cream	¾ cup corn flake crumbs
⅓ cup sugar	2 tablespoons sugar
1 cup butter, melted	2 tablespoons butter, melted

Prepare noodles according to package directions; drain.

Beat egg whites and sour cream at medium speed with an electric mixer. Add sugar, butter, and cream cheese; beat until smooth. Add egg yolks; beat until blended. Fold in noodles.

Pour noodle mixture into a lightly greased 13- x 9-inch baking dish.

Combine crumbs, sugar, and butter; sprinkle on noodles. Cover and refrigerate 8 hours or overnight.

Preheat oven to 350°.

Remove from refrigerator and let stand 45 minutes. Bake for 1¼ hours.

Yield: 10 to 12 servings.

CHEESE NOODLE RING

8 ounces fine noodles	1 pint sour cream
1 pound farmer cheese, softened	1 cup sugar
	4 large eggs, lightly beaten
1 (8-ounce) package cream cheese, softened	Ground cinnamon

Preheat oven to 350°.

Cook noodles according to package directions; drain and cool.

Beat farmer cheese, cream cheese, sour cream, sugar and eggs in a large bowl. Stir in noodles.

Spoon noodle mixture into a buttered and floured Bundt pan. Sprinkle with cinnamon.

Bake 1 hour or until a toothpick inserted in center comes out clean. Invert onto a serving platter and sprinkle with cinnamon. Let stand several minutes before slicing.

Yield: 10 to 12 servings.

Tomato Tart

Dairy

" **I** got this recipe from a friend who is a fabulous cook. I know any recipe I get from her will look and taste amazing. This one is no exception. Be sure to serve the tart hot out of the oven or the cheese won't stay melted and the dish loses its texture. If you want to prepare it for a buffet, keep it on a warming tray. I like to make the dough in a food processor, but you can easily make it by hand. You can make the dough in advance. Place the dough in the tart pan, cover, and refrigerate until ready to fill and bake. Use a tart pan with a removable bottom. The tart is easier to slice and you will have a prettier presentation."

1¾ cups all-purpose flour	¼ cup Dijon mustard
1 tablespoon sugar	2 cups (8 ounces) shredded mozzarella cheese
½ teaspoon salt	
¾ cup margarine or butter, chilled and cut into pieces	1 tablespoon minced garlic
	5-10 ripe plum tomatoes, sliced Olive oil
¼ cup cold water	

Combine flour, sugar, and salt in the container of a food processor fitted with a plastic dough blade. Pulse until blended. Pulse in butter until it resembles coarse crumbs. Sprinkle with water; process until mixture forms a ball.

Place dough on a lightly floured surface. Roll to ⅛-inch thickness. Transfer dough to a 10-inch tart pan with removable bottom. Lightly press into sides; trim excess pastry. Refrigerate 10 minutes.

Preheat oven to 400°.

Brush bottom of the tart with mustard. Sprinkle with mozzarella and garlic. Top with tomato slices placed in concentric circles, overlapping edges. Brush with olive oil.

Bake, uncovered, for 40 minutes.

Yield: 4 to 6 servings.

Mimosas...a splendid way to begin a brunch.

Mimosas

Parve

3 ounces (about ⅓ cup) fresh orange juice

5 ounces (about ⅔ cup) Champagne or sparkling wine

Garnish: mint leaf, fresh raspberry

Pour orange juice into a Champagne flute. Add Champagne and garnish with a mint leaf or raspberry.

Yield: 1 cup.

CRÈME BRÛLÉE FRENCH TOAST

. . . . .

Dairy

*C*ross French toast and a rich caramel roll and you get this incredible, rich brunch dish that your family and friends will love. It's convenient because you can prepare it a day ahead, but that's not why you'll make it. We have no doubt that this recipe is sure to become one of your all-time favorites.

½	cup unsalted butter	5	large eggs
1	cup firmly packed dark brown sugar	1½	cups half-and-half
2	tablespoons light corn syrup	1	teaspoon vanilla extract
6	(1-inch thick) slices day-old challah bread	1	teaspoon Grand Marnier or orange flavored liqueur
		¼	teaspoon salt

Combine butter, brown sugar, and corn syrup in a heavy saucepan over medium heat. Cook, stirring constantly, until melted and smooth. Pour into a 13- x 9-inch baking dish.

Trim crusts from the bread and arrange in one layer in the baking dish.

Whisk together eggs, half-and-half, vanilla, Grand Marnier, and salt in a large mixing bowl. Pour evenly over bread. Cover and refrigerate 8 hours or overnight.

Preheat oven to 350°.

Remove dish from refrigerator and let come to room temperature.

Bake, uncovered, for 35 to 40 minutes or until puffed and edges are light golden brown. Serve immediately with individual pieces turned over with caramel on top.

Yield: 8 to 10 servings.

PUFFY STRAWBERRY PANCAKES

Dairy

2 tablespoons butter, divided
4 large eggs, lightly beaten
1 cup milk
1 cup all-purpose flour
2 tablespoons sugar
½ teaspoon vanilla extract
1 pint strawberries, quartered
1 tablespoon powdered sugar
Maple syrup (optional)

Preheat oven to 425°.

Melt 1 tablespoon butter in each of two, 9-inch deep-dish pie plates. You must use deep-dish pie plates or the batter will not rise properly.

Combine eggs, milk, flour, sugar, and vanilla.

Remove pie plates from oven and pour half of the batter into each. Sprinkle each with a handful of strawberries. Do not use too many, or berries will weigh the batter down.

Bake 20 minutes or until puffy and golden brown. The pancake will rise a few inches above the rim of the pie plate.

Sprinkle with powdered sugar and serve with maple syrup and remaining strawberries.

Yield: 4 to 6 servings.

ZUCCHINI CASSEROLE

Dairy

3 cups sliced zucchini, unpeeled
2 cups (8 ounces) shredded mozzarella cheese
1 small onion, chopped
1 cup buttermilk or all-purpose baking mix
2 tablespoons Parmesan cheese
4 large eggs, lightly beaten
½ cup vegetable oil
½ teaspoon salt
½ teaspoon dried oregano
Pepper

Preheat oven to 350°.

Combine zucchini, mozzarella cheese, onion, baking mix, Parmesan cheese, eggs, oil, salt, oregano, and pepper in a large bowl, mixing well.

Spoon into a lightly greased 13- x 9-inch baking dish.

Bake 40 minutes or until golden brown.

Yield: 10 servings.

Make any brunch or party special with sparkling Champagne Punch.

CHAMPAGNE PUNCH
Parve

2 (2-liter) bottles of ginger ale

1 (6-ounce) or 2 (3-ounce) containers frozen orange juice concentrate, thawed

1 pint strawberries, sliced

1 pint lemon sorbet

1 bottle Champagne or sparkling wine

Garnish: lemon and orange slices

Combine ginger ale, orange juice concentrate, strawberries, and sorbet in a large punch bowl. Stir in Champagne just before serving. Garnish with lemon and orange slices.

Yield: 5½ quarts.

FEATHERBED EGGS

Dairy

This recipe was donated by a beautiful inn in Spring Lake, New Jersey. Featherbed Eggs is their signature dish. The recipe is always prepared the night before, making it an excellent choice for a busy morning when serving a full house. The inn has listed their favorite variations, but they recommend you experiment with your own creation.

8 cups cubed Italian or French bread, crusts removed (about 1½ loaves)	1½ cups milk
	1½ cups half-and-half
	Salt
	Pepper
14 large eggs	Dried herbs

Place bread cubes in a buttered 13- x 9-inch baking dish.

Beat eggs in a large bowl until frothy. Add milk and half-and-half; pour over bread.

Sprinkle with salt, pepper and dried herbs. Cover and refrigerate 6 to 8 hours or overnight.

Preheat oven to 350°.

Bake, covered, for 1½ hours or until lightly brown and puffed.

Yield: 7 to 10 servings.

Variations:

Spoon ingredients into egg-and-bread mixture after it is assembled in the pan.

1. Sautéed sliced mushrooms, fresh rosemary, thyme, and sage

2. Shredded cheddar, mozzarella, and Swiss cheese

3. Dollops of salsa and sour cream with fresh cilantro and shredded cheddar or Monterey Jack cheese

4. Blanched broccoli florets and shredded Swiss cheese

5. Slivered sun-dried tomatoes, fresh basil, and shredded mozzarella cheese

CALIFORNIA SPICY VEGETARIAN CHILI

Dairy

2 tablespoons vegetable oil
2 large onions, chopped
4 large cloves garlic, minced
2 jalapeño chiles, minced
2 (28-ounce) cans plum tomatoes, undrained
½ cup tomato paste
2 green peppers, chopped
2 large carrots, peeled and chopped
1 tablespoon ground cumin
¾ teaspoon salt
½ teaspoon cayenne pepper
2 (15-ounce) cans chickpeas, rinsed and drained
2 (15-ounce) cans kidney beans, rinsed and drained
2 small zucchini, unpeeled and diced
Chopped onions
Shredded cheddar cheese
Fat-free sour cream

Heat oil in a large soup pot over medium heat. Add onions, garlic and chiles; sauté 5 minutes or until onions are translucent.

Drain tomatoes, reserving 1 cup juice; dice. Add tomatoes, reserved juice, tomato paste, green peppers, carrots, cumin, salt, and cayenne pepper to onion mixture.

Bring to a boil, reduce heat and simmer 20 minutes, stirring frequently.

Add chickpeas and kidney beans; cook 15 minutes. Add zucchini; cook 5 minutes, stirring occasionally.

Ladle into bowls and serve with chopped onions, shredded cheese, and fat-free sour cream on the side.

Yield: 12 cups.

EGGPLANT CHEESE STRUDEL

Dairy

1 medium eggplant, peeled and cubed	½ cup dry bread crumbs
½ cup water	¼ cup chopped fresh parsley
2 tablespoons margarine	1 teaspoon salt
1 onion, chopped	½ teaspoon dried basil
1 large clove garlic, pressed	½ teaspoon dried oregano
2 large eggs, lightly beaten	8 sheets phyllo dough
1½ cups (6 ounces) shredded Swiss cheese	½ cup margarine, melted

Combine eggplant and water in a large saucepan over medium-high heat. Bring to a boil, reduce heat and simmer until tender; drain.

Melt 2 tablespoons margarine in a large skillet over medium-high heat. Add onion and sauté 5 minutes or until tender. Add garlic and sauté 3 minutes.

Combine eggplant and onion mixture in a large bowl; mash eggplant with a fork until well blended. Stir in eggs, cheese, bread crumbs, parsley, salt, basil, and oregano.

Preheat oven to 375°.

Brush an 8- x 8-inch baking pan with the melted margarine. Brush one phyllo sheet with margarine and place in pan with edges of phyllo extending over edge of pan. Repeat with three more sheets of phyllo.

Spoon in eggplant mixture, smoothing top flat. Fold phyllo sheets over filling. Brush remaining sheets of phyllo with margarine and place over filling. Fold in edges of the phyllo to fit inside pan with last sheet of phyllo tucked down into the edge of the pan. Brush with margarine. Score phyllo sheets into 4-inch squares.

Yield: 4 servings.

ASPARAGUS QUICHE

Dairy

1   (9-inch) deep-dish pie shell
4   large eggs, lightly beaten
½   cup half-and-half
3   tablespoons all-purpose
      flour
1   teaspoon paprika
1   teaspoon salt

½   teaspoon brown or honey
      mustard
2   cups (8 ounces) shredded
      Swiss cheese
10 asparagus spears,
      trimmed and divided
1-2 plum tomatoes, sliced

Preheat oven to 375°.

Partially bake pie shell according to package directions to a very light golden brown.

Beat eggs, half-and-half, flour, paprika, salt, and mustard. Stir in cheese.

Slice 5 asparagus spears into 1-inch pieces and place on the bottom of the pie shell; pour in egg mixture.

Bake for 20 minutes; remove from oven. Arrange remaining 5 asparagus spears on top to resemble a wagon wheel and place tomato slices between each spear.

Bake 20 to 30 minutes or until puffed in center and knife inserted near center comes out clean.

Yield: 6 servings.

QUESADILLA

Dairy

1   tablespoon oil
1   clove garlic, chopped
1   poblano chili pepper, diced
1   red bell pepper, diced
2   scallions, finely sliced
6   sprigs cilantro, chopped
1   cup frozen corn kernels,
      thawed

8   (6-inch) flour tortillas
2   cups (8 ounces) shredded
      Monterey Jack cheese
      Vegetable cooking spray
      Best Ever Guacamole
      (page 34)
      Salsa

Heat oil in a large skillet over medium-high heat. Add garlic, peppers, scallions, and cilantro. Sauté until tender; let cool.

Stir corn into garlic mixture.

Place four tortillas on a work surface; sprinkle each with ½ cup cheese. Top cheese evenly with corn mixture. Top with remaining tortillas.

Heat a skillet, coated with cooking spray, over medium-high heat. Cook tortillas, one or two at a time, until golden brown on both sides. Cut into quarters and serve immediately with guacamole and salsa.

Yield: 4 servings.

FRUIT AND FLORAL CENTERPIECES

This concept can be done combining any fruits, vegetables, or herbs with flowers.
Try red grapes with sunflowers. Apples with hydrangea, Black Magic Roses and Oseana Roses.
Artichokes and eggplants with dried hydrangea, flat seeded Eucalyptus and oncidium orchids.

You will need:

4 pints of strawberries

15 pink peonies

3 dozen large-headed pink roses
(such as Anna roses)

3 to 4 dozen pink spray roses
and/or short stemmed
variegated pink roses

15 to 20 geranium leaves

18 5-inch green wood
floral stakes

Set aside 18 large strawberries.
Slice tops off remaining
strawberries, and line 10-inch-
diameter bowl with the
trimmed strawberries. Slowly
pour water into the bowl.
Place the peonies in the water,
then make small clusters of the
large-headed roses and place
them among the peonies.
Repeat with clusters of the
remaining roses, then place the
geranium leaves among the
flowers. Insert the pointed end
of a floral stake into each
reserved strawberry; arrange
the berries in clusters of three
among the flowers.

Mushroom and Cheese Frittata

Dairy

"On a previous visit, a 'snooty' cousin was dismayed that I did not have a whisk in my possession. On her latest visit, I was determined to impress her with my egg-cooking prowess. Whisk in hand, I began to prepare the ultimate omelette. When I lost it on the 'flip', I knew I had to think fast. By lowering the flame, then popping it under the broiler for a few minutes, a new taste sensation was born at our house—frittata for everyone."

2 tablespoons butter	Salt
6 ounces mushrooms, sliced	Pepper
6 large eggs, lightly beaten	2 (2-ounce) slices Swiss
2 scallions, sliced	cheese

Preheat oven to broil with rack 6 inches from heat.

Heat butter in a heavy 10-inch ovenproof skillet over medium heat. Add the mushrooms and sauté 6 to 8 minutes or until golden brown. Reduce heat to medium-low.

Combine eggs and scallions in a bowl, beating until well blended. Stir in salt and pepper. The eggs should be beaten only until yolks and whites are mixed. If more, the frittata will be too light and airy.

Pour egg mixture over mushrooms and stir briefly. Let the eggs begin to set around the edges. Lift the edges and tilt the pan so the uncooked egg flows under the cooked portions.

Cook 30 seconds (the center should remain moist and pale). Arrange cheese slices on top.

Broil 2 minutes or until cheese is melted and bubbly. Transfer frittata to a serving platter.

Yield: 4 servings.

Hints for the perfect frittata:

The eggs should be beaten only until the yolk and whites are mixed. Pour egg mixture into a greased pan that has been heated to medium-low to avoid burning the eggs. Cook eggs until the bottom is a light golden color.

STRAWBERRY MUFFINS

Parve

2 cups all-purpose flour	¾ teaspoon salt (optional)
1 cup whole-wheat flour	2 large eggs, lightly beaten
1 cup sugar	1 egg white, lightly beaten
4½ teaspoons baking powder	1 cup apple cider or juice
1½ teaspoons ground cinnamon	½ cup vegetable oil
	2 cups sliced strawberries, divided

Preheat oven to 400°.

Combine flours, sugar, baking powder, cinnamon, and salt.

Combine eggs, apple cider, and oil. Add the egg mixture to the flour mixture, stirring just until moistened.

Set aside 24 slices of strawberry and fold remaining slices into batter. Spoon batter into greased muffin pans, filling two-thirds full. Top each muffin with reserved strawberry slices.

Bake for 25 minutes. Remove from pans immediately and cool on wire racks.

Yield: 2 dozen.

BANANA–CHOCOLATE CHIP MUFFINS

Dairy

1½ cups all-purpose flour	1 cup sour cream
⅓ cup sugar	1 large egg, lightly beaten
1½ teaspoons baking powder	1 teaspoon vanilla
¼ teaspoon baking soda	¾ cup semi-sweet chocolate morsels
¼ teaspoon salt	2 ripe bananas, chopped
½ cup unsalted butter, melted	

Preheat oven to 400°.

Combine flour, sugar, baking powder, baking soda, and salt in a large bowl.

Whisk butter, sour cream, egg, and vanilla, blending well. Add the butter mixture to the flour mixture, stirring just until moistened. Fold in chocolate morsels and banana.

Spoon batter into a greased muffin pan, filling two-thirds full.

Bake for 20 minutes or until toothpick inserted in center comes out clean. Remove from pans immediately and cool on wire rack.

Yield: 1 dozen.

If you beat muffin batter too long, the muffins will turn out tough and dense. Always mix by hand, stirring only long enough to moisten the dry ingredients. The batter will not be creamy smooth; it may even have lumps in it.

BRAN SURPRISE MUFFINS

Dairy

"*These muffins are best when they are fresh and piping hot out of the oven. The batter and filling will keep in the refrigerator for a week, so you can make the muffins as you need them. They appear to rise better after the batter has been refrigerated as well. Tasty and thoughtful– now that's our kind of muffin!*"

Vegetable cooking spray
1 (8-ounce) package cream cheese, softened
⅓ cup sugar
2 tablespoons all-purpose flour
1 teaspoon vanilla extract
2½ cups all-purpose flour
2 cups sugar
1 tablespoon ground cinnamon
2½ teaspoons baking soda
1 teaspoon salt
½ teaspoon freshly grated nutmeg
3½ cups raisin bran cereal
2 large eggs, lightly beaten
2 cups buttermilk, well shaken
½ cup vegetable oil
½ cup raisins

Preheat oven to 400°. Spray muffin pans with cooking spray; set aside.

Combine cream cheese, sugar, 2 tablespoons flour, and vanilla in a small bowl; set aside. This filling mixture can be covered and refrigerated up to 1 week.

Combine flour, sugar, cinnamon, baking soda, salt, and nutmeg in a large bowl. Stir in cereal.

Combine eggs, buttermilk, oil and raisins. Add the egg mixture to the flour mixture, stirring just until moistened. This batter mixture can be covered and refrigerated up to 1 week.

Spoon 1 heaping tablespoon of batter into prepared muffin pans and top with 2 teaspoons of cream cheese mixture. Spoon 1 heaping tablespoon of batter over filling, spreading to completely cover the filling. Repeat with remaining batter and filling.

Bake for 20 to 25 minutes or until toothpick inserted in center comes out clean. Remove from pans immediately, and cool on wire racks.

Yield: 2 dozen.

BUTTERMILK CORNBREAD

Dairy

1 cup stone ground yellow cornmeal	¼ teaspoon salt
1 cup unbleached all-purpose flour	1 large egg, lightly beaten
⅓ cup sugar	1 cup buttermilk
2½ teaspoons baking powder	6 tablespoons unsalted butter, melted

Preheat oven to 400°.

Combine cornmeal, flour, sugar, baking powder, and salt in a bowl.

Combine egg, buttermilk, and butter. Stir the egg mixture into the cornmeal mixture, stirring just until moistened. A few lumps or dry spots are better than overmixing the batter.

Spoon batter into a greased 9- x 9-inch baking pan and level with a spatula.

Bake for 25 minutes or until a toothpick inserted in the center comes out clean and the edges are lightly browned.

Cut into 3-inch squares and serve immediately.

Yield: 9 servings.

CRUSTLESS SPINACH QUICHE

Dairy

2 large eggs, lightly beaten	3 tablespoons cake meal
½ cup milk	2 cups (8 ounces) shredded cheddar cheese
½ cup mayonnaise	2 cups (8 ounces) shredded mozzarella cheese
1 small onion, chopped	
2 (10-ounce) packages frozen chopped spinach, thawed and drained	

Preheat oven to 350°.

Combine eggs, milk, mayonnaise, onion, spinach, cake meal, and cheddar cheese in a large bowl.

Pour into a greased 9-inch round or 8- x 8-inch baking dish. Sprinkle with mozzarella cheese.

Bake 30 to 45 minutes or until puffed in center and knife inserted near center comes out clean.

Yield: 9 servings.

Use carambola flowers to decorate a serving platter. Choose carambola (star fruit) that does not have too many blemishes. Pare down the points to remove tough or discolored parts. Slice ¼-inch thick. Lay the "flower" flat on a platter. Use chives to form stems and herbs to make leaves.

CINNAMON-RICOTTA CREAM
CHOCOLATE CRÊPES
. . . .

Dairy

½ cup all-purpose flour
¼ cup cocoa
¼ cup sugar
1 cup milk
2 large eggs
¼ cup butter, melted and
     divided

1   teaspoon vanilla extract
1¼ cups ricotta cheese
2   tablespoons sugar
¼   teaspoon ground
      cinnamon

Combine flour, cocoa, sugar, milk, eggs, 2 tablespoons melted butter, and vanilla in the container of a blender. Process for 30 seconds.

Brush bottom of an 8-inch crêpe pan or heavy skillet lightly with melted butter; place skillet over medium heat until just hot, but not smoking.

Pour 3 tablespoons batter into pan; quickly tilt pan in all directions to batter covers pan with a thin film. Cook 1 minute.

Life the edge of the crêpe to test for doneness. Crêpe is ready to turn when it can be shaken loosen from pan. Flip crêpe, and cook 30 seconds on other side. Repeat with remaining batter.

Combine ricotta cheese, 2 tablespoons sugar, and cinnamon in a small bowl. Spread filling evenly in the center of the crêpes. Fold bottom and sides of crêpe over filling and roll up.

Yield: 12 to 18 crêpes.

SPINACH–RICOTTA TART

Dairy

1 (9-inch) deep-dish pie
   shell
3 tablespoons butter
1 small onion, minced
2 (10-ounce) packages
   frozen chopped spinach,
   thawed and drained
½ teaspoon salt
   Pepper

3 large eggs, lightly beaten
1 (15-ounce) container
   ricotta cheese
1 cup light cream or
   half-and-half
½ cup grated Parmesan
   cheese
1 cup (4 ounces) shredded
   Swiss cheese

Preheat oven to 350°.

Partially bake pie crust according to package directions to a very light golden brown.

Heat butter in a large skillet over medium-high heat. Add onion and sauté until tender. Stir in spinach, salt, and pepper; remove from heat.

Combine eggs, ricotta, cream, and Parmesan cheese in a large bowl. Stir in spinach mixture.

Sprinkle Swiss cheese in bottom of prepared pie shell. Pour spinach mixture over cheese.

Bake 50 minutes or until lightly browned and puffed in center and knife inserted near center comes out clean.

Yield: 6 to 8 servings.

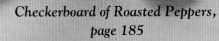

Checkerboard of Roasted Peppers,
page 185

SIDE DISHES

VEGETABLE MEDLEY

Parve

⅓ cup olive oil
1 large white onion, thinly sliced
2 carrots, peeled and sliced into disks
2 cloves garlic, chopped
2 large tomatoes, coarsely chopped
1 large zucchini, sliced into disks

1 red bell pepper, cut into 1-inch squares
1 orange bell pepper, cut into 1-inch squares
1 yellow bell pepper, cut into 1-inch squares
1 tablespoon chopped fresh parsley
Salt
Pepper

Heat oil in a medium pot over medium-high heat. Add onion and sauté until tender. Add carrots; cover and reduce heat to low. Cook for 10 minutes.

Stir in garlic, tomatoes, zucchini, bell peppers, and parsley. Cook over low heat, stirring occasionally, for 45 minutes. Drain excess liquid, if necessary. Season to taste with salt and pepper.

Yield: 6 to 8 servings.

STIR-FRIED SNOW PEAS

Meat or Parve

It's not as easy as ordering in, but the recipe is relatively simple and equally delicious.

2 tablespoons peanut oil
2 cups snow peas, trimmed
¼ cup sliced scallions
½ cup chicken broth or bouillon
1 tablespoon sugar
1 teaspoon peeled and minced fresh ginger or ½ teaspoon ground ginger

1 (8-ounce) can water chestnuts, drained and chopped
1 (8-ounce) can baby corn, sliced into thick pieces (optional)
2 tablespoons cornstarch
2 tablespoons water

Heat oil in a wok or large skillet over high heat. Add snow peas and scallions; stir-fry for 1 to 2 minutes. Add broth, sugar, and ginger. Reduce heat to medium, and cook 3 minutes. Stir in water chestnuts and baby corn.

Combine cornstarch and water; stir into vegetable mixture. Cook 1 minute or until thickened and bubbly. Serve immediately.

Yield: 4 to 6 servings.

CHECKERBOARD OF ROASTED PEPPERS

Parve

The photo on our section cover is a single serving, two-color variation on this recipe. Once you get the hang of roasting the peppers, you can experiment with how you arrange the various colors and shapes. The recipe makes enough to fill a large oval serving platter.

6 bell peppers (a combination of red, green, and yellow)	12 black olives, pitted and halved
½ cup olive oil	5 scallions, sliced into small disks
¼ cup red wine vinegar	1 clove garlic, minced
Salt	
Fresh ground pepper	

Preheat oven to broil with rack 5 inches away from heat.

Cut peppers in half; discard seeds. Place peppers, skin side up, on a foil-lined baking sheet. Broil (with electric oven door partially open) about 5 minutes or until peppers look blistered and blackened.

Place peppers in a paper bag; seal, and let stand 10 minutes to loosen skins. (You do not need to get off every speck of black; it only adds to the flavor.) Place in a large bowl.

Whisk together oil and vinegar. Add salt and pepper; pour over peppers. Cover and refrigerate at least 30 minutes or overnight.

Remove peppers from marinade and trim the edges to make squares of equal size.

Arrange pepper squares on a large, flat platter, alternating colors to resemble a checkerboard of two or three colors. Place scallion slices where the corners of the peppers meet and place olives at either end of the platter. (You may also place olives over uneven corners and use whole scallion strips to make crisscross shapes over the peppers.)

Sprinkle the platter with garlic. Cover and refrigerate until ready to serve. Let stand for 15 minutes at room temperature before serving.

Yield: 10 servings.

VEGETABLE RIBBONS

Parve or Dairy

This pretty vegetable dish is fun and easy to make. Be sure to select squashes that are unblemished and have a uniform thickness. The vegetables are lightly cooked in a garlic sauce and make a great accompaniment to any fish or meat dish.

4 zucchini	2 scallions, minced
4 yellow squash	2 cloves garlic, minced
2 tablespoons margarine or butter	½ teaspoon salt

Cut off ends of zucchini and discard. Cut zucchini lengthwise with a vegetable peeler and discard piece that is covered with skin. Turn over onto a flat surface. Cut long strips or "ribbons" from zucchini using the vegetable peeler, including the edges of skin. Cut slowly to avoid breaking ribbons. Turn zucchini over when you reach sections that are seedy and continue to slice ribbons. Trim edges with a sharp knife.

Cut off ends of yellow squash and repeat procedure.

Heat margarine or butter in a large skillet over medium-low heat. Add the scallions and garlic; sauté 1 minute, stirring frequently, or until tender.

Increase heat to medium. Add squash ribbons and sprinkle with salt. Sauté 5 minutes, stirring frequently, or until vegetables are tender. (Do not overcook.) If the skillet is too small, cook vegetables in batches using additional margarine, if necessary.

Yield: 8 servings.

PECAN NOODLE RING

Parve

Try this mouthwatering twist on a traditional Jewish side dish. The presentation of the kugel is lovely as it conforms to the shape of the Bundt pan. The topping forms a sweet, nutty crown. We know your family will request this recipe again and again.

1 cup chopped pecans
½ cup firmly packed dark
   brown sugar
½ cup margarine, melted
   Vegetable cooking spray
1 (16-ounce) package extra
   wide noodles

6 large eggs, lightly beaten
1 cup sugar
1 teaspoon salt
1 teaspoon ground
   cinnamon

Preheat oven to 350°.

Combine pecans, brown sugar, and margarine and spoon into Bundt pan coated heavily with cooking spray.

Cook noodles according to package directions. Drain and transfer into a large bowl.

Add eggs, sugar, salt, and cinnamon, stirring well. Pour into noodles. Mix well with spoon. Pour into prepared pan.

Bake for 1 hour. Remove from oven and let cool on wire rack for 10 minutes. Turn out onto a serving plate.

Yield: 8 to 10 servings.

Broccoli and Cauliflower with Horseradish Bread Crumbs

Parve

This is a lovely and healthy side dish. The piquant flavor of the horseradish makes it a fine accompaniment to roast beef or brisket.

How to make fresh bread crumbs:

Fresh bread crumbs really add flavor and texture to stuffings and other dishes calling for any type of bread crumb. Packaged bread crumbs can taste somewhat stale and are void of texture.

Preheat oven to 200°. Spread slices of any type of fresh bread on a baking sheet in a single layer. Bake for about 20 to 30 minutes or until bread gets a little dry and toasted. Turn oven off, but keep the door closed. Leave the bread in the oven for another 15 minutes until completely dry. Cut the crusts off the bread and cut into squares. Place the bread into the container of a food processor fitted with a knife blade. Process until finely and evenly chopped. You may prepare fresh bread crumbs up to 3 days ahead; keep in an airtight container.

1 large bunch broccoli, cut into florets
1 large head cauliflower, cut into florets
3 tablespoons margarine, divided
1 tablespoon vegetable oil
2 cups very coarse, fresh bread crumbs (see sidebar)
2 tablespoons prepared white horseradish, drained
Salt
Pepper

Blanch broccoli and cauliflower in boiling water to cover for 3 to 4 minutes or until crisp-tender. Plunge into ice water to stop the cooking process; drain and set aside. (You may prepare the broccoli and cauliflower up to a day ahead. Cover and refrigerate in zip-top bags until ready to use.)

Heat 2 tablespoons margarine and oil in a large skillet over medium-high heat. Add bread crumbs and sauté, stirring constantly, until golden brown. Stir in horseradish and salt, to taste. Cook, stirring constantly, until crisp; set aside.

Preheat oven to 350°.

Heat remaining 1 tablespoon margarine over medium-high heat. Toss with vegetables and season to taste with salt and pepper.

Place vegetables in a lightly greased 13- x 9-inch baking dish and sprinkle with bread crumbs, tossing to combine.

Bake, uncovered, for 10 to 15 minutes or until thoroughly heated.

Yield: 6 servings.

ROASTED ROOT VEGETABLES

Parve

This healthy side dish is a tasty addition to a brisket or turkey. The colors and textures of the vegetables make any meal picture perfect. You can change the amounts and type of the vegetables to suit your family's taste. The recipe is easy since, with the exception of the turnips, you do not have to peel the vegetables. You will find any leftovers are just as good, if not better, on the second day.

2 leeks
5 cloves garlic, unpeeled
5 carrots, cut into 2-inch pieces
4 onions, cut into 1-inch pieces
2 turnips, peeled and cut into chunks
1 parsnip, cut into chunks

2 sweet potatoes, unpeeled and cut into chunks
2 potatoes, unpeeled and cut into chunks
2 acorn squash, unpeeled and cut into chunks
⅓ cup olive oil
Kosher salt

Preheat oven to 400°.

Wash leeks thoroughly and cut off tough outer leaves. Cut off roots, leaving bulb intact to hold leaves together.

Place leeks on the bottom of a very large, shallow roasting pan that has been coated with oil. (Leeks should remain on the bottom to avoid burning.)

Add remaining vegetables and olive oil, tossing to coat. Sprinkle with salt.

Bake, uncovered, for 1½ to 2 hours or until vegetables are tender. Stir occasionally to distribute oil. Although the vegetables are fragrant and delicious alone, you can season the vegetables with sage, rosemary or thyme, if desired.

Yield: 12 to 18 servings.

Zucchini with Garlic and Tomato

Parve

¼ cup olive oil
½ cup thinly sliced onion
1½ teaspoons chopped garlic
1½ pounds unpeeled
    zucchini, sliced ⅜-inch
    thick
½ pound unpeeled yellow
    squash, sliced ⅜-inch
    thick

1 cup chopped plum
    tomatoes
2 tablespoons flat leaf
    parsley, snipped with
    kitchen scissors
1 tablespoon fresh basil, cut
    into slivers
1 teaspoon salt
½ teaspoon pepper

Heat oil in a large skillet over medium heat. Add onion and garlic; sauté until translucent. Stir in zucchini, squash and tomatoes; cover and cook 8 minutes. Stir in parsley, basil, salt, and pepper; cook 2 minutes.

Yield: 4 to 6 servings.

Fresh Green Beans Al Pomodoro

Parve

This recipe is a healthy alternative to carbohydrate-rich side dishes. It is low in cholesterol and fat, which makes it heart-friendly as well as delicious.

1½ pounds thin green beans,
    trimmed
⅓ cup olive oil
1 small onion, chopped
1 clove garlic, chopped

6 ripe tomatoes, peeled,
    seeded and chopped
    (see sidebar page 153)
Salt
Freshly ground pepper

Cook green beans in boiling, salted water for 5 minutes or just until tender. Drain, reserving ½ cup of cooking water. Plunge into ice water to stop the cooking process; drain.

Heat oil in a saucepan over medium-high heat. Add onion and garlic; sauté 5 minutes or until tender.

Add tomatoes and season to taste with salt and pepper. Cook 5 minutes.

Stir in ½ cup reserved water and green beans. Reduce heat to medium-low and cook, covered, for 20 minutes.

Yield: 6 servings.

Green Beans with Port-Mushroom Sauce

Dairy

This exotic and savory dish goes very well with any fish.

3	tablespoons butter, divided	3	tablespoons chopped shallots, divided
12	ounces wild mushrooms (such as shiitake or oyster), stemmed and sliced	½	cup port wine or sherry
		1	cup heavy whipping cream
¾	teaspoon dried thyme	1½	pounds green beans, trimmed

Heat 2 tablespoons butter in a large skillet over medium-high heat. Add mushrooms and thyme; sauté for 5 minutes. Add 2 tablespoons shallots; sauté 3 minutes or until mushrooms are tender.

Add wine and cook 2 minutes or until liquid evaporates. Stir in the cream and cook 2 minutes or until slightly thickened; set aside.

Cook green beans in boiling, salted water for 5 minutes or just until tender. Plunge into ice water to stop the cooking process; drain.

Sauce and beans may be prepared up to 6 hours ahead. Cover and refrigerate separately until ready to serve. Reheat before serving.

To serve, heat 1 tablespoon butter in a skillet over medium heat. Add beans and remaining tablespoon shallots; sauté until thoroughly heated. Season to taste with salt and pepper. Place beans on a platter and top with mushroom sauce.

Yield: 6 servings.

ASPARAGUS WITH
HONEY-GARLIC SAUCE

Parve

1	pound fresh asparagus, trimmed	1	clove garlic, minced
¼	cup Dijon mustard	¼	teaspoon dried thyme, crushed
¼	cup dark ale or beer	¼	teaspoon salt
3	tablespoons honey		

Cook asparagus, covered, in boiling, salted water for 3 minutes or until barely tender; drain. Place on serving platter.

Combine mustard, beer, honey, garlic, thyme, and salt. Pour over asparagus and serve.

Yield: 3 to 4 servings.

CREAMY MASHED POTATOES

Parve

	Vegetable oil	¼	cup margarine, melted
3	pounds yellow onions, thinly sliced	1	cup non-dairy creamer
5	pounds potatoes (Yukon Gold or red)		Salt
			White pepper

Pour oil to a depth of ¼-inch into a large, heavy skillet. Fry onions, covered, in hot oil over medium-low heat 30 to 40 minutes or until golden brown. Uncover, and stir occasionally to prevent overcooking. Set aside.

Peel potatoes and cut into 1-inch pieces. Place potatoes in a large pot with water to cover. Bring to a boil, and cook, partially covered, for 20 minutes or until tender. Drain, reserving ¼ cup of cooking water, and transfer to a large mixing bowl. Add reserved water and margarine.

Using a slotted spoon, spoon onions into potato mixture, reserving pan drippings. Add non-dairy creamer.

Beat at medium speed with an electric mixer until smooth and fluffy. Add pan drippings from onion mixture, if necessary. Season to taste with salt and pepper.

Yield: 8 to 10 servings.

Add height to the plate for an exciting three-dimensional effect. Place the mashed potatoes in a pastry bag and squeeze the potatoes into a tall cone. Cross long strands of fresh chives vertically across potatoes.

Another way to add height to the plate is by tying carrots into a stack with a strand of chive or leek blanched in boiling water for a minute or two until pliable.

ASPARAGUS TERIYAKI

Parve

1 pound asparagus, trimmed
⅓ cup olive oil
⅓ cup low-sodium soy sauce
¼ cup sugar
1 tablespoon sesame seeds

Cook asparagus, covered, in boiling, salted water for 3 minutes or until barely tender; drain. Place on serving platter.

Combine oil, soy sauce, sugar, and sesame seeds in a cruet or jar. Cover tightly and shake vigorously. Pour over asparagus and serve.

Yield: 3 to 4 servings.

ROASTED GARLIC MASHED POTATOES

Dairy

1 head garlic, unpeeled
16 medium red potatoes, unpeeled
2 tablespoons butter, softened
½ cup reduced-fat sour cream
½ cup buttermilk
2 tablespoons olive oil
1 tablespoon chopped fresh chives
½ cup grated Parmesan cheese
Salt
Freshly ground white pepper

Preheat oven to 400°.

Cut a ¼-inch slice from top of garlic and discard; wrap the remaining head in foil.

Bake for 40 to 50 minutes or until very soft; cool. Squeeze pulp from garlic cloves and set aside.

Place potatoes in a large pot with water to cover two inches above potatoes. Bring to a boil, reduce heat to medium, and simmer for 30 minutes or until tender. Drain (do not peel) and transfer to a large mixing bowl.

Add butter; beat at low speed with an electric mixer until mashed. Add sour cream, buttermilk, chives, and oil and beat at medium speed until light and fluffy. Add Parmesan cheese, reserved garlic, salt, and pepper; beat until smooth.

Yield: 6 to 8 servings.

CRUSTY GARLIC AND ROSEMARY POTATOES

Parve

1 pound small red potatoes (or medium red potatoes, cut into 1½-inch pieces)	1 tablespoon chopped fresh rosemary or ½ teaspoon dried and crumbled rosemary
¼ cup olive oil	1 tablespoon dried minced onion
8 cloves garlic, unpeeled	½ teaspoon kosher salt
3 cloves garlic, minced	Freshly ground pepper

Preheat oven to 350°.

Combine potatoes and olive oil in a large plastic zip-top bag. Add garlic cloves, minced garlic, rosemary, onion, salt, and pepper; toss to coat.

Place potato mixture into a baking pan. Bake 1 hour or until potatoes are tender. Increase heat to 400°, if necessary, to cook potatoes to a golden brown.

Yield: 4 servings.

CAJUN SWEET POTATO FRIES

Parve

There's no need to travel to New Orleans to satisfy your craving for Cajun food. This "hot" recipe is a great alternative to traditional fries at your next barbecue.

1 teaspoon salt	½ teaspoon garlic powder
1 teaspoon paprika	2 sweet potatoes, peeled and cut into thin strips
½ teaspoon cayenne pepper	
½ teaspoon pepper	Canola oil

Combine salt, paprika, cayenne, pepper, and garlic powder in a plastic zip-top bag.

Add the sweet potatoes, tossing to coat.

Pour oil to a depth of 2 to 3 inches in a large, heavy skillet over medium-high heat. Fry sweet potato fries until crispy. Drain on paper towels.

Yield: 4 servings.

At your next outdoor party, add gentle light with pretty artichoke candle holders. Cut a thin slice off the bottom of an artichoke so it will be level when placed on a table. Trim the sharp points from the leaves and scoop out the center. Place a votive in the center and use this unique presentation to add soft light on each table or around your buffet table.

(see photo page 122)

PESTO POTATO CAKE

Parve or Dairy

This recipe is versatile; make the potatoes from scratch or use leftover mashed potatoes. The pesto and tomato sauce can be homemade or store bought.

½ tablespoon olive oil	3 tablespoons pesto
3 cups mashed potatoes, room temperature	(see sidebar)
1 large egg, lightly beaten	Chunky tomato sauce

Preheat oven to 475°. Brush an 8-inch round cake pan with oil.

Combine potatoes and egg in a medium bowl, mixing until well blended. Layer half of the potato mixture and half of the pesto in the prepared pan. Repeat with remaining potatoes and pesto.

Bake for 15 minutes or until golden brown. Let stand for 5 minutes; cut into wedges and serve with tomato sauce on the side.

Yield: 4 to 6 servings.

ZUCCHINI KUGEL

Parve

1 (17.3-ounce) package frozen puff pastry (2 sheets)	2-3 tablespoons oil
	6 eggs or 12 egg whites
	4 heaping tablespoons flour
8-10 zucchini, peeled and sliced into thin discs	3 tablespoons instant soup mix (chicken flavored)
5 large Vidalia onions, sliced into thin rings	Salt and pepper to taste
	1 egg lightly beaten

Preheat oven to 350°. Roll out one puff pastry sheet and place it into the bottom and a little up the sides of a 9- x 13-inch glass casserole dish. Bake for 10 minutes until dough is lightly golden and puffed. Remove from oven and set aside. Turn oven off.

In a large pot over a medium flame heat the oil. Add the onions and sauté until soft but not brown. Stir occasionally to make sure they are cooking evenly, about 20 to 25 minutes. Add the zucchini and cook until soft, about 15 to 20 minutes, stirring occasionally. Do not drain the liquid. Let cool for about an hour.

Preheat oven to 350°. Add eggs, flour, soup mix, salt and pepper. Pour the zucchini mixture into the puff pastry. Roll out the second puff pastry sheet and cut into strips. Lay the strips across the top of the kugel in a diagonal fashion and then crisscross pastry the other way for a lattice effect. Carefully brush the pastry strips with beaten egg. Bake uncovered for 60 minutes or until lightly golden. Cut into squares and serve warm.

Yield: 12 servings.

PESTO

Parve or Dairy

Pesto is a wonderful topping or sauce for pasta, bread, potatoes- really almost anything!

2 cups fresh basil leaves

½ cup pine nuts

4 cloves garlic

1 cup olive oil, divided

1 cup grated Parmesan cheese (optional for dairy meals)

Salt

Pepper

Combine basil, pine nuts, garlic, and a few tablespoons of olive oil in the container of a food processor fitted with a knife blade. Process until finely chopped, stopping once or twice to scrape down sides. With processor running, pour salt, pepper, and remaining oil through food chute until a thick paste forms. Add Parmesan cheese, if desired, pulsing until well blended.

Yield: 2 cups.

ASPARAGUS KUGEL

Parve

Looking for a quick and easy side dish with ingredients found in your pantry? This is a great one.

2 (15-ounce) cans asparagus, drained	½ cup mayonnaise
1½ tablespoons all-purpose flour	½ cup non-dairy creamer
1 tablespoon chopped onion	Pepper
3 large eggs, lightly beaten	1½ tablespoons margarine, melted
	Corn flake crumbs

Preheat oven to 350°.

Mash asparagus with a fork in a medium bowl. Add flour, onion, eggs, mayonnaise, creamer, and pepper, blending well.

Pour into a lightly greased 8- x 8-inch baking pan. Top with melted margarine and sprinkle with corn flake crumbs.

Bake for 1 hour.

Yield: 4 to 6 servings.

POTATO KUGEL MUFFINS

Parve

2 tablespoons oil	1½ tablespoons salt
3 onions, chopped	½ teaspoon pepper
5 pounds russet potatoes, peeled and grated	Vegetable cooking spray
5 large eggs, lightly beaten	1-2 teaspoons paprika

Preheat oven to 400°.

Heat oil in a skillet over medium-high heat. Add onions and sauté until translucent and golden brown.

Squeeze out excess liquid from potatoes and place in a large bowl. Add eggs, salt, and pepper, stirring until well blended. Stir in sautéed onions.

Coat muffin pans very well with cooking spray; pour mixture into muffin pans, filling each ¾ full. Sprinkle evenly with paprika.

Bake for 5 minutes; reduce heat to 350° and bake 30 to 40 minutes or until medium brown.

Yield: 2 dozen.

CARROT KUGEL

Parve

Try this kid-friendly, user-friendly kugel you can make ahead.

4 large carrots, cut into
   3- to 4-inch pieces
   Vegetable cooking spray
1 cup all-purpose flour
½ cup firmly packed dark
   brown sugar

½ cup sugar
1½ teaspoons baking powder
½ cup oil or ½ cup
   applesauce
2 large eggs
1 teaspoon vanilla extract

Combine carrots and water to cover in a large saucepan over high heat. Boil 25 minutes or until carrots are tender. Drain and place in a large mixing bowl. Mash carrots with a fork.

Preheat oven to 350°. Coat a 9-inch non-stick springform pan with non-stick cooking spray. (You can also use a tart pan with a removable bottom. Be sure sides are at least 2 inches high.) Set aside.

To the carrots, add flour, sugars, baking powder, oil, eggs, and vanilla. Beat at medium speed with an electric mixer until well blended (can also be mixed by hand). Do not overbeat so batter will have small pieces of carrot for texture.

Pour mixture into prepared pan. Bake for 45 minutes or until a toothpick inserted in the center comes out clean. Cut into wedges.

Yield: 12 servings.

If you don't have the time to boil fresh carrots you can substitute 8 ounces of baby food carrots. Beat them in with the rest of the ingredients.

This recipe can be made into muffins. Insert paper liners into muffin tins. Pour batter to fill each compartment three-fourths full. Bake 30 minutes.

Yield: 20 to 22 muffins.

TRI-COLOR VEGETABLE SOUFFLÉ

Parve

4½	tablespoons margarine
4½	tablespoons all-purpose flour
1½	cups non-dairy creamer
1½	cups mayonnaise
9	large eggs
1	(1½-ounce) package onion soup mix
1¼	pounds fresh or frozen broccoli
1¼	pounds fresh or frozen cauliflower
1¼	pounds fresh or canned carrots
	Crumbled corn flakes

Preheat oven to 350°.

Heat margarine in a saucepan over medium-high heat. Add flour, whisking until blended. Gradually whisk in non-dairy creamer until thickened. Remove from heat and stir in mayonnaise, eggs, and soup mix; set aside.

Cook broccoli in boiling water to cover until tender; drain. Place broccoli in the container of a food processor fitted with a knife blade; process until almost smooth. Stir in 2 cups of egg mixture.

Pour broccoli mixture into a lightly greased 9-inch springform pan.

Bake for 20 to 25 minutes.

Cook cauliflower in boiling water to cover until tender; drain. Place cauliflower in the container of a food processor fitted with a knife blade; process until almost smooth. Stir in 2 cups of egg mixture. Spread evenly over broccoli layer.

Bake 20 to 25 minutes.

Cook carrots in boiling water to cover until tender; drain. Place carrots in the container of a food processor fitted with a knife blade; process until smooth. Stir in remaining 1½ cups egg mixture. Spread evenly over cauliflower layer. Sprinkle top with crumbled corn flakes.

Bake 20 to 25 minutes. Release carefully from the springform pan and serve.

Yield: 12 to 14 servings.

BARLEY PILAF
WITH CARAMELIZED ONIONS

Meat

⅓ cup pecan halves	¾ cup dried cherries or
2 tablespoons olive oil	blueberries, chopped
2 large onions, finely	¾ teaspoon salt
chopped	½ teaspoon dried sage
2 cloves garlic, minced	½ teaspoon freshly ground
1 cup pearl barley (not	pepper
quick cooking)	1 cup water
1½ cups chicken broth	Garnish: chopped fresh
	parsley

Preheat oven to 350°.

Place pecans in a single layer on a baking sheet. Bake 5 to 7 minutes or until lightly toasted. Do not overbake. Cool; coarsely chop and set aside. Keep oven on.

Heat oil in a Dutch oven or heavy skillet over medium heat. Add onions and sauté 10 minutes, stirring frequently, or until golden brown. Add garlic and sauté 1 to 2 minutes.

Stir in barley. Add broth, dried fruit, salt, sage, pepper, and 1 cup water. Bring mixture to a boil. Cover and transfer carefully to the oven.

Bake 30 minutes or until barley is tender and all liquid is absorbed. Stir in toasted pecans and sprinkle with parsley.

Yield: 4 servings.

COUSCOUS WITH
ROASTED PEPPERS AND ARTICHOKES

Parve

2 cups water
1 vegetable or chicken
   flavored bouillon cube
1 tablespoon olive oil
½ teaspoon salt
1 (10-ounce) package
   couscous
1 (7-ounce) jar roasted red
   peppers, drained and
   cut into thin strips

1 (6-ounce) jar marinated
   artichoke hearts,
   drained and chopped
1½ tablespoons fresh lemon
   juice
2 tablespoons olive oil
   Salt
   Pepper

Combine water, bouillon, oil, and salt in a medium saucepan over high heat. Bring just to a boil. Stir in couscous and cover. Remove from heat; let stand 5 minutes.

Fluff couscous lightly with a fork. Add peppers, artichoke hearts, lemon juice, and oil, tossing to coat. Season to taste with salt and pepper.

Yield: 4 servings.

SESAME NOODLES

Parve

"*Over the years I have tried many sesame noodle recipes. Most I encountered were laden with peanut butter and just unappealing. Then I stumbled on this recipe. After serving it, I headed over to my recipe file and tore up all of the other sesame noodle recipes I had amassed over the years.*"

1 (16-ounce) package
   linguine
6 cloves garlic, minced
6 tablespoons sugar
6 tablespoons safflower oil
6 tablespoons rice vinegar
6 tablespoons soy sauce

2 tablespoons sesame oil
1-2 teaspoons hot Chinese
   chili sauce or crushed
   red pepper flakes
6 scallions, sliced
1 teaspoon sesame seeds,
   toasted

Cook linguine according to package directions; drain and transfer to a large serving bowl.

Combine garlic, sugar, oil, vinegar, soy sauce, sesame oil, and chili sauce in a saucepan over medium-high heat. Bring mixture to a boil, stirring constantly, until sugar dissolves.

Pour over linguine, tossing to coat. Sprinkle with scallions and sesame seeds.

Yield: 6 to 8 servings.

CRANBERRY RELISH

Parve

"**M**y mother-in-law serves this tasty treat in an elegant gravy boat. It is fabulous with turkey- even when it's not Thanksgiving!"

1 (12-ounce) package fresh cranberries, rinsed and drained	½ cup raisins
¾ cup sugar	1½ cups water
¾ cup dried dates, cut into pieces	¼ cup lemon juice
	¼ teaspoon ground cinnamon
	¼ teaspoon ground ginger

Combine cranberries, sugar, dates, raisins, water, lemon juice, cinnamon, and ginger in a medium saucepan over medium-high heat. Bring mixture to a boil, reduce heat, and simmer, stirring occasionally, for 10 minutes. Cover and chill before serving.

Yield: 1 quart.

Quick Variation: Substitute 2 cans whole-berry cranberry sauce for fresh cranberries. Mash cranberry sauce with a fork and combine with remaining ingredients omitting the sugar and the water. Cook as directed.

OATMEAL BERRY BAKE

Parve

"**T**his sweet side dish has traditionally been served along with the main course. Recently, however, my family has been having this recipe do double-duty, both as a side dish and delicious dessert."

1 cup all-purpose flour	½ cup margarine, melted
1 cup oatmeal	1 (16-ounce) can whole-berry cranberry sauce
⅔ cup firmly packed light brown sugar	1 (20-ounce) can crushed pineapple, drained
1 heaping teaspoon ground cinnamon	

Preheat oven to 350°.

Combine flour, oatmeal, brown sugar, and cinnamon in a bowl. Add margarine, stirring until well blended.

Pour half of the oatmeal mixture into a lightly greased 8- x 8-inch baking dish.

Combine cranberry sauce and pineapple and spoon on top of oatmeal mixture. Top with remaining oatmeal mixture.

Bake, uncovered, for 45 minutes.

Yield: 4 to 6 servings.

Floral Ice Bowls

Impress your guests with a stunning ice bowl. Use it to hold a pretty side dish like Cranberry Relish, a crisp green salad, or a cold dessert like fresh berries or ice cream.

2 freezer-proof glass or aluminum bowls of the same shape, one about 2 inches smaller than the other
Water
Assorted edible flowers
Scotch tape

Pour 1 inch of water into the larger bowl. Place the bowl in the freezer, making sure it is standing perfectly flat. When the water has frozen remove the bowl from the freezer. Place the smaller bowl inside the larger one resting on the ice. Tape the bowls together using Scotch tape to make sure they don't shift. Pour water into the gap between the two bowls. Have it come halfway up the side. Stick the edible flowers into the water all the way around the perimeter of the bowl. Use a pencil or skewer to push the flowers down if necessary. Place the bowls in the freezer again, until the water has frozen. Remove the bowls and add another layer of water so it reaches the top. Freeze again. When the ice bowl is frozen solid, remove the bowls from the freezer. Remove the tape. Try to separate the bowls. If necessary, run under tepid water just until the bowls release. Place the ice bowl back into the freezer until needed. Serve the bowl on a chilled glass plate or tray to catch drips. You can try this concept with foil confetti, herbs, or slices of citrus fruit.

SCALLOPED POTATOES
WITH RED ONION AND ROSEMARY

Parve or Meat

2 tablespoons parve margarine or olive oil

¼ pound red onion, thinly sliced

1 tablespoon fresh rosemary or 1 teaspoon dried rosemary

Freshly ground pepper

Paprika

2 pounds potatoes, sliced paper thin

Salt

2 cups chicken stock (page 39) or bouillon

Preheat oven to 350°.

Heat 1 teaspoon margarine in a skillet over medium-high heat. Add onion and sauté until tender. Add rosemary, pepper, and paprika to color and cook 1 minute.

Layer one-third of potatoes in the bottom of a 5½- x 7½-inch loaf pan greased with 2 teaspoons margarine.

Top potatoes with half of onions and sprinkle with salt. Repeat with one-third of potatoes and remaining onions. Add remaining potatoes, overlapping neatly on top.

Add broth until you reach the top layer of potatoes. Melt remaining margarine and drizzle over top.

Bake covered for 1½ hours. Remove cover and bake an additional 20 to 30 minutes until golden brown and liquid is absorbed. Cut into squares to serve.

Yield: 6 servings.

SWEET POTATO PIE

Parve

1 cup graham cracker
   crumbs
½ cup melted margarine
2 cups fresh cooked or
   canned sweet potato
3 large eggs, lightly beaten
¾ cup non-dairy creamer

2 tablespoons melted
   margarine
½ cup firmly packed light
   brown sugar
1 teaspoon ground
   cinnamon
½ teaspoon salt
1 cup mini marshmallows

Here is an alternate topping for the marshmallows:

½ cup corn flake
crumbs

3 tablespoons
margarine, softened

3 tablespoons
brown sugar

Mix all ingredients
together and sprinkle
on top of pie before
baking as directed.

Preheat oven to 450°.

Combine cracker crumbs and ½ cup melted margarine in a small bowl. Press into the bottom and slightly up the sides of a 9-inch springform pan.

Combine sweet potato, eggs, creamer, 2 tablespoons margarine, brown sugar, cinnamon, and salt in a mixing bowl. Beat with an electric mixer on medium speed until well blended. Pour sweet potato mixture into the crust.

Bake for 10 minutes. Reduce temperature to 350°; bake for 45 minutes.

Preheat oven to broil with rack 6 inches from heat.

Top pie with marshmallows and broil for 1 minute, watching carefully so topping doesn't burn.

Yield: 1 (9-inch) pie.

MAPLE-ROASTED SWEET POTATOES

Dairy or Parve

3 large sweet potatoes
   (about 3 pounds), peeled
   and cubed
1 (12-ounce) package fresh
   or frozen cranberries

½ cup butter or margarine,
   melted
½ cup maple syrup
½ cup chopped pecans,
   toasted

Preheat oven to 375°.

Place sweet potatoes and cranberries in a large, lightly greased roasting pan.

Combine butter and maple syrup. Pour over sweet potatoes and cranberries, stirring to coat. Cover tightly with foil.

Bake 30 to 35 minutes or until potatoes are tender. Spoon into a serving dish and sprinkle with pecans.

Yield: 6 to 8 servings.

PINE NUT RELISH

Parve

This relish goes nicely with chicken or turkey.

½ cup (3 ounces) dried apricots, chopped	2 teaspoons chopped jalapeño pepper, with seeds
⅓ cup chopped onion	⅔ cup chopped tomatoes, seeded
3 tablespoons drained and chopped sun-dried tomatoes (packed in oil)	3 tablespoons pine nuts, toasted
2½ tablespoons honey	1 tablespoon chopped fresh cilantro leaves
1 tablespoon peeled and minced fresh ginger	Salt
	Pepper

Combine apricots, onion, sun-dried tomatoes, honey, ginger, and pepper in a large bowl. Cover and refrigerate 8 hours or overnight.

Stir in tomatoes, pine nuts, and cilantro. Season to taste with salt and pepper. Cover and refrigerate. Bring to room temperature before serving.

Yield: 2 cups.

PASTRAMI FRIED RICE

Meat

2 tablespoons vegetable oil, divided	6 ounces sliced smoked turkey, shredded into thin strips
4 large eggs, lightly beaten	
1 bunch scallions, chopped	6 cups cooked white rice (page 209)
2 cloves garlic, chopped	
12 ounces sliced pastrami, shredded into thin strips	½-1 tablespoon soy sauce, divided

Heat 1 tablespoon oil in a large skillet over medium-high heat. Add eggs and cook, stirring constantly. Remove from pan and chop into small pieces; set aside.

Heat remaining 1 tablespoon oil in the skillet. Add scallions, garlic, pastrami, and turkey and sauté until scallions are tender. Remove from heat.

Stir in rice and reserved egg mixture. Stir in soy sauce to taste.

Yield: 10 to 12 servings.

BULGUR, PINE NUT AND RED PEPPER PILAF

Parve or Meat

1 tablespoon vegetable oil
1 small onion, finely chopped
1 cup plus 2 tablespoons chicken stock (page 39) or bouillon
¾ cup bulgur

3 tablespoons finely diced red bell pepper
2 tablespoons pine nuts, lightly toasted
2 tablespoons minced fresh chives
Salt
Pepper

Heat oil in a saucepan over medium heat. Add onion and sauté until tender. Stir in broth, bulgur, and red bell pepper.

Bring to a boil, reduce heat, and simmer, covered, for 12 minutes or until the liquid is absorbed. Remove from heat and let stand, covered, for 5 minutes.

Stir in pine nuts, chives; season to taste with salt and pepper.

Yield: 2 to 3 servings.

WILD MUSHROOM RISOTTO

Parve or Meat

¼ cup margarine
3 cloves garlic, chopped
1 shallot, chopped
8 ounces shiitake mushrooms, sliced

8 ounces cremini mushrooms, sliced
2 cups Arborio rice
2 cups dry white wine
2 cups chicken stock (page 39) or bouillon

Preheat oven to 350°.

Heat margarine in a skillet over medium-high heat. Add garlic, shallots, mushroom, salt, and pepper. Sauté for 2 minutes. Add rice and sauté until slightly brown. (There will be a nutty aroma.) Set aside.

Combine wine and stock in a saucepan over high heat. Bring to a boil; remove from heat.

Combine rice mixture and wine mixture in a lightly greased 2½-quart baking dish. Cover tightly and bake 35 to 40 minutes or until liquid is absorbed and rice is creamy.

Yield: 6 servings.

TABBOULEH

Parve

This dish is light and refreshing—a real summer side dish that goes well with fish or meat. Plan to prepare it a day or two ahead so the couscous grains have time to soften and absorb flavor.

1⅓ cups couscous, uncooked	⅓ cup chopped fresh flat leaf parsley
4 large tomatoes, coarsely chopped	2-3 tablespoons chopped fresh mint
1 green bell pepper, coarsely chopped	⅓ cup fresh lemon juice
1 red onion, finely chopped	¼ cup olive oil
1 clove garlic, pressed	Salt
½ cucumber, coarsely chopped	Freshly ground pepper

Combine couscous, tomatoes, bell pepper, onion, garlic, cucumber, parsley, mint, lemon juice, olive oil, salt and pepper in a large bowl. Stir until well blended.

Cover and refrigerate 12 to 48 hours. Adjust seasonings before serving.

Yield: 6 to 8 servings.

CONFETTI RICE PILAF

Parve

This colorful rice dish is a beautiful complement to any chicken or meat entrée. A wonderful summer side dish when served at room temperature.

1 (7-ounce) package rice pilaf mix	½ cup green olives, sliced
½ cup chopped onion	½ cup black olives, sliced
2 scallions, chopped	¼ cup vegetable oil
2 tomatoes, diced	2 tablespoons lemon juice
¾ cup raisins	2 teaspoons mustard

Prepare rice pilaf according to package directions. Stir in onion, scallions, tomatoes, raisins, and olives.

Combine oil, lemon juice, and mustard. Pour over pilaf, tossing to coat.

Yield: 4 servings.

Acorn Squash with Wild Rice and Orzo

Parve or Meat

4 small acorn squash, cut
   in half and seeded
   Salt
   Freshly ground pepper
1 cup wild rice, rinsed and
   drained
2 tablespoons shallots,
   minced

3 cups chicken stock
   (page 39) or bouillon
1 cup orzo
1 teaspoon coarse kosher salt
2 tablespoons olive oil
3 tablespoons unsalted
   margarine, divided
2 bunches scallions, sliced
¼ cup chopped fresh parsley

Place squash halves, cut side down, in a large glass baking dish. Cover tightly with plastic wrap; pierce plastic wrap to let steam escape. Microwave on HIGH for 10 minutes.

Uncover and turn squash halves cut side up. Loosen and mash pulp with a fork, leaving it in the shell; season with salt and pepper.

Combine wild rice, shallots and chicken stock in a heavy saucepan over high heat. Bring to a boil, stir, and reduce heat. Simmer, covered, for 50 minutes or until tender. Remove from heat and uncover. Set aside for 10 minutes and drain off half of liquid from rice.

Cook orzo in boiling water with 1 teaspoon kosher salt for 8 minutes or until al dente. Drain and set aside.

Heat oil and 1 tablespoon margarine in a large saucepan over medium heat. Add scallions and sauté 1 minute or until tender.

Add reserved rice with remaining water, orzo, and parsley, stirring to blend. Season with salt and pepper to taste. Reduce heat to low; cook 5 minutes or until thoroughly heated.

Preheat oven to 425°.

Spoon wild rice and orzo mixture into squash halves. Dot with remaining 2 tablespoons margarine. Cover and chill until ready to bake.

Bake 25 minutes or until thoroughly heated.

Yield: 8 servings.

FRENCH–FRIED ORZO

Meat or Parve

If a recipe gets points for ease, this one is the hands-down winner. The simple directions and few ingredients don't detract from the delicious flavor of the dish. Orzo is a pasta product, similar in shape to rice.

¼ cup margarine
1 (16-ounce) package orzo
4 cups chicken stock
    (page 39) or bouillon

1 (2.8-ounce) can French
    fried onions

Preheat oven to 350°.

Heat margarine in a skillet over medium heat. Add orzo and cook until golden brown; remove from heat.

Bring chicken broth to a boil. Add to orzo mixture. Pour into a lightly greased 2-quart casserole dish or loaf pan and sprinkle with onions.

Bake, uncovered, for 45 minutes or until pasta is tender.

Yield: 8 servings.

SAFFRON RICE

Meat

2½ cups chicken stock
     (page 39)
     Pinch saffron
1-2 teaspoons margarine

1 small onion, finely chopped
1¼ cups long grain rice, rinsed
     Salt

Combine broth and saffron; cover and refrigerate 8 hours or overnight. (You may also heat broth in a small saucepan and stir in saffron. Let stand 1 hour.)

Heat margarine in a saucepan over medium-high heat. Add onions and sauté until golden brown. Stir in rice and sauté 30 seconds. Stir in broth mixture.

Bring rice mixture to a boil, stirring once. Remove from heat, cover tightly, and set aside for 25 minutes or simmer over very low heat for 15 to 20 minutes until rice is tender.

Yield: 4 cups.

PERFECT WHITE RICE

Parve

American grown rice is clean and does not need rinsing before or after cooking. Rinsing simply washes away nutrients. Long grain rice remains separate and not sticky. Short grain rice is sticky and is the best rice to use for sushi and stir-fries.

1 cup regular long grain rice	1 teaspoon salt
2 cups water	1 teaspoon oil

Combine rice, water, salt, and oil in a 2- to 3-quart saucepan. Bring mixture to a boil, stirring only once to distribute the salt and oil through the mixture.

Boil rapidly until rice rises above the water. Reduce heat, cover, and simmer 15 minutes. Do not stir. If rice is not quite tender or liquid is not absorbed, cook, covered, 2 to 4 additional minutes. Fluff with a fork to allow steam to escape and the grains to separate.

Yield: 3 cups.

Short Grain Rice

Prepare rice as directed in recipe, decreasing water by ¼ cup to 1¾ cups water. When cooked, do not fluff with fork.

PERFECT WILD RICE

Parve

1 cup (6 ounces) wild rice	4 cups water

Rinse rice thoroughly in a colander or wire mesh strainer.

Combine rice and water in a heavy saucepan; bring to a boil. Reduce heat and simmer, loosely covered, for 45 to 60 minutes or until rice puffs and most of the liquid is absorbed. Remove from heat.

Fluff rice with a fork. Cover tightly and let stand for 5 minutes. Drain off any excess water. Add flavor by serving with margarine, butter, salt, or spices.

Yield: 4 cups.

BLACK AND WHITE RICE MOLD

Meat or Parve

This side dish makes a stunning presentation when taken out of the pan. Use it as a centerpiece for your dinner table. Both long grain and short grain rice will work in this recipe.

2 cups extra long or short grain white rice	¼ cup margarine, cut into pieces
1 (6-ounce) box long grain and wild rice mix	Salt
4 cups chicken stock (page 39) or bouillon	Pepper
2⅓ cups water	1 teaspoon vegetable oil
4 bay leaves	10 ounces mushrooms, chopped
¼ cups chopped fresh parsley (optional)	1 large onion, chopped
	3 cloves garlic, chopped

Combine white rice, long grain and wild rice with seasoning packet, stock, water, bay leaves, parsley and margarine in a large soup pot over high heat. Bring mixture to a boil; reduce heat to low. Cover and simmer for 20 minutes or until all of the liquid is absorbed. Remove from heat. Remove bay leaves and discard. Season to taste with salt and pepper.

Preheat oven to 300°.

Heat oil in a large skillet over medium-high heat. Add mushrooms and onion; sauté for 10 minutes or until tender. Add garlic and sauté 3 to 4 minutes. Season to taste with salt and pepper. Stir mushroom mixture into rice mixture.

Spoon rice mixture into a well greased Bundt pan, pressing to pack mixture tightly.

Cover and bake for 20 minutes. Turn out rice mold onto a serving plate. Let stand a few minutes before cutting.

Yield: 8 to 10 servings.

DESSERTS

Blueberry-Raspberry Tart,
page 213

LEMON TART IN ALMOND CRUST

Parve

Crust:

½ cup margarine, softened
5 ounces ground almonds
3 tablespoons sugar

1½ cups all-purpose flour
1 medium egg
½ teaspoon vanilla extract

Filling:

1 (2¾-ounce) package
   lemon pudding and pie
   filling mix (not instant)
1½ cups water
¾ cups sugar

3 egg yolks
3 lemons
   Garnish: fresh raspberries
   or other berries

Preheat oven to 350°. Grease a 10-inch round or square tart pan with removable bottom; set aside.

Beat the margarine at medium speed with an electric mixer in a large mixing bowl. Add almonds, sugar, flour, egg, and vanilla, beating well after each addition. (Dough will be crumbly.)

Press dough in bottom and up sides of prepared pan. Bake for 20 to 30 minutes or until golden brown.

Combine pudding mix, water, sugar, and yolks in a small saucepan. Cut lemons in half and squeeze juice into saucepan, stirring well. Place 4 of the lemon halves in saucepan so flavor will be extracted during the cooking process. Bring mixture to a boil. Reduce heat to low and simmer, stirring constantly, until the mixture thickens. Remove lemon halves, scraping out any filling inside. Pour filling into prepared pastry. Cover and refrigerate until chilled. Remove sides of pan before serving.

Garnish with fresh raspberries or other colorful berries.

Yield: 8 servings.

An alternate way to present this tart is to make a batch of Meringues (page 257) and place one large spiraled meringue in the middle with berries coming out of it like spokes, or scatter small meringue mounds in a decorative fashion.

BLUEBERRY–RASPBERRY TART

Parve

Dough:

1½ cups all-purpose flour

3 tablespoons sugar

¾ cup margarine

1½ tablespoons vinegar

Filling:

3 pints fresh blueberries

½ cup sugar

2 tablespoons all-purpose flour

½ teaspoon ground cinnamon

1 pint fresh raspberries

Preheat oven to 400°.

For dough: Combine flour and sugar in the container of a food processor fitted with a plastic dough blade; pulse 3 or 4 times until combined. Add margarine, pulsing 5 or 6 times or until mixture is crumbly.

With processor running, slowly add vinegar; process just until pastry begins to form a ball and leaves sides of bowl. This dough can also be made by hand or with an electric mixer.

With lightly floured hands, press dough into the bottom and sides of an 11-inch tart pan with a removable bottom.

For filling: Sort blueberries and place the plumpest, prettiest ones to fill three-fourths of one of the pint boxes; set aside. Wash remaining blueberries, shaking off excess water. (Do not towel dry. A little moisture will enable the sugar to stick to the berries.)

Combine washed blueberries, sugar, flour, and cinnamon in a bowl, tossing to blend.

Spoon berry mixture into tart pan. There should be a small mound of berries in the center; it will flatten as the blueberries bake.

Bake for 1 hour or until the berries are bubbly. Remove from oven and let stand 5 minutes.

Starting from the outside, place remaining fresh blueberries and raspberries in concentric circles, lightly pressing each berry into the tart. Remove sides of pan before serving.

Yield: 8 servings.

LINZER TORTE PIE

Parve

½ cup whole almonds
½ cup margarine
¾ cup sugar
1 large egg
1½ cups all-purpose flour

1 teaspoon cinnamon
¼ teaspoon salt
¾ cup raspberry or apricot
   jam
   Powdered sugar

Preheat oven to 375°.

Spread almonds in a single layer on a baking sheet. Bake for 8 to 10 minutes or until golden brown; cool slightly.

Place almonds in the container of a food processor fitted with a knife blade; process until finely ground, but not pasty. Set aside.

Beat margarine at medium speed with an electric mixer until fluffy; gradually add sugar, beating well. Add egg, beating well.

Combine ½ cup ground almonds (save extra for other uses), flour, cinnamon, and salt; stir into margarine mixture.

Press two-thirds of dough mixture into the bottom and sides of a 10-inch tart pan with removable bottom. Spread jam over dough.

Roll remaining one-third of dough on a lightly floured surface forming a 10- x 6-inch rectangle. Cut dough into 10- x ½-inch strips. Arrange 4 or 5 strips of dough lengthwise across the tart. Arrange remaining strips of dough across tart, pressing ends of all strips into the edge of the crust.

Bake 25 to 30 minutes or until crust is golden brown. Cool completely on wire rack. Remove side of tart pan and sprinkle with powdered sugar.

Yield: 8 servings.

STRAWBERRY–RHUBARB PIE

Parve or Dairy

*T*his pie is a delightful combination of sweet and tart. A lovely dish that can be served room temperature or warm, with ice cream or a dollop of whipped cream.

Dough:

1¼ cups all-purpose flour	3 tablespoons cold water
¼ teaspoon salt	1 tablespoon lemon juice
½ cup margarine or butter	

Filling:

1 cup sugar	3 cups frozen rhubarb, cut into 1-inch pieces
½ tablespoon cornstarch	
⅓ cup all-purpose flour	1 tablespoon margarine, cut into small pieces
2 tablespoons orange juice	
3 cups fresh strawberries, hulled	1 egg white, lightly beaten

Preheat oven to 400°.

Combine 1¼ cups flour and salt; cut in margarine with a pastry blender or fork until mixture is crumbly. Combine water and lemon juice; sprinkle, 1 tablespoon at a time, evenly over flour mixture. Stir with a fork until dry ingredients are moistened.

Divide dough into 2 equal pieces. Roll each piece on a floured surface into a 12-inch circle. Fit one circle into a 9-inch pie pan; allow excess dough to hang off sides.

In a large bowl combine sugar, cornstarch, and ⅓ cup flour. Stir in orange juice. Fold in strawberries and rhubarb; spoon into pastry. Dot with margarine.

Place remaining pastry over filling. Fold edges under, and crimp. Trim and flute edges, if desired. Cut slits in top crust for steam to escape. Brush with egg white.

Bake for 1 hour; shield edges of pastry with foil to prevent excessive browning, if necessary.

Yield: 8 servings.

BLUEBERRY BUCKLE

Parve or Dairy

"*This is a marvelous tasting cake. Every summer we go blueberry picking and use our 'bounty' to make this wonderful dessert.*"

Cake:

- ¼ cup unsalted margarine or butter
- ¾ cup sugar
- 1 large egg
- 1 teaspoon vanilla
- 2 cups all-purpose flour
- 2 teaspoons baking powder
- ½ teaspoon salt
- ½ cup non-dairy creamer or milk
- 1 tablespoon all-purpose flour
- 1 pint blueberries

Topping:

- ½ cup sugar
- ⅓ cup all-purpose flour
- ½ teaspoon ground cinnamon
- ¼ cup margarine or butter, softened
- Non-dairy whipped topping or whipped heavy cream

Preheat oven to 375°. Grease an 8-inch springform pan.

Beat butter at medium speed with an electric mixer until fluffy; gradually add sugar, beating well. Beat in egg and vanilla.

Combine 2 cups flour, baking powder, and salt; add to butter mixture alternately with milk, beginning and ending with the flour mixture.

Combine 1 tablespoon flour with blueberries (to keep them from sinking to the bottom) and fold into batter. Pour batter into prepared pan.

Combine sugar, flour, and cinnamon in a small bowl. Cut in butter with a pastry blender or fork until crumbly; sprinkle on batter.

Bake for 1 hour or until a toothpick inserted in center comes out clean. Cool in pan on a wire rack. Run a knife along the edge of pan and remove sides. Serve with whipped cream.

Yield: 6 to 8 servings.

DECADENT CHOCOLATE CAKE

Dairy

1 cup boiling water	2 large eggs, separated
3 ounces unsweetened chocolate, cut into pieces	1 teaspoon baking soda
½ cup unsalted butter, softened	½ cup sour cream
	2 cups all-purpose flour
1 teaspoon vanilla extract	1 teaspoon baking powder
2 cups sugar	Chocolate Frosting

Preheat oven to 350° with rack in the center. Grease and flour a 10-inch tube pan; set aside.

Combine water, chocolate, and butter in a large bowl; let stand until melted. Stir in vanilla and sugar. Whisk in eggs yolks, one at a time, blending well after each addition. Combine baking soda and sour cream; stir into chocolate mixture.

Combine flour and baking powder; add to chocolate mixture, stirring well.

Beat egg whites at high speed with an electric mixer until stiff peaks form. Do not overbeat. Stir one-fourth of eggs into batter until completely blended. Gently fold in remaining egg whites until just blended.

Pour batter into prepared pan. Bake 40 to 50 minutes or until edges pull away from the sides. Cool in pan for 10 minutes; remove from pan and let cool on a wire rack.

Spread Chocolate Frosting on top and sides of cooled cake.

Yield: 12 servings.

CHOCOLATE FROSTING:
Dairy

6 tablespoons unsalted butter	¾ cup semi-sweet chocolate morsels
6 tablespoons heavy whipping cream	1¼ cup powdered sugar
	1 teaspoon vanilla extract

Combine butter, cream, chocolate morsels, sugar, and vanilla in a heavy saucepan over low heat. Cook, whisking constantly, until smooth. Cool slightly. Add more powdered sugar, if necessary.

Chocolate Curls

Soften a bar of semi-sweet chocolate with the heat of your hand or in a barely warm oven. Slowly and firmly, pull a vegetable peeler across the wide side of the chocolate for wide curls or along the thin side for thin curls. The softer the chocolate, the better it will curl. Don't pick up chocolate curls with your hands as they are very fragile. Hang the curl off a toothpick and place it on top of the cake.

ENCLOSED APPLE TART WITH CARAMEL SAUCE

Parve or Dairy

Crust:

2 cups all-purpose flour
¾ cup powdered sugar
½ cup unsalted margarine or butter, chilled

2 large egg yolks, lightly beaten
3 tablespoons parve or dairy heavy whipping cream

Filling:

6 Granny Smith apples, peeled, cored, and cut into ⅓-inch thick slices
½ cup sugar
¼ cup golden raisins

2 tablespoons all-purpose flour
1 teaspoon sugar
   Caramel Sauce

Combine flour and sugar; cut in margarine with a pastry blender or fork until mixture is crumbly. Stir in egg yolks and cream, kneading until dough is smooth.

Divide dough into 2 pieces, with one slightly larger than the other. Form each piece into a flattened disk. Cover with plastic wrap and refrigerate for 30 minutes. This may be done a day ahead; let soften at room temperature before proceeding with recipe.

Preheat oven to 375°.

Roll out larger pastry on a floured surface into a 12-inch circle. Press into the bottom and 2 inches up the sides of a greased 9-inch springform pan.

Combine apple slices, sugar, raisins, and flour; spoon into prepared pastry.

Roll remaining pastry on a floured surface into a 9-inch circle. Place pastry over filling; fold edges under and crimp.

Sprinkle 1 teaspoon sugar over top of tart and cut 5 slits in top crust to let steam escape.

Bake for 1 hour or until golden brown. Place tart under a broiler, if desired, for 1 to 2 minutes for a darker golden brown. Cool completely on a wire rack. Release sides and serve with warm Caramel Sauce.

Yield: 8 servings.

CARAMEL SAUCE:

1   cup sugar
½   cup water

1   cup parve or dairy heavy
    whipping cream

Combine sugar and water in a heavy saucepan over low heat. When sugar dissolves, increase heat to medium-high. Cook, without stirring, until syrup turns a deep amber color. Brush down the sides of the pan with a wet pastry brush so sugar crystals do not form. Swirl pot occasionally (do not stir) for at least 10 minutes, until caramel colored. Reduce heat to low and add cream. Whisk to dissolve any hard bits. Let stand 5 minutes. Serve warm.

*Sauce works best when made dairy.

Yield: 2¼ cups.

APPLE CRISP

Parve or Dairy

½-¾ cup currants (optional)
1   cup boiling water
5   Golden Delicious apples,
     peeled, cored, and
     coarsely chopped
1   cup chopped pecans
¾   cup all-purpose flour
⅓   cup sugar
⅓   cup firmly packed light
     brown sugar

½   teaspoon ground
     cinnamon
½   cup unsalted margarine
     or butter, chilled and
     cut into pieces
     Non-dairy whipped
     topping or whipped
     heavy cream

If you are using the currants, place them in a small heatproof bowl. Pour the boiling water over them and let stand for 10 minutes or until currants plump; drain.

Preheat oven to 375°. Grease a 9-inch square baking dish; set aside.

Combine apples and currants; spoon into prepared dish.

Combine pecans, flour, sugar, brown sugar, and cinnamon in a small bowl; cut in margarine with a pastry blender or fork until mixture is crumbly. Sprinkle over apples.

Bake for 40 minutes or until topping is brown and apples are tender. Serve with whipped cream.

Yield: 6 servings.

Ultimate Chocolate Cake

Parve or Dairy

What makes this the ultimate chocolate cake is its versatility. It can be made in 5 minutes, into any shape– round, square, muffins, or Bundt. It can be made in advance, freezes with ease, and is always a favorite at the table.

2	cups sugar	1	cup non-dairy creamer or milk
1¾	cups all-purpose flour		
¾	cup cocoa	½	cup vegetable oil
1½	teaspoons baking soda	2	teaspoons vanilla extract
1½	teaspoons baking powder	2	large eggs, lightly beaten
1	teaspoon salt	1	cup boiling water

Preheat oven to 350°. Grease and flour the pan of your choice: one 13- x 9-inch pan, two 8-inch round or square pans, or a Bundt pan.

Combine sugar, flour, cocoa, baking soda, baking powder, and salt in a large mixing bowl, stirring until well blended.

Add milk, oil, vanilla, and eggs; beat at medium speed with an electric mixer for 2 minutes, occasionally scraping down the sides of the bowl.

Fold in boiling water with a spoon or rubber spatula. Pour into prepared pan(s).

Bake for 25 to 50 minutes or until toothpick inserted in the center comes out clean. (The more shallow the baking pan, the less time it will take to bake.)

Yield: 8 to 12 servings.

Decorate your cake platter with frosted fruit. Select strawberries, grapes, cranberries or other fruits individually or in clusters. Beat an egg white until slightly foamy. Use a pastry brush to lightly coat each berry or fruit with the egg white. Immediately roll the fruit in granulated sugar to coat. Place the sugar frosted fruit on waxed paper lined baking sheets and air dry at least 3 hours. Frosted fruit can also be used to decorate cheesecakes or pies.

KAHLÚA ICED CHOCOLATE CAKE

Parve

2 cups boiling water	1 teaspoon baking soda
2 teaspoons instant coffee	1 teaspoon salt
2½ cups sugar	2 teaspoons vanilla extract
1 cup vegetable oil	1-2 ounces semi-sweet
4 large eggs	chocolate, melted
3 cups all-purpose flour	10 whole coffee beans
1 cup cocoa	Kahlúa Frosting
1 tablespoon baking powder	

Preheat oven to 350°. Grease and flour two 9- x 3-inch round cake or springform pans; set aside.

Combine water and coffee, stirring until dissolved; cool and set aside.

Beat sugar, oil, and eggs in a large mixing bowl at medium speed with an electric mixer until well blended.

Combine flour, cocoa, baking powder, baking soda, and salt; stir until well blended.

Add flour mixture alternately with coffee, beginning and ending with coffee. Beat at low speed until blended after each addition. Stir in vanilla.

Pour into prepared pans and bake 20 to 25 minutes or until a toothpick inserted in the center comes out clean. Cool in pans on wire racks for 10 minutes; remove from pans and cool on wire racks.

Spread Kahlúa Frosting between layers and on top and sides of cake. Drizzle with melted chocolate and garnish the edges with coffee beans.

Yield: 12 servings.

KAHLÚA FROSTING:

1 teaspoon instant coffee	1 (16-ounce) package
1 teaspoon boiling water	powdered sugar plus
1 (8-ounce) container	more as needed
frozen parve whipping	2 teaspoons vanilla extract
cream, thawed	4-5 teaspoons Kahlúa
½ cup margarine, softened	

Combine coffee and water, stirring until dissolved.

Beat whipping cream, margarine, and powdered sugar until soft peaks form.

Beat in vanilla, coffee, and Kahlúa to taste. Add more powdered sugar if the frosting is too thin.

Yield: about 4 cups.

YELLOW CAKE

Parve

This is a versatile cake that can be decorated in many ways. We've included two icings, but this cake can handle almost any you choose. You may also add 1 cup of "M&M's"® Chocolate Mini Baking Bits to the batter to make a cake your kids will love.

3 cups all-purpose flour	1 cup vegetable oil
2 cups sugar	1 cup orange juice
1 tablespoon baking powder	1 teaspoon vanilla extract
½ teaspoon coarse salt	4 large eggs
	White or Chocolate Icing

Preheat oven to 325°. Grease a 13- x 9-inch baking pan; set aside.

Combine flour, sugar, baking powder, and salt in a large mixing bowl, stirring until well blended.

Add oil, orange juice, vanilla and eggs; beat at medium speed with an electric mixer until well blended, occasionally scraping down the sides of the bowl.

Pour into prepared pan and bake for 50 minutes or until a toothpick inserted into the center comes out clean; cool. (Cover and freeze, if desired.)

Frost top of cooled cake with White or Chocolate Icing.

Yield: 15 servings.

WHITE ICING:
Parve

½ cup vegetable shortening	2 tablespoons warm water
2 cups powdered sugar	½ teaspoon vanilla extract

Beat shortening at medium speed with an electric mixer until creamy; gradually add sugar, beating until light and fluffy. Add water; beat until spreading consistency. Stir in vanilla.

Yield: 1½ cups.

Decorate this cake with fresh flowers. It makes a great showpiece as long as you keep the flowers fresh. To achieve this, cut a 3-inch piece from a drinking straw. Bend one end up and secure with tape. Fill the straw halfway with water. Cut the flower stem so that it is only about 3-inches long. Stick the flower stem into the straw. Arrange the flowers by sticking them, in their straw "vases" into the cake and pushing them in so only the blossoms show. You can completely cover the top of the cake with flowers or make your own design. Remove before eating.

Chocolate Icing:
Parve

⅓ cup margarine
2 cups powdered sugar
½ cup cocoa

5 tablespoons boiling water
2 teaspoons vanilla extract

Beat margarine at medium speed with an electric mixer until creamy. Combine powdered sugar and cocoa, stirring to blend. Add gradually to margarine, beating until light and fluffy. Add water; beat until spreading consistency. Stir in vanilla.

Yield: 1½ cups.

When making this yellow cake recipe, try this variation:

Blueberry Streusel Cake

1 pint blueberries

1 cup all-purpose flour

½ cup firmly packed dark brown sugar

1 teaspoon ground cinnamon

½ cup margarine, cut into small pieces

Fold blueberries into cake batter.

Combine flour, brown sugar, and cinnamon in a small bowl. Cut in margarine with a pastry blender or fork until mixture is crumbly. Sprinkle on top of cake batter. Bake as directed.

Apricot Mini Strudels
Dairy

1 cup butter, softened
2 cups all-purpose flour
1 egg yolk
½ pint sour cream
1 cup apricot jam

Ground cinnamon
Sugar
1 cup chopped walnuts
1 egg white
½ cup butter, melted

Combine butter, flour, egg yolk, and sour cream and mix by hand until it forms a dough. Cover and refrigerate 1 to 2 hours or overnight.

Preheat oven to 350°.

Divide the dough into 8 sections and place on a work surface very lightly dusted with flour. Roll each section into a very thin rectangle or oblong shape.

Brush on a thin layer of apricot jam and sprinkle evenly with cinnamon, sugar, and chopped walnuts. Drizzle with butter.

Starting from the long side, roll up each piece of dough jelly roll fashion. Brush with egg white. Place mini strudels, seam side down, on a lightly greased baking sheet.

Bake 40 to 50 minutes or until golden brown.

Cut each roll into 1-inch pieces.

Yield: 4 to 5 dozen.

DEEP-DARK CHOCOLATE TRUFFLE TART
Dairy

This is an incredibly smooth chocolate fantasy. There are only two ingredients in the truffle filling–cream and chocolate–so make sure you are using fresh and first quality of both.

Dough:

6 tablespoons butter	¼ cup plus 2 tablespoons sifted cocoa
½ cup sugar	
¾ teaspoon vanilla extract	¾ cup all-purpose flour
⅛ teaspoon salt	

Filling:

10 ounces bittersweet or semi-sweet chocolate, cut into small pieces (not unsweetened or morsels)	1¼ cups heavy whipping cream
	2 tablespoons cocoa

Beat butter, sugar, vanilla, and salt at medium speed with an electric mixer until smooth. Stir in cocoa to form a dark paste. Add flour and beat on low speed just until blended. (Dough may be made in a food processor.)

Form dough into a flattened disk. Cover with plastic wrap and refrigerate at least 30 minutes. (Dough may be prepared up to three days in advance.)

Remove dough from refrigerator and let stand at room temperature for 20 minutes or until pliable enough to roll.

Roll the dough out between two pieces of plastic wrap. Press dough firmly in bottom and sides of a 9½-inch tart pan with removable bottom. Refrigerate pastry for 30 minutes.

Preheat oven to 375°.

Remove pastry from refrigerator and prick all over with a fork. Bake for 12 to 14 minutes. (Pastry may look a little undercooked in center.) Cool completely on a wire rack.

Place chocolate in a metal or glass bowl.

Heat cream in a saucepan over medium-high heat to just under the boiling point. Immediately pour cream over chocolate and let stand for 30 seconds. Stir slowly and gently until chocolate is melted and mixture is smooth.

Pour chocolate mixture through a wire mesh strainer into cooled pastry. Refrigerate for 4 hours or until set. The tart may be prepared up to two days ahead. Cover and refrigerate until serving.

Place a doily or stencil over chilled tart. Place cocoa in a wire mesh strainer and shake over tart. Carefully remove doily. Refrigerate in a covered container until ready to serve. Let stand at room temperature for 45 minutes to soften to a perfect consistency. Remove sides of pan before serving.

Yield: 14 servings.

CHOCOLATE TORTE

Dairy or Parve

10 ounces bittersweet or semi-sweet chocolate, chopped	5 large eggs
1 cup butter or margarine, cut into pieces	1¼ cups sugar
	5 tablespoons flour
	1½ teaspoons baking powder
	Powdered sugar

Preheat oven to 325°. Grease and flour a 10-inch springform pan.

Heat chocolate and butter in a double boiler until mixture is melted and smooth.

Beat eggs and sugar in medium mixing bowl until slightly thickened. Combine flour and baking powder and stir into egg mixture.

Fold chocolate mixture into flour mixture. Pour into prepared pan.

Bake for 20 minutes then cover with foil. Bake 30 minutes or until toothpick inserted in center comes out with moist crumbs. Cool on a wire rack; release sides.

Yield: 6 to 8 servings.

Place a stencil or doily over the chocolate torte. Pour powdered sugar into a sieve or wire mesh strainer and shake over the doily or stencil. When you remove it, the sugar will have formed a pretty design.

Another nice idea is to decorate a plain white dessert plate. Place a fork on one side of the plate. Pour cocoa into a sieve and shake over the fork. Carefully remove the fork from the plate. Place a slice of torte or cake in the center of the plate, next to the imprint of the fork.

FLOURLESS CHOCOLATE CAKE

Parve

"This is our family's favorite parve dessert. It is a smooth, dense slice of heaven. It is best served at room temperature and looks beautiful sliced and garnished with fresh mint leaves and fresh raspberries. Due to its low flour content, this recipe can be used for Passover. Simply substitute 4 teaspoons of Passover cake meal for the flour."

16 ounces semi-sweet chocolate (not morsels), cut into pieces	4 large eggs, separated
½ cup margarine	4 teaspoons sugar
	4 teaspoons all-purpose flour

Preheat oven to 425°. Lightly grease a 9- x 5- x 3-inch loaf pan. Cut a rectangle out of parchment or waxed paper and press into the bottom of the pan; set aside.

Heat chocolate in a double boiler until melted and smooth; stir in margarine and set aside.

Beat egg whites at high speed with an electric mixer until stiff peaks form; set aside. (Egg whites will whip better at room temperature.)

Beat egg yolks at high speed until thick and pale yellow. Gradually add sugar, beating constantly. Add flour to the yolk mixture and beat until just blended. Stir in chocolate mixture.

Fold chocolate mixture into egg whites with a wire whisk. Spoon into prepared pan.

Place in oven and reduce heat immediately to 350°. Bake for 25 minutes. Cool completely on a wire rack. Refrigerate at least 4 hours or overnight. Serve at room temperature.

Yield: 10 servings.

Mango and Raspberry Sauces

Serve this cake on a plate decorated with raspberry and mango sauces. Cut the flesh from 2 mangoes; place in a blender and process until smooth. You can also place the mangoes in a cup and process with an immersion blender. Add a few tablespoons of sugar, as needed. Follow the same directions with a pint of raspberries, but pass the raspberries through a strainer to remove the seeds.

Place the sauces in squeeze bottles and zigzag across the plate. If you don't have squeeze bottles, place each sauce in a heavy-duty zip-top bag and snip the corner. Use the plastic bag like a pastry bag. Place a thin slice of cake on top of sauces and scatter a raspberry or blackberry on top and place a mint sprig next to it.

BETTER-THAN-DRAKES COFFEE CAKE

Dairy or Parve

A delicious, crumb-topped coffee cake that's a real crowd pleaser.

2	large eggs	4	teaspoons baking powder
1	cup milk or non-dairy creamer	1	teaspoon salt
3	cups all-purpose flour	1	cup butter or margarine, melted
1½	cups sugar		Cinnamon-Crumb Topping

Preheat oven to 350°. Grease a 13- x 9-inch baking dish; set aside.

Beat eggs and milk in a small bowl; set aside.

Combine flour, sugar, baking powder, and salt; stir in margarine. Stir in egg mixture, beating until just combined.

Pour batter into prepared pan; sprinkle with topping. Bake for 45 to 50 minutes or until a toothpick inserted in the center comes out clean. Cool in pan on a wire rack for 10 minutes. Remove from pan, and cool on a wire rack. This cake freezes well.

Yield: 12 servings.

CINNAMON-CRUMB TOPPING:

Dairy or Parve

2½	cups all-purpose flour	1	cup butter or margarine, melted
2	cups sugar		
¼	cup ground cinnamon	1	tablespoon vanilla extract

Combine flour, sugar, and cinnamon in a large bowl, stirring until well blended. Add margarine and vanilla, stirring until mixture is crumbly.

Yield: 5½ cups.

MOIST APPLE OR PEACH COFFEE CAKE

Parve

2-3 apples, peeled and thinly
    sliced or 3-4 peaches,
    unpeeled and sliced
    Ground cinnamon
    Sugar
1 cup vegetable oil
4 large eggs

2 cups sugar
3 cups all-purpose flour
1 tablespoon baking
    powder
1 teaspoon salt
¼ cup orange juice
1 tablespoon vanilla extract

Preheat oven to 350°. Grease a 10-inch tube pan; set aside.

Place apples or peaches in a small bowl and stir in a generous amount of cinnamon and sugar; set aside.

Beat oil and eggs at medium speed with an electric mixer; gradually add sugar, beating well. Combine flour, baking powder, and salt; add to egg mixture, stirring until well blended. Stir in orange juice and vanilla.

Pour half of batter into the prepared pan. Layer apples over batter, making sure apples do not touch the sides of the pan or they will stick. Pour remaining batter over apples.

Bake for 1¼ hours. Let cool in pan for 20 minutes. Remove from pan and cool on wire rack.

Yield: 8 servings.

In the active stock market of the '90's, there was no greater excitement than having advance knowledge of an impending IPO. But that excitement did not even come close to the frenzy that was created in the kosher community when news leaked out that OREO® cookies and M&M® candies might soon become kosher. The kosher community frantically searched for the source of this insider information as they would for a great stock market tip. Was it a reliable rumor? For years people who kept kosher would enviously watch their non-kosher counterparts savor the delicious treats.

Expectations ran high and the excitement built to a fever pitch. Then, like stock that bursts onto the scene and skyrockets, the cookies and candies suddenly appeared on the supermarket shelves bearing a kosher symbol. Our joy knew no bounds, and we all cashed in very quickly and continue to do so as OREO® cookies and M&M® candies continue to give us all many happy returns. (See pages 229 and 247 for some delicious recipes using these products.)

OREO® RIPPLE COFFEE CAKE

Dairy

24 OREO® cookies, coarsely chopped
⅓ cup all-purpose flour
¼ cup butter or margarine, melted

⅓ cup miniature semi-sweet chocolate morsels
1 (16-ounce) package pound cake mix
¾ cup water
2 large eggs

Glaze:
1 cup powdered sugar

4 teaspoons milk

Preheat oven to 350°. Grease a 9- or 10-inch tube pan; set aside.

Combine chopped cookies, flour, and butter in a medium bowl. Stir in chocolate morsels and set aside.

Prepare cake mix according to package directions using water and eggs. Pour half of the batter into the prepared pan. Sprinkle 2 cups of the cookie mixture evenly over the batter. Top with remaining batter and cookie mixture, pressing the cookie mixture gently into the batter.

Bake for 45 to 50 minutes or until a toothpick inserted near the center comes out clean. Cool in the pan on a wire rack for 10 minutes. Remove from pan; invert cake. Cool completely.

Combine powdered sugar and milk; drizzle over cake.

Yield: 12 servings.

SOUR CREAM COFFEE CAKE

Dairy

Cake:

1¼ cups sour cream	1½ teaspoons vanilla extract
1½ teaspoons baking soda	3 cups all-purpose flour
1 cup margarine	2 teaspoons baking powder
1½ cups sugar	1½ teaspoons salt
3 large eggs	

Topping:

1 cup sugar	2½ teaspoons ground
¾ cup chopped walnuts	cinnamon
	Powdered sugar

Combine sour cream and baking soda in a small bowl. Let stand at room temperature for 1 hour. (The mixture will bubble.)

Preheat oven to 350°. Grease a 9- or 10-inch springform pan; set aside.

Beat margarine at medium speed with an electric mixer until fluffy; gradually add 1½ cups sugar, beating well. Add eggs, 1 at a time, beating until blended after each addition. Stir in vanilla. Add sour cream mixture, beating well.

Combine flour, baking powder, and salt. Stir into sour cream mixture.

Prepare the topping: combine 1 cup sugar, walnuts, and cinnamon in a small bowl.

Pour one-third of cake batter into prepared pan and top with one-third of topping mixture. Repeat twice with remaining ingredients, ending with topping. Bake for 1 hour. Let cool in pan for 20 minutes. Release from pan and cool completely on a wire rack. Dust with powdered sugar.

Yield: 10 to 12 servings.

Use a three-tiered cake stand to display two different desserts. For the top level, soak a round piece of floral foam and place it on the cake stand. Cut down the stems of light colored carnations to about 2-3 inches. Push them into the foam forming a soft mound. Cut out sprigs of baby's breath and push these in among the carnations. Fill any gaps with pieces of moss. This formal crown will add a simple elegance to your dessert table.

WHITE CHOCOLATE MOUSSE

Dairy

It is important to use real white chocolate– look for cocoa butter in the ingredient list. Avoid using white chocolate morsels or white candy coating.

½ cup sugar	9 ounces white chocolate, finely grated
¼ cup water	2 cups heavy whipping cream
4 large egg whites	

Combine sugar and water in a saucepan over medium heat. Bring mixture to a boil, stirring frequently. Set a candy thermometer in place and cook without stirring for 10 minutes until the temperature reaches 248° or firm-ball stage.

Place grated chocolate in a small bowl; rest this bowl inside a bowl of boiling water. Do not allow water to touch chocolate. Stir until melted; set aside.

Beat egg whites at high speed with an electric mixer until stiff peaks form. With mixer running at medium speed, pour hot syrup in a thin stream into beaten egg whites, beating until just blended.

Gradually add melted chocolate, stirring until mixture is smooth.

Beat whipping cream until stiff peaks form. Fold whipped cream into white chocolate mixture. Cover and refrigerate at least 2 hours to set the mousse.

Yield: about 7 cups.

Serve scoops of this mousse on Crispy Chocolate Chip cookies (page 242) and drizzle with Fresh Berry Sauce.

FRESH BERRY SAUCE
Parve

2 cups fresh raspberries, blueberries, or blackberries

¾ cup sugar

1 tablespoon cornstarch

⅛ teaspoon salt

Place berries in a blender; process until smooth. Pour mixture through a wire mesh strainer; remove and discard seeds. Heat the berry purée in a small saucepan over medium-high heat. Bring mixture to a boil.

Combine sugar, cornstarch, and salt; stir into berry mixture. Cook, stirring constantly, until thickened and bubbly.

Yield: about 1¼ cups.

CRÈME BRÛLÉE

Dairy

*C*ool, silky cream, a hint of vanilla, and a whisper of wafer thin caramelized sugar, this dessert is an elegant dream. The custard can be prepared hours in advance, but wait until just before serving to caramelize the sugar.

1 cup milk	6 large egg yolks
¼ cup plus 1 tablespoon sugar	2 cups heavy cream
1 vanilla bean, split in half lengthwise	½ cup raw sugar or firmly packed light brown sugar

Combine milk, sugar, and vanilla bean in a saucepan over medium heat. Heat to just below the boiling point, stirring until sugar dissolves. Remove from heat and let mixture stand for 15 minutes to infuse milk with vanilla flavor. Remove vanilla bean.

Preheat oven to 300°. Place 4 (1-cup) ramekins or shallow baking dishes in a large roasting pan; set aside.

Whisk egg yolks until light and fluffy; stir in cream. Gradually stir about one-fourth of hot milk mixture into yolk mixture; add remaining milk mixture to egg mixture. Strain through a wire mesh strainer to remove any cooked egg pieces.

Pour into prepared ramekins. Pour enough hot water into the roasting pan to come halfway up the sides of the ramekins. (See sidebar on water baths on page 233.)

Bake for 30 to 35 minutes until mixture is just set in the middle. (Custard will not be completely firm in the center.) Remove ramekins from pan. Cover and refrigerate at least 3 hours or up to 2 days.

Remove custards from refrigerator 20 minutes before serving. Sprinkle with raw sugar in a thin, even layer.

Preheat oven to broil with rack 3 inches from heat. Place ramekins on a baking sheet and broil 30 seconds to 2 minutes or until sugar caramelizes. Do not burn.

You may also light a hand held blow torch and hold it just touching the surface of the sugar. Start at the center and fan across sugar until caramelized. Serve immediately.

Yield: 4 servings.

 The best way to coat the top of crème brûlée is to force the brown sugar through a fine sieve by rubbing your fingers over it. This will give a nice even coat.

TRIPLE LAYER CHEESECAKE

Dairy

Crust:

1 cup OREO® cookie crumbs

2 tablespoons sugar
2 tablespoons butter, melted

Filling:

4 (8-ounce) packages cream cheese, softened
1¾ cups sugar
1 teaspoon vanilla extract
Pinch salt
4 large eggs

1 teaspoon instant espresso powder
1 tablespoon hot water
3 ounces unsweetened chocolate, coarsely chopped

Water Baths

The heat of an oven can be very uneven. Baking cheesecakes in a water bath allows them to cook evenly and slowly, resulting in a more uniform texture. Water baths prevent the outside from cooking before the inside and the rising steam creates a moist environment that eliminates brown edges.

The best way to make a water bath is to bring a kettle of water to a boil while preheating your oven. Wrap the springform pan tightly in foil to prevent leaks. Set a roasting pan on the oven rack. Set the uncooked cheesecake in the empty pan. Pour the boiling water into the pan until it comes halfway up the sides of the springform pan. Since the pan is already in oven, you reduce the risk of getting scalded by splashing water.

Preheat oven to 350°. Butter bottom and sides of a 9-inch springform pan. Cover outside tightly with 2 to 3 layers of heavy-duty foil; set aside.

Combine cookie crumbs and sugar in a small bowl. Stir in butter until mixture is evenly moistened.

Press crumbs on bottom of prepared pan. Bake for 10 minutes; cool on a wire rack. Turn oven off.

Beat cream cheese in a large mixing bowl at medium-high speed with an electric mixer until light and fluffy. Gradually add sugar, beating well. Reduce speed to medium and beat in vanilla and salt. Add eggs, 1 at a time, beating until blended after each addition.

Dissolve espresso powder in hot water in a large bowl. Spoon 2 cups of cream cheese mixture into espresso, blending with a rubber spatula. Spoon into crust and freeze 1 hour until firm.

After first layer is firm, melt chocolate in top of a double boiler. Add 1¾ cups cream cheese mixture, stirring until well blended. Spoon over espresso layer and freeze 20 minutes.

Preheat oven to 350°.

Spread remaining filling over chocolate layer. Place cheesecake in a larger baking pan on oven rack. Pour enough hot water into larger pan to come 1-inch up the side of the springform pan. Bake 1½ hours or until center is just set.

Remove cheesecake from water bath. Cool completely on a wire rack. Remove foil from pan. Cover and refrigerate overnight. Remove side of pan just before serving. Drizzle with melted chocolate and garnish with coffee beans.

Yield: 12 to 16 servings.

FUDGE SAUCE

Dairy

½ cup milk

5 ounces bittersweet or semi-sweet chocolate, chopped (not unsweetened)

¼ cup heavy whipping cream

1 tablespoon unsalted butter

3 tablespoons sugar

Pour milk into a heavy saucepan over medium-high heat; bring to a boil. When milk boils, remove it from the heat and add chopped chocolate, whisking to blend. Set aside.

Combine the cream, butter, and sugar in a heavy 1-quart saucepan over medium-high heat. Bring to a boil, stirring occasionally. The butter should be completely melted and sugar dissolved.

Pour the cream mixture into the chocolate mixture. Bring to a boil, whisking constantly. Mixture will thicken slightly as it cooks. Remove from heat just as sauce begins to boil. Serve warm.

Yield: 1½ cups.

WHITE CHOCOLATE SNICKERS® CHEESECAKE

Dairy

Crust:

⅔ cup graham cracker crumbs

⅔ cup sugar

1 teaspoon ground cinnamon

3 tablespoons unsalted butter, softened

6 large Snickers® candy bars, chilled and finely chopped

Filling:

4 (8-ounce) packages cream cheese, softened

⅔ cup sugar

3 large eggs

1 teaspoon vanilla extract

6 ounces white chocolate (not morsels or coating)

¾ cup heavy whipping cream

Fudge Sauce (see sidebar)

Preheat oven to 350°. Cover the outside of a 10-inch springform pan tightly with 2 to 3 layers of heavy-duty foil to make sure no water touches the crust while baking; set aside.

Combine crumbs, sugar, cinnamon, and butter in a small bowl; mix well. Press crumb mixture into the bottom of the prepared pan. Place half of the chopped candy bars in a large mound in the center of the crust.

Beat cream cheese for 5 minutes or until fluffy, stopping to scrape down sides of bowl; gradually add sugar, beating well. Add eggs, 1 at a time, beating until blended after each addition. Stir in vanilla.

Heat chocolate in the top of a double boiler. Add cream, stirring until well blended. Slowly add melted chocolate to cream cheese mixture, stirring until well blended.

Pour filling into crust. Place cheesecake in a larger baking pan on oven rack. Pour hot water into the larger pan to a depth of 1 inch. Bake 1½ hours or until center is just set.

Remove cheesecake from water bath. Cool completely on a wire rack (about 2 hours). Remove foil from pan. Remove side of pan just before serving. Top with Fudge Sauce and sprinkle evenly with remaining chopped candy bars.

Yield: 12 to 16 servings.

CHILEAN TRIFLE DESSERT

Dairy

*T*alk about advanced planning! This recipe needs to be made 3 to 4 weeks in advance or up to a year! Due to the vodka, it never really freezes, but uses the time to soak up all of the flavors. It has an intriguing list of ingredients, but we promise it is an absolutely-to-die-for-recipe.

5 (14-ounce) cans sweetened condensed milk, unopened	¼ cup vodka
40 ounces pitted prunes	2½ cups crushed walnuts
Hot water	22 ounces tea biscuits, crushed

Place the unopened condensed milk cans into a large pot of water over medium-high heat. Bring to a boil; boil for 3 hours. You will need to replace the water as it evaporates. The milk will caramelize in the cans. Let the cans cool in cold water until you can touch them with your hands, or the cans may explode.

Soak prunes in hot water to cover for at least 1 hour; set aside.

Open cooled cans of milk and combine with walnuts and vodka. Split prunes in half, using your hands.

Layer one-fourth of crushed biscuits in the bottom of a round, glass container with high sides. Top with one-fourth of prunes, skin side up and flesh facing the crushed biscuits. Pour one-fourth of milk mixture on top. Repeat layers with remaining ingredients. Cover tightly and freeze for 3 to 4 weeks. Keep frozen until serving.

Yield: 20 servings.

Banana Split Brownie Pizza

Dairy

1 (19.02-ounce) package
   brownie mix*
   Parchment paper
2 (8-ounce) packages
   cream cheese, softened
⅔ cup sugar
1 banana, sliced
   Sliced strawberries
   Sliced kiwi

1 (8-ounce) can crushed
   pineapple, drained
   (optional)
½ cup chopped nuts
1 ounces semi-sweet
   chocolate morsels,
   melted
1 tablespoon butter or
   margarine, melted

Preheat oven to 375°. Place a large sheet of parchment paper on a 15-inch pizza stone. (You must use parchment or the batter will run off the stone.)

Mix brownie batter according to package directions. Spoon batter on parchment and spread into a 14-inch circle. Bake for 15 to 20 minutes; cool.

Beat cream cheese at medium speed with an electric mixer until fluffy, scraping down sides of bowl. Add sugar, beating well. Spread cream cheese mixture over crust.

Arrange banana, strawberry, kiwi, and pineapple in concentric circles. Sprinkle with nuts.

Combine chocolate and butter, stirring until well blended. Drizzle over fruit.

Refrigerate pizza; slice into wedges.

Yield: 12 servings.

Note: you can experiment with homemade brownie recipes, but the mix gives the right consistency needed to support the "pizza" while many homemade brownies do not.

LINZER TARTS

Parve

These cookies come out very professional, even for "non-bakers." The raspberry jelly peeks out from the hole in the top cookie like a sparkling jewel. If you want to try for a romantic cookie, use a mini heart shaped cookie cutter instead of a thimble to cut out the center.

1 cup margarine	1 teaspoon vanilla
½ cup sugar	Seedless raspberry preserves
1 large egg	Powdered sugar
2 cups all-purpose flour	

Preheat oven to 350°.

Beat margarine at medium speed with an electric mixer until creamy; gradually add sugar, beating well. Add egg and vanilla, beating until blended. Add flour, beating at low speed until blended.

Roll dough into small balls and place on greased cooked sheets, 2 inches apart. Flatten dough balls with a flat-bottomed cup wrapped in a damp paper towel.

Dip a thimble or small round cutter in flour and cut out a small circle in the center of exactly half of the cookies.

Bake for 8 to 10 minutes or until set. (The cookies will be pale. The cut out halves will bake faster so watch closely.) Transfer carefully to wire racks to cool.

Spread raspberry preserves on top of solid cookies. Top with remaining cookies, bottom sides down, to make sandwiches. Sift powdered sugar over tops of cookies.

Yield: 2 dozen.

Make a floral centerpiece the center of your dessert buffet. Take a beautiful antique china or floral teapot and fill with flowers that accent the teapot's design. Place it on a low cake stand and surround it with a variety of flavored tea bags and scattered flower petals.

BLACK AND WHITE BUTTER COOKIES

Dairy

As you can see in the photo, the stark black and white designs make these cookies stand out on any cookie platter. The cookies are delicious and buttery and make a show-stopping presentation for both your eyes and palate.

½ cup plus 2 tablespoons
    unsalted butter, softened
½ cup sugar
1 egg yolk
1 teaspoon vanilla extract

¼ teaspoon salt
2 cups all-purpose flour
    White Chocolate Glaze
    Dark Chocolate Glaze

Beat butter at high speed with an electric mixer until light and fluffy; gradually add sugar, beating well. Add egg yolk, vanilla, and salt, beating at low speed after each addition. Gradually beat in flour until well blended.

Divide the dough in half and form each piece into a flattened disk. Cover in plastic wrap and refrigerate until firm. You can prepare dough a few days in advance.

Preheat oven to 350°.

Place each dough disk between two sheets of waxed paper. Roll each one out to ⅛-inch thickness. Refrigerate until firm.

Cut dough into 2-inch circles with a cookie cutter, re-rolling and chilling scraps as necessary. Place cookies on a baking sheet. Using a sharp knife, lightly score about one-fourth of the cookies with a vertical line.

Bake 9 to 10 minutes on an ungreased cookie sheet until light golden brown. Let cool on baking sheet for 2 minutes; transfer to wire rack to finish cooling. Separate the scored cookies from the unscored cookies and place sheets of waxed paper under the wire racks to catch any glaze drips.

Spread White Chocolate Glaze with a small spatula over half of each scored cookie using the center line as a guide. Hold the cookie over the bowl of glaze to catch drips. Use a clean spatula to coat the other half with the Dark Chocolate Glaze. Repeat with remaining scored cookies. Let dry at room temperature for a few hours.

Pour each glaze into separate zip-top bags. Snip a corner off the bags. Drizzle White and Dark Chocolate Glazes over the remaining cookies in dot, spiral, lattice, and zigzag patterns. Let dry at room temperature for a few hours.

Yield: about 3½ dozen.

If the dough is too crumbly to roll out or work with, knead in a few drops of milk.

You can sandwich two cookies together for an elegant jelly cookie. In a small saucepan combine:

1 cup seedless preserves

2 teaspoons cornstarch

Bring to a boil then cook over medium heat for 3 minutes. Cool to room temperature. Spoon a rounded teaspoonful on one cookie and top with another. Decorate as per recipe.

WHITE CHOCOLATE GLAZE:
Dairy

3   ounces white chocolate,
    chopped (not coating or
    morsels)

1½   teaspoons pure vegetable
     shortening

Place white chocolate and shortening in a small glass bowl. Microwave at 30% for 1 minute. Stir. Microwave at 30% at 10-second intervals, stirring in between if needed to melt chocolate.

Yield: ¼ cup.

DARK CHOCOLATE GLAZE:
Parve

3   ounces semi-sweet
    chocolate, chopped
1   tablespoon pure vegetable
    shortening

Place chocolate and shortening in a small glass bowl. Microwave at 70% for 1 minute. Stir. Microwave at 70% at 20 second intervals, stirring in between if needed to melt chocolate.

Yield: ¼ cup.

DEEP CHOCOLATE
WHITE CHUNK COOKIES

Dairy

"These are, in a word, incredible. An ultimate indulgence. The deep-dark chocolate is a backdrop for the smooth, creamy white chocolate chunks. Use only good quality white chocolate. If shavings come off the bar as you are cutting chunks, add them into the batter as well. I like to keep the dough prepared in my freezer, wrapped in parchment and aluminum foil. Then, at the end of a hard day, or a good day, or a tiring day, or a momentous day–actually, any day in mind calls for these sweet rewards, I pop a few in the oven and eat them warm and melty."

1¼ cups butter, softened	1¾ cups all-purpose flour
1¼ cups sugar	1¼ cups cocoa
¾ cup firmly packed light brown sugar	2 teaspoons baking soda
2 large eggs	10 ounces white chocolate, cut into ¼-inch chunks

Preheat oven to 350°.

Beat butter at medium speed with an electric mixer until light and fluffy; gradually add sugars, beating well. Add eggs, 1 at a time, beating until blended after each addition.

Combine flour, cocoa, and baking soda; add to butter mixture, beating at low speed until well blended.

Fold in white chocolate chunks with a spatula.

Drop dough in tablespoon-sized balls on buttered cookie sheets 2 inches apart. (A mini ice cream scoop helps get uniformly sized cookies, but is not necessary.)

Bake for 8 to 10 minutes. The cookies will be puffed, but will set when cooled. Cool slightly for 5 to 10 minutes on baking sheet; remove to wire racks to cool completely.

Yield: 5 dozen.

The quality of the white chocolate will greatly affect the quality of your baking. Good quality white chocolate contains cocoa butter as its only source of fat. Look for it in the ingredient list. If cocoa butter is not listed, the product is confectionery coating, which tends to be very white.

White chocolate can't take high heat. When melting, do so in a microwave on Low or 30% power for 1 minute per ounce.

CHOCOLATE DIPPED BUTTER COOKIES

Dairy or Parve

Hard to believe that a butter cookie could be delicious parve? Bake a batch of these in its parve version for your next meat meal and you won't be disappointed. Needless to say, they are fabulous when made dairy.

1	cup butter or margarine	¼	teaspoon salt
⅔	cup sugar	6	ounces semi-sweet chocolate morsels
1	egg yolk		
1	teaspoon vanilla extract	3	tablespoons butter or margarine
2⅓	cups all-purpose flour		
1	cup finely chopped unblanched almonds	1	tablespoon hot water Chopped almonds

Beat butter at medium speed with an electric mixer until light and fluffy; gradually add sugar, beating well. Add egg yolk and vanilla, beating until blended.

Combine flour, almonds, and salt; add to butter mixture, beating at low speed until well blended.

Shape dough into 2 rolls, 1½-inches in diameter. Cover in plastic wrap or foil and refrigerate for 2 hours.

Preheat oven to 350°.

Cut dough with a sharp knife into ¼-inch slices and place 1-inch apart on greased cookie sheets. Bake 10 minutes or until light brown; transfer to wire racks to cool.

Heat chocolate morsels and butter or margarine in a small saucepan over low heat, stirring until melted. Stir in hot water.

Dip half of each cookie into chocolate mixture. Sprinkle with chopped almonds.

Yield: 6 dozen.

CRISPY CHOCOLATE CHIP COOKIES

Dairy

1 cup butter, softened
1 cup sugar
1 cup firmly packed light
   brown sugar
2 large eggs
1 teaspoon baking soda

1 teaspoon vanilla extract
¼ teaspoon salt
2 cups all-purpose flour
1 (12-ounce) bag semi-
   sweet chocolate morsels

Preheat oven to 350°.

Combine butter, sugar, and brown sugar in the container of a food processor fitted with a plastic dough blade. Process until light and fluffy. Add eggs, baking soda, vanilla, and salt; process until smooth. Add flour and pulse just until blended.

Transfer dough to a bowl and stir in chocolate chips.

Drop dough by heaping teaspoonsful 1½ inches apart on greased baking sheets. (Re-grease baking sheets before baking a new batch.)

Bake 10 to 12 minutes or until just beginning to brown at edges. Cool on sheets 1 minute; carefully transfer with a spatula to a serving platter to cool.

Yield: 6 dozen.

CHEWY CHOCOLATE CHIP COOKIES

Dairy

   Vegetable cooking spray
½ cup unsalted butter
6 tablespoons sugar
6 tablespoons dark brown
   sugar
½ teaspoon vanilla extract

1 large egg
1 cup plus 2 tablespoons
   all-purpose flour
½ teaspoon baking soda
1 cup semi-sweet chocolate
   morsels

Preheat oven to 350°. Lightly spray 2 baking sheets with vegetable cooking spray.

Beat butter at medium speed with an electric mixer until creamy; gradually add sugar, brown sugar, and vanilla. Beat in egg.

Combine flour and baking soda; add to butter mixture, beating at low speed until blended. Stir in morsels.

Form the cookies into small balls and place 2 inches apart on prepared pans.

Bake 2 sheets of cookies at a time. After 5 minutes, take the sheets out and bang them on the counter. Return baking sheets to oven with original top sheet on the bottom and original bottom sheet on the top rack. Continue baking for 5 minutes.

Transfer immediately to a wire rack to cool.

Yield: 2 dozen.

OATMEAL–RAISIN COOKIES

Parve

1 cup raisins
¾ cup margarine
1 cup granulated brown
  sugar
½ cup sugar
1 large egg
2 tablespoons water
1 teaspoon vanilla extract

⅔ cup all-purpose flour
1 teaspoon ground
  cinnamon
½ teaspoon salt
½ teaspoon baking soda
3 cups quick-cooking oats
6 ounces semi-sweet
  chocolate morsels

Preheat oven to 375°.

Soak raisins in water to cover in a small bowl. Let stand 10 minutes; drain.

Beat margarine at medium speed with an electric mixer until fluffy; gradually add sugars, beating well. Add egg, water, and vanilla, beating until well blended.

Combine flour, cinnamon, salt, and baking soda; add to margarine mixture, beating at low speed until blended. Combine raisins, oats, and morsels; fold into batter.

Drop cookies by rounded teaspoonsful on greased baking sheets.

Bake for 10 minutes or until edges are light golden brown. Transfer to wire racks to cool.

Yield: 6 dozen.

GINGER CRINKLES

Dairy

" I thought these were my son's favorite cookie. Last summer, he kept writing home asking me to bake batches and send them up to camp. Every few days, a new postcard was waiting for me requesting another batch. My poor homesick child was comforted by the taste of his mom's homemade cookies. A tear came to my eye as I baked the batch I would be bringing up on visiting day. When we arrived at camp, I got the best hug from my son, I know he must have appreciated the hours I spent in the kitchen baking all those Ginger Crinkles. As the wonderful day drew to a close and it was time for parents to leave, one of my son's bunk mates came over to me and said, 'Lady, you gotta drop the price of those cookies, I spent half of my trip and canteen money on them!' My son was selling my cookies!"

1 cup butter	1¾ teaspoons ground cinnamon
1¾ cups sugar	1¾ teaspoons ground ginger
1 large egg	1¼ teaspoons baking soda
⅓ cup mild molasses	½ teaspoon salt
2¾ cups all-purpose flour	Sugar

Preheat oven to 350°.

Beat butter at medium speed with an electric mixer until fluffy; gradually add sugar, beating well. Add egg and molasses, beating until blended after each addition.

Combine flour, cinnamon, ginger, baking soda, and salt in a small bowl; gradually add to butter mixture, beating at low speed until blended.

Form the dough into walnut-sized balls; roll in sugar and place on ungreased baking sheets.

Bake for 12 minutes. The cookies will be puffed, very light golden brown, and cracked on top. Remove from oven and let cool on pans for 2 minutes. Transfer to a wire rack to completely cool. (Cookies will flatten slightly.)

Yield: 3 dozen.

COCOA PECAN CRESCENTS

Parve

1 cup margarine	⅓ cup Dutch cocoa
⅔ cup sugar	⅛ teaspoon salt
1½ teaspoons vanilla extract	1½ cups ground pecans
1¾ cups all-purpose flour	Powdered sugar

Beat margarine at medium speed with an electric mixer until light and fluffy; gradually add sugar, beating well. Stir in vanilla.

Combine flour, cocoa, and salt; add to margarine mixture, beating at low speed until blended.

Stir in pecans.

Roll into a log and wrap in parchment; refrigerate at least 1 hour.

Preheat oven to 375°.

Roll a scant tablespoon of dough into a 2½-inch long log; shape into a crescent and place on greased cookie sheets.

Bake for 13 to 15 minutes; cool slightly on baking sheets. Transfer to a wire rack to cool completely. Roll cooled cookies in powdered sugar.

Yield: 5 dozen.

SNICKER DOODLES

Dairy or Parve

½ cup butter or margarine	½ teaspoon baking soda
¾ cup sugar	¼ teaspoon salt
1 large egg	1 tablespoon sugar
1¼ cups all-purpose flour	1 tablespoon ground
1 teaspoon cream of tartar	cinnamon

Beat butter at medium speed with an electric mixer until fluffy; gradually add sugar, beating well. Beat in egg.

Combine flour, cream of tartar, baking soda, and salt in a small bowl; gradually add to butter mixture, beating on low speed until blended.

Cover and refrigerate for 1 hour.

Preheat oven to 375°.

Combine sugar and cinnamon in a small bowl. Form the dough into walnut-sized balls; roll in cinnamon mixture and place on ungreased baking sheets.

Bake for 10 to 12 minutes or until cookies are flat and edges are brown. Transfer to a wire rack to cool completely.

Yield: 30 cookies.

LACE COOKIES

Parve

"These are a pretty toffee-like cookie. If you are baking for a crowd, you may want to avoid sandwiching the chocolate between two cookies. You can get more servings out of the batch by leaving the cookies single and drizzling the chocolate on top."

½ cup margarine
½ cup light corn syrup
⅔ cup firmly packed brown sugar
1 cup all-purpose flour

1 cup walnuts, chopped
1 (12-ounce) package semi-sweet chocolate morsels

Preheat oven to 325°.

Combine margarine, syrup, and sugar in a heavy saucepan over medium-low heat. Bring mixture to a boil; remove from heat.

Combine flour and nuts; stir into syrup mixture.

Drop dough by ½ teaspoonful 3 inches apart on greased baking sheets. (The cookies spread a lot.)

Bake 8 to 10 minutes. Cool 1 minute on pan, then transfer with a thin metal spatula to a wire rack to cool. The cookies will be soft and hard to handle, but will harden when cool.

Melt chocolate in top of a double boiler. Spread a thin layer of chocolate onto the smooth side of one cookie. Cover with the smooth side of another cookie to make sandwiches. Repeat with remaining cookies and chocolate. These cookies freeze well.

Yield: 2 dozen.

Quick Melted Chocolate

To melt chocolate chips quickly without using a double boiler, put them in a heavy duty zip top bag, seal, and drop the bag in very hot water (135° to 140°) for a few minutes. When the chocolate feels soft, dry the outside of the bag carefully, cut a very small hole in one corner of the bag and squeeze out the chocolate to write a greeting on a cake or drizzle over cookies.

CHOCOLATE–RASPBERRY THUMBPRINTS

Dairy or Parve

"M&M's"® Chocolate Mini Baking Bits make these fun-to-make cookies, fun to eat!

½ cup butter or margarine, melted	2 cups all-purpose flour
½ cup sugar	½ teaspoon baking powder
½ cup firmly packed light brown sugar	1¼ cups "M&M's"® Chocolate Mini Baking Bits, divided
1 large egg	Powdered sugar
1 teaspoon vanilla extract	½ cup raspberry jam

Combine butter, sugar, and brown sugar in a large bowl, mixing well. Stir in egg and vanilla.

Combine flour and baking powder; stir into butter mixture. Stir in 1¼ cups "M&M's"® Chocolate Mini Baking Bits. Cover and refrigerate dough for 1 hour.

Preheat oven to 350°.

Roll the dough into 1-inch balls and place about 2 inches apart on greased baking sheets. Make an indentation with your thumb in the center of each ball.

Bake 8 to 10 minutes; remove from oven and press thumb in center of cookie again, if necessary. Transfer to wire racks. Lightly dust warm cookies with powdered sugar. Fill each indentation with raspberry jam and sprinkle with remaining ½ cup "M&M's"® Chocolate Mini Baking Bits. Cool completely and dust with additional powdered sugar, if desired. Store in a tightly covered container.

Yield: 4 dozen.

MINI COCONUT CAKES

Parve

This is a very impressive dessert. It is not difficult, but requires a lot of patience and planning as you wait for each step to cool before proceeding with the recipe.

Cake:

4	large eggs	1½	cups all-purpose flour
1¼	cups sugar	2	teaspoons baking powder
1	packet vanilla sugar		

Topping:

10	egg whites	1	packet vanilla sugar
1½	cups sugar	3	cups flaked coconut

Garnish:

4	ounces semi-sweet chocolate, chopped	½	cup apricot jelly
		24	whole almonds

Preheat oven to 350°.

Combine eggs, sugar, vanilla sugar, flour, and baking powder in a large bowl, mixing well. Press evenly into a lightly greased baking pan.

Bake for 30 minutes. Remove from oven and place pan on wire rack to cool. Decrease heat to 300°. After cake has cooled 15 minutes, begin to prepare the topping.

Beat egg whites at high speed with an electric mixer until foamy. Add sugar and vanilla sugar, 1 tablespoon at a time, beating until stiff peaks form and sugar dissolves. (When you slash the egg whites with a knife, the slash mark will stay in place.)

Gently fold in coconut with a rubber spatula.

Spread the egg white mixture on top of the slightly cooled cake.

Bake for 30 minutes. Remove from oven and place on a wire rack to cool completely. (Cake must be completely cool before proceeding.)

Cut circles from the cake with a 1½-inch round cookie cutter or small juice glass.

Place chocolate in a small heavy-duty, zip-top bag; seal. Submerge in hot water until chocolate melts. Snip a tiny hole in 1 corner of the bag, and drizzle chocolate over the tops of the mini cakes in zigzag fashion.

Heat jelly in a small saucepan; remove from heat. Roll the almonds in the jelly and place one on top of each cake at an angle, slightly off center.

Yield: 2 dozen.

MANDEL STICKS

Parve

Vegetable cooking spray
½ cup vegetable oil
1 cup sugar
2 large eggs
1 teaspoon vanilla extract
2 cups all-purpose flour
1 teaspoon baking powder
¼ teaspoon salt
½-¾ cup chopped pecans or almonds
2 teaspoons sugar
½ teaspoon ground cinnamon

Preheat oven to 350°. Coat 2 baking sheets with vegetable cooking spray; set aside.

Combine oil and 1 cup sugar in a large bowl, stirring to blend. Stir in eggs and vanilla.

Combine flour, baking powder, and salt; gradually add to egg mixture. Stir until well blended. Stir in nuts.

Divide dough into 4 pieces and form into 4 loaves. Place two loaves on each prepared baking sheet.

Combine 2 teaspoons sugar and cinnamon; sprinkle evenly on loaves.

Bake for 30 to 40 minutes; turn off oven. Remove from oven and cool for 10 minutes; slice. For harder mandel, return to turned off oven after slicing. Mandel Sticks freeze well.

Yield: 3 to 5 dozen.

MANDELBROT

Parve

The combination of nuts and oats along with their two-step baking process gives these cookies a nice texture and crunch. They freeze very well.

Vegetable cooking spray
4 large eggs
1¼ cups vegetable oil
1½ cups sugar
1 teaspoon vanilla extract
1 teaspoon almond extract
½ teaspoon imitation liquid butter

3½ cups all-purpose flour
1 teaspoon baking powder
1 teaspoon ground cinnamon
2 cups sliced almonds
1 heaping cup old-fashioned oats

Preheat oven to 350°. Coat 2 baking sheets with cooking spray; set aside.

Combine eggs, oil, and sugar in a large bowl, mixing well with a spoon. Stir in vanilla, almond extract, and imitation butter.

Combine flour, baking powder, and cinnamon; stir into egg mixture.

Stir in almonds and oats.

Form dough into 2 loaves about 4 inches wide and 1 inch high; place on prepared baking sheets.

Bake for 35 minutes. Slice and place each piece on its side on baking sheets.

Bake for 20 to 30 minutes until golden brown.

Yield: 5 dozen.

CHOCOLATE CHIP STICKS

Parve

Vegetable cooking spray
½ cup vegetable or canola
  oil
½ cup sugar
½ cup firmly packed light
  brown sugar

1 large egg, lightly beaten
1 teaspoon vanilla
1½ cups all-purpose flour
½ teaspoon baking soda
½ teaspoon salt
½ cup chocolate morsels

Preheat oven to 350°. Coat 2 baking sheets with cooking spray.

Combine oil, sugar, and brown sugar in a large bowl, mixing well. Stir in egg and vanilla.

Combine flour, baking soda, and salt tossing with a fork. Stir into egg mixture, blending well. Fold in chocolate morsels.

Form dough into two 3- to 4-inch wide logs. Place on the prepared baking sheets.

Bake for 20 to 30 minutes, checking after 20 minutes, or until edges are golden brown.

Cool 10 minutes; cut slightly warm into sticks.

Yield: 2 dozen.

CHINESE ALMOND COOKIES

Dairy or Parve

2¾ cups sifted all-purpose
  flour
1 cup sugar
½ teaspoon baking soda
1 cup butter or margarine,
  cut into pieces

1 large egg, lightly beaten
1 teaspoon almond extract
⅓ cup whole unblanched
  almonds

Preheat oven to 325°.

Combine flour, sugar, and baking soda in a bowl, mixing well. Cut in butter or margarine with a pastry blender or fork until mixture resembles corn meal. Add egg and almond extract; mix well.

Shape dough into 1-inch balls and place 2 inches apart on an ungreased baking sheet. Place an almond on top and press to flatten slightly.

Bake for 15 to 18 minutes; transfer to wire racks to cool.

Yield: 2½ dozen.

LEMON SQUARES

Parve or Dairy

Crust:

1 cup unbleached all-purpose flour	½ cup margarine or butter, softened
¼ cup powdered sugar	

Filling:

2 large eggs	2 tablespoons all-purpose flour
¾ cup sugar	½ teaspoon baking powder
3 tablespoons grated lemon rind	Powdered sugar
¼ cup fresh lemon juice (not bottled)	

Preheat oven to 350°.

Combine flour and sugar in a bowl. Cut in margarine with a pastry blender or blend with fingers until mixture is crumbly. Crust may also be prepared in a food processor fitted with a plastic dough blade.

Press crust evenly into an 8-inch square baking pan. Bake for 20 minutes or until golden; cool.

Beat eggs at medium speed with an electric mixer until frothy. Gradually add sugar and beat until mixture becomes light-colored and foamy. Beat in rind and juice.

Combine flour and baking powder; stir into egg mixture, blending well.

Spread filling over crust. Bake for 25 minutes until filling is set; cool. Cut into 2-inch squares. Sprinkle with powdered sugar.

Yield: 16 small squares.

When a recipe calls for lemon peel, rind, or zest, use only the thin, yellow layer of skin, not the spongy white part that is bitter. Grate fresh lemons using a sharp zester or fine grater. Grate just before needed because the peel dries out very quickly.

Amaretto Cheesecake Squares

Dairy

1 cup all-purpose flour
⅓ cup firmly packed dark brown sugar
6 tablespoons butter, softened
1 (8-ounce) package cream cheese, softened
¼ cup sugar
1 large egg
¼ cup amaretto
½ teaspoon vanilla extract
¼ cup chopped almonds

Serve individual squares surrounded by fresh berries.

Preheat oven to 350°.

Combine flour and brown sugar in a bowl; cut in margarine with a pastry blender or fork. Knead until mixture forms uniform crumbs.

Set aside a scant 1 cup of crumb mixture. Press remaining crumb mixture into the bottom of an ungreased 8-inch square baking pan.

Bake for 12 to 15 minutes or until light brown.

Beat cream cheese and sugar at medium speed with an electric mixer until fluffy. Add egg, amaretto, and vanilla, beating well. Spread batter into partially baked crust.

Combine almonds with reserved crumb mixture; sprinkle over batter.

Bake 20 to 25 minutes. Cool; cut into 2-inch squares.

Yield: 16 squares.

Watermelon Sherbert

Parve

2 ¼ pounds fresh watermelon, seeded and in small pieces
1 cup sugar
Juice of 1 lemon
½ cup cold water
2 egg whites
Mint leaves, to decorate

This pretty pink sherbert makes a light and refreshing dessert after a long meal or can be served before the main dish to cleanse the palate at a grand dinner. Serve in scoops decorated with mint leaves.

Puree ¾ of the watermelon in a food processor or blender. Mash ¼ of the watermelon on a plate–this will give the sherbert more texture. Stir the sugar with the lemon juice and cold water in a saucepan over very low heat, until the sugar dissolves and the syrup is clear. Mix all the watermelon and syrup in a large bowl and transfer the mixture to a freezer container. Freeze for 1 to 1½ hours, until the edges begin to set. Beat the mixture, return container to freezer and freeze for another hour. When the hour is up, beat the egg whites to form a soft peak. Beat the iced mixture again and then fold in the egg whites. Return to freezer for another hour, then beat once more and freeze until firm. Transfer the sherbert from the freezer to the refrigerator for 20 to 30 minutes before serving.

Peanut Butter and Chocolate Bonbons

Parve

*T*hese candies can be prepared in advance and then placed in decorative baskets, tins, or platters.

½ cup unsalted margarine, melted
1½ cups creamy peanut butter
1 (16-ounce) box powdered sugar

1 teaspoon vanilla extract
1 (12-ounce) package semi-sweet chocolate morsels
3 tablespoons vegetable shortening

Combine margarine, peanut butter, sugar, and vanilla in a large bowl; mix until smooth.

Shape mixture into 1-inch balls and place on a foil-lined baking sheet. Freeze for 1 hour.

Melt chocolate and shortening in top of a double boiler, stirring constantly until well blended.

Place a toothpick in the center of each ball and dip halfway into chocolate mixture. Return to baking sheet, chocolate side down, and freeze until ready to serve. To serve, place each ball in a candy-size paper cup and place on a serving platter. Can be stored in the freezer up to 1 month.

Yield: 7 to 8 dozen.

Chocolate Dipped Pretzels

Parve

1 (12.5-ounce) box pretzel rods
1 (12-ounce) package semi-sweet chocolate morsels, melted

Shredded coconut
Chopped peanuts or almonds
Multi-color or chocolate sprinkles

Dip each pretzel in melted chocolate and roll in coconut, nuts, or sprinkles. Place on waxed paper-lined tray and refrigerate until ready to serve.

Yield: 3 dozen.

BAKED APPLES WITH PECANS

Parve

9   Rome or Granny Smith
    apples
½   cup applesauce
½   cup dark raisins
⅓   cup chopped pecans
½   cup sugar, divided

1   tablespoon fresh lemon
    juice
½   teaspoon ground
    cinnamon, divided
4   teaspoons unsalted
    margarine

Preheat oven to 375°.

Partially peel 8 apples, leaving the bottom half of fruit intact. Remove core with a melon baller. Cut a thin slice from bottom of apples, if necessary, to stand upright. Place apples in a baking dish; set aside.

Peel remaining apple and cut into ½-inch dice. Combine diced apple, applesauce, raisins, pecans, ⅓ cup sugar, lemon juice, and ¼ teaspoon cinnamon in a medium bowl. Toss gently to combine.

Combine remaining sugar and cinnamon in a small bowl.

Fill apples with stuffing mixture. Place ½ teaspoon margarine on top of each apple. Sprinkle with 1 teaspoon cinnamon mixture.

Add water to baking dish to a depth of ½ inch.

Bake for 1 hour or until tender, basting occasionally with pan juices. Add water if necessary. Serve warm or at room temperature.

Yield: 8 servings.

SIMPLE AND ELEGANT POACHED PEARS

Parve

1   cup cold water
1   cup white wine
¾   cup sugar
8-10 cinnamon sticks

6-8 firm Anjou or Bartlett
     pears, peeled, with stem
     attached

Combine water, wine, sugar, and cinnamon in a large pot over medium-high heat. Bring to a boil, reduce heat, and simmer until sugar is dissolved and syrupy.

Place the pears stem side up in the pot and reduce heat. Cover and simmer 20 to 30 minutes or until pears are tender.

Refrigerate pears in the syrup until chilled and ready to serve.

To serve, stand each pear on a plate cutting a thin slice from the bottom, if necessary, to keep upright. Serve in a pool of syrup and garnish with 1 cinnamon stick per pear.

Yield: 6 to 8 servings.

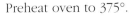

The Poached Pears can be served with a delicious chocolate sauce.

COCOA SAUCE
Parve

¼ cup cocoa

½ cup sugar

Pinch salt

⅓ cup hot water

1 teaspoon vanilla extract

1 tablespoon pear liqueur (optional)

Combine the cocoa, sugar, and salt in a small saucepan. Gradually stir in water until smooth. Bring to a boil over medium heat. Reduce heat and simmer, stirring occasionally, for 3 minutes.

Remove from heat and stir in vanilla and liqueur. Serve warm or chilled. Place a puddle of sauce in the center of the plate and place pear on top of sauce.

Yield: 1 cup.

CHOCOLATE PALETTE OF SORBETS

Parve

A s you can see from the cover photo, this eye-catching dessert is colorful and stunning.

16 ounces semi-sweet chocolate, tempered (see sidebar)
1 (16- x 24-inch) piece of (.003 weight) acetate or parchment paper
4 seedless grapes, halved
5 different flavors of creamy sorbet (do not use fat-free)
Raspberry Sauce (see sidebar page 226)
Mango Sauce (see sidebar page 226)

Spread a ⅛-inch layer of tempered chocolate onto acetate or parchment. (Acetate works best because it makes the chocolate shine.) Let chocolate set 4 to 5 minutes. The chocolate should be firm enough to cut, but not hard.

Photocopy the palette template (page 257) onto cardstock or heavy paper; cut out.

Trace the palette template onto the chocolate with the tip of a sharp paring knife, making sure to cut all the way through the chocolate. Cut out a finger hole with a 1-inch round cutter. Cut 5 holes for the sorbet "paints" with the end of a ½-inch plain decorating tip as shown on the template. Repeat to make a total of 8 chocolate palettes.

Cover chocolate with a large piece of parchment and carefully flip over. Peel off the acetate or parchment. Remove the cut palettes and set aside until ready to assemble.

Prop each palette up with a grape half on individual serving plates. Scoop balls of sorbet with a ½-inch ice cream scoop and place them in the "paint" holes of the palette.

Drizzle plates with Raspberry and Mango Sauces.

Yield: 8 servings.

PALETTE TEMPLATE:

MERINGUE KISSES

Parve

3 large egg whites	¾ cup sugar
⅛ teaspoon cream of tartar	½ teaspoon vanilla extract

Preheat oven to 275°. Line a baking sheet with foil; set aside.

Beat egg whites and cream of tartar at high speed with an electric mixer until soft peaks form. Add sugar, 2 tablespoons at a time, beating 2 to 4 minutes until stiff peaks form and sugar dissolves. Beat in vanilla.

Spoon meringue into a large decorating bag fitted with a large star tip. Pipe the cookies into small spiral mounds about 1½ inches in diameter on the prepared baking sheet.

Bake 20 to 30 minutes until the color is just beginning to turn (do not let meringues darken). Immediately turn the oven off, leaving the meringues in the oven overnight to completely dry.

Remove from oven and store in an airtight container.

Yield: 4 dozen.

Instead of piping spirals, pipe small mounds using a writing or plain tip. Shape the meringue into a nest with the back of a spoon. Bake as directed.

When ready to serve, fill meringue nests with ice cream or whipped cream and top with a variety of different colored berries.

Pour chocolate sauce into a plastic squeeze bottle and make chocolate swirls and zigzags across each plate. Lay a piece of dessert in the center and add a dollop of whipped cream or parve vanilla ice cream.

CHOCOLATE SAUCE
Parve

1 cup semi-sweet chocolate, chopped
½ cup light corn syrup
¼ cup non-dairy creamer
1 tablespoon margarine
1 teaspoon vanilla extract

Combine chocolate and corn syrup in a 1-quart saucepan over low heat, stirring until chocolate melts.
Remove from heat; add cream, margarine, and vanilla, stirring until mixture is smooth.

Yield: 1¾ cups.

If the Chocolate Sauce is not used right away it may become too thick to squeeze out of the bottle. If this happens, set the bottle in a cup of hot water. After a few minutes, the sauce will warm and become easier to use.

PECAN PIE BARS
Parve

Crust:

  2 *cups all-purpose flour*
  ½ *cup firmly packed light brown sugar*

  ½ *teaspoon salt*
  ¾ *cup margarine, cut into ½-inch pieces*

Topping:

  ½ *cup margarine*
  1 *cup firmly packed light brown sugar*
  ⅓ *cup honey*

  2 *tablespoons non-dairy creamer*
  2 *cups chopped pecans*

Preheat oven to 350°.

Combine flour, ½ cup brown sugar, and salt in the container of a food processor fitted with a knife blade; pulse to blend. Add ¾ cup margarine and pulse until mixture is crumbly.

Press crust into bottom of a 13- x 9-inch baking pan, using a metal spatula to press evenly across the bottom.

Bake for 20 minutes or until light golden brown.

Heat ½ cup margarine in a heavy saucepan over medium heat, stirring until melted. Add 1 cup brown sugar, honey, and cream, stirring until blended.

Bring mixture just to a boil, reduce heat, and simmer, stirring occasionally, for 1 minute. Stir in pecans. Pour pecan mixture over hot crust and spread evenly.

Bake for 20 minutes until bubbling. Place on wire rack and cool completely in pan. Cut into 24 bars. Keep covered at room temperature.

Yield: 2 dozen.

TRADITIONAL

*Ultimate Handmade
Gefilte Fish,
page 282*

SHABBAT

Shabbat is a very special time in the Jewish home. Beginning at sundown on Friday evening, and concluding when the stars come out on Saturday night, this is the day we rest, in commemoration of God's resting on the seventh day of creation. However, the "rest" of Shabbat has much to do with religious activities like prayer (and abstention from prohibited activities) and little to do with sleep. We rest from our ordinary activities, and remember this day as God had commanded us to. Meals are an important aspect of Shabbat observance. The concept of *Oneg Shabbat* instructs us to enjoy the Shabbat in various ways, including eating especially delicious foods.

The Friday dinner and Saturday lunch are the most significant Shabbat meals. Families eat together and often invite guests. The table is beautifully set and everything about the meal reflects the sanctity and beauty of Shabbat. After we light the Shabbat candles, we begin the meal by making Kiddush (the blessing over the Shabbat wine) and Hamotzi (the blessing over the challah).

SAVORY CROCK-POT CHOLENT

Meat

You may vary the proportions of the barley and beans to your family's taste, but keep the total amount at 1 cup.

4-5	beef bones		Salt
¾	cup barley		Pepper
¼	cup cholent bean mix or mixture of kidney and white beans	1	(1.3-ounce) packet onion soup mix
1	large onion, sliced	6-8	medium potatoes, peeled and cubed
2	tablespoons paprika	1-1½	pounds cubed beef
	Garlic powder	1	kishka roll

Place bones, barley, cholent, onion, paprika, garlic powder, salt, pepper, soup mix, potatoes, beef, and kishka in a large crock-pot in the order listed.

Add water to cover ingredients.

Cover and cook on HIGH for 1 hour, then turn heat setting to LOW and cook overnight or until ready to serve. Remove bones before serving.

Yield: 6 to 8 servings.

GOLDEN CHICKEN SOUP WITH LIGHT AND FLUFFY MATZOH BALLS

Meat

2½ quarts water
1 (3- to 4-pound) whole chicken
1 large onion
3 stalks celery, sliced
3 large carrots, peeled and sliced into disks
2 parsnips, peeled and sliced into disks
1 large or 2 small sweet potatoes, peeled and cut into large pieces
2 teaspoons salt
1½ teaspoons coarsely ground pepper
Light And Fluffy Matzoh Balls batter

Bring water to boil in a large soup pot. Remove liver and giblets from chicken; save for other uses or discard. (If the whole chicken will not fit in the pot, cut into smaller pieces.)

Add chicken, onion, celery, carrots, parsnips, sweet potatoes, salt, and pepper; bring to a boil. Reduce heat and gently simmer, covered, for 3 to 4 hours.

Remove onion and discard. Transfer chicken to a platter; cool slightly. Remove meat from bones; set aside.

Bring soup to a rolling boil. Wet hands slightly with water and form heaping tablespoons of the matzoh mixture into balls. Drop into boiling soup. Cover tightly and reduce heat to a low boil. Boil 30 to 40 minutes. Or alternatively, drop matzoh balls into a pot of salted boiling water or chicken stock. When they fluff, remove them and place into soup. (This keeps the matzoh balls from "drinking" up all the soup.)

Return chicken to soup. Cook over medium-high heat until thoroughly heated.

Serve hot and include chicken, carrots, parsnips, and sweet potato in each serving.

Yield: 6 to 8 servings.

LIGHT AND FLUFFY MATZOH BALLS
Parve

1 cup matzoh meal

4 large eggs, lightly beaten

¼ cup canola or light vegetable oil

¼ cup water

2 teaspoons salt

Combine matzoh, eggs, oil, water, and salt in a medium bowl and mix with a fork until well blended.

Cover and refrigerate or freeze for 30 minutes.

Yield: 2½ cups (enough for 12 to 14 matzoh balls)

Use a food processor for quick and easy preparation.

SMOOTH POTATO KUGEL

Parve

6 potatoes, peeled and cut
   into pieces
1 onion, quartered
1 dry or frozen stale
   challah roll

3 large eggs
½ cup oil
1 tablespoon salt
1 teaspoon baking powder
   Pepper

Preheat oven to 375°.

Combine potatoes, onion, roll, and eggs in the container of a food processor fitted with knife blade. Process until smooth. (Process in batches, if necessary.)

Combine potato mixture, oil, salt, baking powder, and pepper in a large bowl.

Pour into a greased 13- x 9-inch baking dish. (Use an 8- x 8-inch pan for a thicker kugel.)

Bake, uncovered, for 1 hour or until golden brown.

Yield: 12 servings.

LACY POTATO KUGEL

Parve

6 large potatoes, peeled
2 onions (1 medium,
   1 large)
4 large eggs, lightly beaten
5 tablespoons oil

2 teaspoons salt
   Pepper
¼ cup potato starch
1 cup boiling water
¼ cup oil

Preheat oven to 500°.

Grate potatoes and onions and place together in a large bowl.

Stir in eggs, 5 tablespoons oil, salt, and pepper. Sprinkle starch on top.

Pour boiling water over starch, and stir thoroughly.

Pour ¼ cup oil into 13- x 9-inch baking pan and place in oven for 1 minute or until hot. (Do not burn.)

Carefully pour potato mixture into pan.

Bake 20 minutes, reduce heat to 400° and bake 40 minutes or until deep golden brown.

Yield: 12 servings.

*For Your
Shabbat Table,
May We Suggest . . .*

Crystal Clear
Chicken Soup

Whole Roasted Chicken

Silver Tip Roast Beef

Grilled Chicken Salad
with Raspberries

Black and White
Rice Mold

Carrot Kugel

Pecan Noodle Ring

Tricolor Vegetable
Soufflé

Chocolate Torte

Poached Pears

Mini Coconut Cakes

HEAVENLY BREAD MACHINE CHALLAH

Parve

*P*lace ingredients in the order recommended by the manufacturer (usually dry ingredients on the bottom).

2¾ cups plus 1 tablespoon bread flour	1 cup water
¼ cup plus 2 heaping tablespoons sugar	2¼ teaspoons yeast
	Vegetable cooking spray
¾ teaspoon salt	1 large egg, lightly beaten
3½ tablespoons vegetable oil	Poppy seeds
3 egg yolks	Sesame seeds

Place flour, sugar, salt, oil, yolks, water and yeast in the bread machine according to manufacturer's directions. (Place yeast in separate yeast holder, if equipped.) Process ingredients in dough cycle. Remove immediately.

Preheat oven to 350°.

Divide dough into 3 equal pieces and roll each portion into a thick rope. Place the three pieces side by side on a baking sheet coated with cooking spray and pinch the top ends together. Braid dough and pinch ends together.

Cover challah with a towel; let stand 30 minutes.

Brush with beaten egg and sprinkle with poppy and sesame seeds.

Bake 30 minutes or until brown and challah sounds hollow when tapped on the bottom. Cool on wire rack.

Yield: 1 challah.

DELICIOUS CHALLAH

Parve

Make this challah once. You will never go back to the bakery again. We got this recipe from a woman who doesn't even live in New Jersey, but her challah's reputation is so incredible, it travels across state boundaries.

4 cups warm water (105° to 115°)	2 cups sugar
2 (2-ounce) bars fresh yeast (not packets of dry yeast)	1½ tablespoons salt
	3 large eggs
1 tablespoon sugar	1½ cups canola or corn oil
1 (5-pound) bag of high gluten flour	Canola or corn oil
	1 large egg, lightly beaten

Preheat oven to 300°. Open oven door.

Combine water and yeast in a medium metal or glass bowl. Stir in 1 tablespoon sugar. Place the mixture on the open oven door (the small amount of heat helps proof the yeast) and let stand for 10 minutes. The mixture will be bubbly. If your yeast mixture isn't bubbly, then something is wrong with it and you must start recipe over again. Turn oven off.

Place flour in a large aluminum bowl; remove 2 cups of flour and set aside for other uses. Stir in 2 cups sugar and salt, mixing well. Push the flour against the sides of the bowl, leaving a well in the center.

Pour the yeast mixture, 3 eggs, and 1½ cups oil into the well; mix with a wooden spoon until you can no longer stir it.

Knead the dough with your hands until it no longer sticks to the sides of the bowl. The dough should be smooth and springy. If the dough is still very sticky, knead in small amount of flour until it is smooth.

Brush the top of the dough with oil. Cover with plastic wrap and a dry towel. Let rise for 1½ hours in a warm room. (If your kitchen or room is cold, preheat your oven to 200°. Turn it off, allowing just enough heat to remove the chill. Place the dough in the oven to rise.)

Turn the dough out onto a lightly floured surface and punch down.* Divide the dough into 5 to 7 sections. Divide each section into 3 equal pieces. Roll each portion into a thick rope. Place the 3 pieces side-by-side on a lightly greased baking sheet and pinch the top ends together. Braid the dough and pinch the bottom ends together. Repeat with remaining dough. Unrisen challot may be placed in a foil pan, wrapped in plastic and foil, and frozen. Remove from the freezer, thaw, and proceed with recipe directions.

Brush challot with beaten egg. Let rise, uncovered, for 45 minutes to an hour.

Preheat oven to 350°.

Bake challot 25 to 35 minutes until golden brown and challah sounds hollow when tapped on the bottom. (After 15 to 20 minutes, reverse

(continued)

the direction of the baking sheet.) Cool on wire racks.

Yield: 5 to 7 challot.

*Note: This is the point at which challah is taken and the blessing is recited.

Shabbat/Mitzvah

A special mitzvah called *hafrashat challah* (separating challah) is one of three mitzvot entrusted specifically to Jewish women. Hafrashat Challah is the separating of a portion of dough which, in the time of the *Beit Hamikdash* (Holy Temple) was given to the *Cohanim* (Priestly Tribe.) Although since the destruction of the Beit Hamikdash we may not bring the separated dough to the Cohanim, the mitzvah of Hafrashat Challah remains as a treasured observance for the Jewish woman.

The ability to fulfill the mitzvah of Hafrashat Challah is dependent on the types of flour and liquid in the recipe, and on the specific amounts of flour and liquid it contains. Flour used should be wheat, rye, barley, oat or spelt, and the liquid (including eggs and oil) should be mostly water. In order to be able to separate challah with the blessing, more than 3 pounds 11 ounces (approximately 12 or more cups unsifted*) flour should be used. If less than 3 pounds 11 ounces but more than 2 pounds 11 ounces (between approximately 9 and 10¼ cups) flour are used, then challah is separated but no blessing is said. Recipes using less than 2 pounds 11 ounces (approximately 7½ cups or less) of flour do not require Hafrashat Challah.

If the mitzvah's very specific requirements are met, then a woman may proceed with the fulfillment of the mitzvah. Before the prepared dough is shaped into individual loaves, a portion (approximately an ounce) is removed from the dough and the following is said:

Harai zeh challah – This is challah. This statement is followed by the blessing:

Baruch atah ado-nai elo-heinu melech ha-olam asher kid'shanu b'mitzvotav v'tzivanu l'hafrish challah.

Blessed are You, Lord our God, King of the Universe, Who has sanctified us with His Commandments and commanded us to separate challah.

Then the separated portion is usually burned.

The recipe for Delicious Challah meets the requirements for the mitzvah of Hafrashat Challah, but only if followed in full. Halving the recipe will cause the mitzvah to be inapplicable.

*The measurements given in cups are approximate in that they leave "buffer" zones to take into account possible measuring inaccuracies.

Rosh Hashanah

Rosh Hashanah, the Jewish New Year, is one of the most significant and joyful of holidays. As Jewish families everywhere look forward to a sweet year full of blessings, we dip challah and apple slices into honey. We eat round challah and sweet dishes such as tzimmes and honey cake, all symbolic of our hopes for a sweet, full (round) and happy new year. In addition to the roundness and sweetness of the coin-shaped carrots in tzimmes, wordplay on the Yiddish word *merren,* which means both "to increase" and "carrots," provides another source for the idea of eating tzimmes on Rosh Hashanah.

The Ten Days following Rosh Hashanah are called the Aseret Y'Mei Teshuvah, The Ten Days of Atonement. These conclude with Yom Kippur, which is a fast day. On Erev Yom Kippur (the day preceding the fast day) two meals are served. One is to be eaten in the early afternoon, and the second, the *Seudah Hamafseket,* is the last meal before the fast. The *Seudah Hamafseket* is usually a lighter meal, and excessively salty or spicy foods should be avoided.

Following the fasting of Yom Kippur, it is traditional for families to gather together to break the fast. Although there are no rules regarding the dishes at this meal, it is common to find bagels, smoked fishes, eggs, and cheeses on the table.

Golden Tzimmes

Parve

6 cups peeled and sliced carrots	⅔ cup firmly packed dark brown sugar or honey
3 cups peeled and sliced canned yams	⅔ cup orange juice
10-14 large pitted prunes	½ cup sherry
1 cup crushed pineapple or chunks with juice	½ teaspoon salt

Preheat oven to 300°.

Cook carrots in boiling water to cover until just tender; drain.

Combine carrots, yams, prunes, and pineapple with juice, brown sugar, orange juice, sherry, and salt and place in a greased 2-quart baking dish.

Bake, covered, for 3½ to 4 hours. This recipe reheats (covered) well.

Yield: 12 to 14 servings.

APPLE SOUFFLÉ

Parve

10-12 firm, crisp apples such as
    Gala, Macintosh, or
    Golden Delicious, peeled
    and sliced
1⅓ cups sugar, divided
1 cup all-purpose flour

1 teaspoon baking powder
½ cup oil
2 teaspoons vanilla extract
4 large eggs, lightly beaten
    Vegetable cooking spray
    Cinnamon-sugar

Preheat oven to 350°.

Combine apples and ⅓ cup sugar in large bowl, tossing to coat; set aside.

Combine remaining 1 cup sugar, flour, baking powder, oil, vanilla, and eggs in a large bowl, mixing into a smooth batter.

Place half of the apple mixture in the bottom of a 13- x 9-inch baking pan coated with cooking spray.

Combine remaining apples with batter; pour over apples in the pan. Sprinkle generously with cinnamon-sugar.

Cover pan with a tent of foil (so foil does not touch top of apple mixture) and bake for 1 hour. Uncover, and bake 10 minutes. Apple Soufflé is best when served warm, but it may also be served at room temperature.

Yield: 10 to 12 servings.

FRUIT AND HONEY GLAZED CHICKEN

Meat

1 (3½- to 4-pound) chicken
2 carrots, peeled and sliced
    into disks
1 onion, sliced
½ cup golden raisins

½ cup pitted prunes
⅓ cup dried apricots
¼ cup dark raisins
⅓ cup oil
1 cup honey

Preheat oven to 400°.

Place chicken in the center of a roasting pan.

Combine carrots, onion, golden raisins, prunes, apricots, dark raisins, and oil in a large bowl. Spoon mixture evenly around chicken.

Pour honey over chicken and vegetable/fruit mixture, lightly coating entire chicken.

Bake for 30 minutes, baste, and reduce heat to 350°. Bake for 1 hour, basting occasionally, or until chicken, vegetables, and fruit are tender and golden brown.

Yield: 4 servings.

APPLE NUT CAKE

Parve

1½ cups oil	½ teaspoon freshly grated nutmeg
1½ cups sugar	
½ cup firmly packed light brown sugar	½ teaspoon salt
	3½ cups peeled and chopped apples, such as Granny Smith or Newton
3 large eggs	
3 cups all-purpose flour	
2 teaspoons ground cinnamon	1 cup coarsely chopped walnuts
1 teaspoon baking soda	2 teaspoons vanilla extract Brown Sugar Glaze

Preheat oven to 325°. Grease and flour a 10-inch tube pan; set aside.

Combine oil, sugar, and brown sugar in a large mixing bowl, beating at medium speed with an electric mixer until well blended.

Add eggs, one at a time, beating well after each addition.

Combine flour, cinnamon, baking soda, nutmeg, and salt. Add flour mixture to egg mixture and blend into a smooth batter. Fold in apples, walnuts, and vanilla.

Spoon batter into prepared pan. Bake for 1 hour and 45 minutes or until toothpick inserted in center comes out clean. Let cool in pan for 20 minutes; turn out on wire rack. Pour glaze over warm cake or dust the top of cooled cake with powdered sugar.

Yield: 14 servings.

BROWN SUGAR GLAZE:
Parve or Dairy

3 tablespoons margarine or butter	3 tablespoons parve or dairy heavy whipping cream
3 tablespoons light brown sugar	
	¼ teaspoon vanilla extract
3 tablespoons sugar	

Combine butter, brown sugar, sugar, cream, and vanilla in a heavy saucepan over medium high heat. Bring to a boil; boil 1 minute.

Yield: ¾ cup.

For Your Rosh Hashanah Table, May We Suggest . . .

Apple Walnut Salad with Cranberry Vinaigrette

Queen Chicken Victoria

Sweet and Sour Brisket

Brisket with Dried Fruits

Oatmeal Berry Bake

Sweet Potato Pie

Baked Apples with Pecans

Lace Cookies

Moist Apple or Peach Coffee Cake

Kahlúa Iced Chocolate Cake

HONEY CAKE

Parve

1 tablespoon instant coffee	3 cups all-purpose flour
1 cup hot water	2 teaspoons baking powder
3 large eggs, lightly beaten	2 teaspoons baking soda
1⅓ cup honey	1 teaspoon ground
½ cup oil	cinnamon
1 cup sugar	½ teaspoon ground nutmeg
2 teaspoons vanilla extract	

Preheat oven to 350°. Grease and flour two 8- x 4-inch loaf pans; set aside.

Combine coffee and water, stirring until dissolved; set aside.

Combine eggs, honey, and oil in a large mixing bowl. Beat at medium speed with an electric mixer until well blended. Stir in dissolved coffee, sugar, and vanilla.

Combine flour, baking powder, baking soda, cinnamon, and nutmeg in a small bowl. Gradually add to egg mixture, beating at low speed until blended.

Pour into prepared pans, filling each halfway.

Bake for 45 minutes or until toothpick inserted in the center comes out clean. Turn off oven; leave cakes in oven for 10 minutes to gradually cool (this will prevent cakes from falling). Remove from pans and place on wire racks to completely cool.

Yield: 12 to 15 servings.

Long taper candles can add height and drama to a beautiful holiday or special occasion floral centerpiece.

Sukkot/Shmini Atzeret/Simchat Torah

Sukkot is a wonderful and festive holiday which involves the whole family, and has special appeal to children. During the seven days of Sukkot, we eat our meals in a sukkah, a temporary dwelling with openings in the roof covering (made of vegetation like leafy branches or bamboo) so that we may see the stars in the sky. Eating in the Sukkah reminds us of our reliance on God, and of the protective clouds of glory with which God surrounded the Jewish people when they resided in temporary dwellings in the desert.

A second theme of Sukkot is the bountiful harvest. This is the time of gathering in the harvest of the vineyards, orchards, and fields. The Sukkah is brightly decorated with hanging gourds, bunches of deeply colored dried ears of corn, and bunches of grapes and other fruits. Meals eaten in the Sukkah are lavish and festive. Traditional dishes for Sukkot include those based on autumn and winter produce, such as Glazed Acorn Squash. In addition, foods that are also warm and filling, like Mushroom and Wild Rice Soup and Kasha Varnishkas, are especially suitable for dinner in the sukkah on a chilly night.

Concluding Sukkot are two more days of Yom Tov, Shmini Atzeret and Simchat Torah. Many follow the custom of eating in the Sukkah on Shmini Atzeret as well. Simchat Torah is a joy-filled holiday on which we read the last weekly portion of the Torah and begin the year-long cycle again. On Simchat Torah we return to eating indoors, but the festival meals should be every bit as special as those eaten in the Sukkah. Stuffed Cabbage is an especially nice choice for Simchat Torah, since its rolled shape resembles the rolled scrolls of the Torah.

Stuffed Cabbage

Meat

This dish freezes beautifully.

2   large heads cabbage
3   tablespoons oil
1½-2 pounds lean ground beef
1   onion, finely chopped
¼   cup white rice, uncooked

2   large eggs, lightly beaten
    Salt
    Pepper
2   onions, sliced

Sauce:

4   (8-ounce) cans tomato
    sauce
¾   cup firmly packed light
    brown sugar

¼   cup raisins
⅓   cup fresh lemon juice

Boil cabbage in water to cover until tender. (You may steam in the microwave with a small amount of water, covered, on HIGH for 20 minutes.)

Coat bottom of large soup pot with oil. Remove outer leaves of cabbage and place in a single layer over oil.

Combine meat, chopped onion, rice, eggs, salt, and pepper in a bowl; set aside.

Core cabbage and remove leaves, one at a time; set aside.

Place 1 to 2 tablespoons of the meat mixture on lower half of each cabbage leaf; fold bottom and sides over meat and roll. Repeat with remaining leaves and meat.

Place rolls, seam side down, in pot and cover with sliced onions.

Combine tomato sauce, brown sugar, raisins, lemon juice, salt, and pepper; pour over cabbage rolls.

Bring mixture to a boil, reduce heat, and simmer, covered, for 1½ hours.

Preheat oven to 350°.

Transfer cabbage rolls carefully to a lightly greased baking dish in a single layer.

Bake 45 to 60 minutes or until lightly browned.

Yield: 6 to 8 servings.

*For Your Sukkot Table,
May We Suggest . . .*

Endive Salad with
Tangerines, Beets,
and Olives

Mushroom and Wild
Rice Soup

Apricot-Glazed
Stuffed Squab

Glazed Corn Beef

Brisket with Dried Fruit

Roasted Root
Vegetables

Sweet and Sour Stuffed
Peppers

Parve Stuffed
Mushrooms

Enclosed Apple Tart
with Caramel Sauce

Apple Crisp

FANCY KASHA VARNISHKES

Meat

1	(16-ounce) package bowtie pasta	1	cup whole kasha
2	cups chicken stock (page 39)	1	large egg, lightly beaten
	Oil	1	teaspoon salt
1	onion, chopped	¼	teaspoon pepper
1	cup mushrooms, chopped	2	tablespoons margarine (optional)

Prepare pasta according to package directions; drain and set aside.

Bring stock to a boil; keep hot.

Heat oil in a 2-quart saucepan over medium-high heat. Sauté onions and mushrooms about 5 minutes until onions are golden brown.

Stir in kasha and egg. Sauté for 2 minutes, stirring constantly until grains no longer stick together.

Pour hot stock over kasha; stir in salt and pepper. Cover tightly and simmer for 20 minutes or until kasha is puffy and dry. (Do not overcook.)

Combine kasha with reserved pasta. Serve immediately or spoon into a casserole dish and dot with margarine; cover tightly.

Yield: 8 servings.

GLAZED ACORN SQUASH RINGS TWO WAYS

Parve

	Vegetable cooking spray	Honey Soy Glaze or
2	(1½ pound) acorn squash	Maple Glaze
		Salt
		Pepper

Preheat oven to 450°.

Cover a baking sheet with foil and coat with vegetable cooking spray.

Cut off both ends of the squash; discard. Cut each squash into 4 rings; scoop out seeds and discard.

Place squash rings on the prepared baking sheet in a single layer. Cover tightly with foil.

Bake for 15 to 20 minutes or until squash begins to soften.

Prepare your choice of glazes; set aside.

Uncover squash and brush with half of glaze mixture; sprinkle with salt and pepper.

Bake, uncovered, for 10 minutes. Brush remaining glaze over squash.

Bake, uncovered for 10 minutes or until squash is brown, tender, and glazed.

Place squash rings on a platter and drizzle with any remaining glaze.

Yield: 8 servings.

HONEY-SOY GLAZE:
Parve

⅓ cup honey	1 tablespoon peeled and
2 tablespoons soy sauce	minced fresh ginger
4 teaspoons rice vinegar	2 cloves garlic, minced

Whisk together honey, soy sauce, vinegar, ginger, and garlic in a small bowl.

Yield: about ⅔ cup.

MAPLE GLAZE:
Parve

⅓ cup pure maple syrup	¼ teaspoon ground
2 tablespoons margarine,	cinnamon
melted	¼ cup pecans, toasted and
½ teaspoon salt	coarsely chopped

Whisk together syrup, margarine, salt, and cinnamon in a small bowl. Before serving sprinkle with pecans.

CHANUKAH

Chanukah is a holiday of miracles. Among them is the miraculous defeat of the Greek Army by a small group of Jews who called themselves the Maccabees. When the Maccabees entered the Beit Hamikdash (Holy Temple), which had been desecrated by the Greeks, they found only enough ritually pure oil to light the menorah for one day. It would take eight days before more oil could be produced. Miraculously, the oil lasted eight full days, until more was available. On Chanukah, in commemoration of the miracle of the oil, we eat foods that are fried in oil. These traditionally include Crisp and Golden Potato Latkes and Sufganiyot (Jelly Doughnuts).

Dairy foods are also appropriate for Chanukah meals, as they remind us of Yehudit, a heroic woman whose act of bravery helped the Maccabees to their victory. Yehudit fed salty cheese, accompanied by strong wine, to the evil Greek general, and then slew him with his own sword as he slept. Fried Brie Sticks, which are both dairy and fried in oil, are a good Chanukah dish.

FRIED BRIE STICKS

Dairy

1 large egg, lightly beaten	1 tablespoon all-purpose flour
2 tablespoons minced fresh parsley	1½ cups plain, dry bread crumbs or fresh, homemade bread crumbs (page 188)
1 tablespoon oil	
½ teaspoon pepper	
10 drops hot pepper sauce	Oil
1 (12-ounce) Brie cheese, well chilled	

Combine egg, parsley, oil, pepper, and hot sauce in a medium bowl, stirring until well blended.

Slice Brie into 3-inch x 1-inch pieces.

Dust cheese with flour, dip into egg mixture, and dredge in bread crumbs. (You may make fresh bread crumbs from day-old white bread with crusts using a food processor.)

Freeze for 30 minutes.

Pour oil into a large, deep pan to depth of 1 to 2 inches and heat over medium-high heat.

Fry Brie for 1½ to 2 minutes or until light brown and crisp. Fry in batches, if necessary, to avoid overcrowding. Drain on paper towels and serve immediately.

Yield: 4 to 6 servings.

CRISP AND GOLDEN POTATO LATKES

Parve

5	medium to large potatoes
2	onions, coarsely chopped
3	large eggs, lightly beaten
2-4	tablespoons all-purpose flour or matzoh meal

1-2	teaspoons salt
½	teaspoon pepper
	Canola oil

Peel and cube potatoes; place in a bowl of cold water until ready to prepare latkes. (The cold water prevents the potatoes from turning dark and allows you to prepare them a few hours ahead.)

Drain potatoes. Place potatoes and onion in the container of a food processor fitted with a knife blade. Pulse until smooth; drain mixture immediately.

Pour potato mixture into a large bowl. Stir in eggs. Add flour or matzoh meal, 1 tablespoon at a time, until the mixture holds together as a wet paste. Season to taste with salt and pepper.

Pour oil into a large, deep pan to depth of 1 to 2 inches and heat over medium-high heat.

Carefully drop several heaping tablespoons of potato mixture into hot oil; flatten slightly. Fry for several minutes on each side until golden brown. Drain on paper towels.

Serve with sour cream and Homemade Applesauce.

Yield: 20 to 30 latkes.

HOMEMADE APPLESAUCE

Parve

The flavor of this applesauce is largely determined by the kind of apple you choose. Macintosh, Royal Gala, and Golden Delicious will all make a flavorful and nicely textured applesauce. Avoid using overripe and mealy fruit, as the texture will not be as good as with firmer apples. Feel free to use combinations of apples for a unique flavor.

12	apples, cored
1	cup water

½	teaspoon ground cinnamon

Pour water into bottom of a large pot. Peel and slice apples, letting slices drop into water as you cut. (For a textured applesauce, do not peel.)

Cook, uncovered, over medium heat for 20 to 30 minutes or until apples are soft enough to mash with a fork. Add more water, if necessary, to avoid scorching the apples. Sprinkle with cinnamon and gently stir.

Transfer apples to a large bowl; gently break up any large pieces with a fork, leaving smaller pieces to enhance texture. Cool before serving.

Yield: about 6 cups.

Sufganiyot (Jelly Doughnuts)

Dairy

¾ cup lukewarm milk
2 tablespoons dry yeast
3½ tablespoons sugar
2½ cups all-purpose flour
2 egg yolks, lightly beaten
Pinch salt
Pinch ground cinnamon

1½ tablespoons margarine, softened
Raspberry or strawberry preserves
Vegetable oil
Powdered sugar

Combine milk, yeast, and 2 tablespoons sugar in a small bowl. Let stand 5 minutes or until dissolved. (The mixture should be bubbly.)

Place flour on a board or work surface and make a well in the center. Pour the yeast mixture in the well and add the yolks, salt, cinnamon, and remaining 1½ tablespoons sugar, mixing well. Knead until smooth. Add margarine and knead until the dough is elastic. Place in a well-greased bowl, turning to grease top.

Cover and let rise in a warm place for 2 hours.

Turn dough out onto a floured work surface. Roll dough to ¼-inch thickness. Cut circles using a 2-inch round cutter or glass. Cover and let rise 15 minutes.

Pour oil to a depth of 2 inches in a large, heavy pot over medium-high heat. Heat to 375°.

Drop doughnuts in hot oil a few at a time. Fry until golden brown on each side; drain on paper towels.

Fill a tiny spoon with preserves. Insert the spoon into the top of the doughnut and carefully revolve it around. Pull spoon carefully out of the same hole.

Roll doughnuts in powdered sugar and serve immediately.

Yield: 2½ dozen.

PURIM

Purim celebrates the survival of the Jewish people despite the plans for their utter destruction by the evil Haman. Though a series of "hidden" miracles, God placed Esther into a position where she could save her people. Both Esther and her uncle, Mordechai, realized that it was through God and Torah that the Jews would be saved. Mordechai led the Jewish people in re-embracing Torah, and Esther asked her people to join her in 3 days of fasting and prayer.

The day before Purim is a fast day called Ta'anit Esther, in remembrance of Esther's fast. But when the day of Purim arrives, there is much celebration and emphasis on food. In addition to the joyful festival meal, which usually begins in the late afternoon, we give gifts of at least two ready-to-eat foods to at least one friend *(mishloach manot)*. Usually among these foods are hamantaschen, triangular cookies with a sweet filling. Their name may derive from the words *mohn* (poppy seeds, a popular filling) and *tashen* (pockets), or that hamantaschen remind us of Haman's triangular hat. At the Purim Seudah (festival meal), it is customary to serve kreplach, as well as hamantaschen (for dessert). The hidden fillings within these foods remind us of the hidden miracles of Purim.

DELICIOUS KREPLACH

Meat

Filling:

5	tablespoons oil, divided		1/4	teaspoon pepper
1	onion, diced		1	large egg, lightly beaten
1	cup cooked ground beef		1	tablespoon matzoh meal
1½	teaspoons salt, divided			

Dough:

2	cups all-purpose flour		2	egg yolks
1½	teaspoons baking powder			Salted water or soup stock
½	cup water			

To prepare filling: heat 2 tablespoons oil in a large skillet over medium-high heat. Add onion and sauté until tender and translucent. Add beef and cook for 5 minutes, stirring frequently, until browned. Stir in 1 teaspoon salt, pepper, whole egg, and matzoh meal; set aside.

To prepare dough: combine flour, baking powder, remaining ½ teaspoon salt, remaining 3 tablespoons oil, water, and egg yolks in a large bowl, kneading until dough forms.

Turn out dough onto a floured surface; roll to a ⅛-inch thickness. Cut out 3-inch circles with a cookie cutter or drinking glass.

Place heaping teaspoons of filling in the center of each circle. Moisten edges of dough with water. Fold over three sides of dough to form a triangle, moistening and gently pressing overlapping dough together.

Heat water or stock in a large soup pot over high heat. Place kreplach in boiling salted water or soup stock, and cook approximately 20 minutes or until kreplach float to the top.

Yield: about 3 dozen.

Kreplach may be fried in oil over medium heat until golden brown on each side.

Hamantaschen

Parve

1 (6-ounce) package dried
   apricots
½ cup water
½ cup margarine
1 cup sugar
1 large egg
⅓ cup orange juice
1 teaspoon vanilla extract

3 cups all-purpose flour
2 teaspoon baking powder
½ teaspoon salt
   Walnut or pecan halves
   (optional)
1 egg white, beaten
   Cinnamon-sugar

Combine apricots and water in a small saucepan over medium-low heat. Cook until apricots are soft and water is absorbed. Mash gently with a fork; set aside.

Preheat oven to 350°.

Beat margarine at medium speed with an electric mixer until creamy; gradually add sugar, beating well. Add egg, orange juice, and vanilla.

Combine flour, baking powder, and salt. Add to margarine mixture; stir into a uniform dough.

Shape dough into a flat disk. Cover in plastic wrap and refrigerate at least 15 minutes (may be made 2 days ahead).

Roll out chilled dough on a lightly floured surface to ⅛-inch thickness. Cut 3-inch circles with a cookie cutter or drinking glass.

Place ½ teaspoon of apricot mixture in the center of each circle. Top with one walnut or pecan half, if desired.

Shape into a triangle by folding 2 sides of the circle to the center and pinch together at the sides. Fold remaining side up to the center and pinch together at the sides. Some of the filling should be visible in the center.

Place hamantaschen 1 inch apart on a greased baking sheet. Brush with egg white and sprinkle with cinnamon-sugar.

Bake for 20 to 35 minutes.

Yield: about 4 dozen.

A great variety of sweet fillings may be used in hamantaschen, so try different fillings for these tasty treats and have fun!

Suggested fillings for hamantaschen:

Prepared Poppy Seed Filling (This is the most traditional)

Apricot Butter

Prune Butter

Apricot Jam

Strawberry Jam

Other Jams and Jellies

Chocolate Chips

Dairy Hamantaschen

Dairy

ue to the need to chill the dough, this recipe is best begun the day before.

1 cup unsalted butter, softened	⅓ cup plus 2 tablespoons sugar
1 (8-ounce) package cream cheese, softened	½ teaspoon vanilla extract
	2 cups all-purpose flour
	Apricot butter

Beat butter and cream cheese at medium speed with an electric mixer until creamy; gradually add sugar, beating well. Stir in vanilla.

Stir in flour, mixing into a smooth dough. Form dough into two balls. Cover in plastic wrap and refrigerate 8 hours or overnight.

Preheat oven to 350°.

Roll chilled dough, one piece at a time, on a floured surface to ½-inch thickness. Cut into 3-inch circles with a cookie cutter or drinking glass.

Place ½ teaspoon of apricot butter in the center of each circle. Shape into a triangle by folding two sides of the circle to the center and pinch together at the corners. Fold remaining side up to the center and pinch together at corners. Some of the filling should be visible in the center.

Place hamantaschen 1 inch apart on a greased baking sheet. Chill in freezer for 15 minutes.

Remove from freezer and, again, pinch corner of each triangle. (This is important or the triangle shape will not hold.)

Bake for 15 to 20 minutes on the middle rack of the oven.

Yield: 2½ to 3 dozen.

Passover

Passover is an eight-day holiday during which we remember and relive our forefathers' enslavement in Egypt, the miracles God did to free them, and their ultimate journey out of Egypt. The most significant food-related laws of Passover are the prohibition of all chometz (leaven) and the requirement to eat matzoh. Chometz includes all things containing wheat, barley, oats, rye or spelt. Additionally, Ashkenazic Jews do not eat kitneot, legumes like peas and beans, and rice.

Passover is by far the most complicated holiday to cook for. In the days and weeks before Passover begins, the entire house, and particularly the kitchen, is cleaned of all chometz. And yet, there are few recipes that are specific to Passover. With exceptions such as matzoh and charoset, the Passover meals strongly resemble other festive meals of the Jewish home, but lacking any ingredients that are chometz. On the first and second night of Passover, the Seder includes the festival meal. The Hagadah (the book of the Seder) guides us through specific mitzvot involving the eating of matzoh, bitter herbs, and other items related to the seder. But when the time comes for the festival meal, endless variations are possible. However, a traditional Seder meal might begin with Handmade Gelfilte Fish, followed by Rich, Golden Chicken Soup with Matzoh Balls, followed by the main course and side dishes. Many people do not eat roasted meat on the first night of Passover because we no longer have the ritual sacrifice of Passover (which was roasted) so they choose a stewed meat or chicken dish for the main course.

Sweet Passover Charoset

Parve

6-8 apples (a combination of Macintosh, Red Delicious, Royal Gala, or Golden Delicious)
1 cup walnuts, coarsely chopped
½ cup golden raisins
½ cup sweet red Passover wine
1 teaspoon ground cinnamon

Core and grate unpeeled apples into a large bowl. Drain off excess juice. Stir in walnuts, raisins, and wine.

Add more wine, one tablespoon at a time, if necessary to make a thick and damp texture (to resemble the mortar with which the Jewish people made bricks in Egypt).

Add cinnamon, stirring until well blended. Cover and refrigerate until ready to serve.

Yield: 3 to 3½ cups.

Ultimate Handmade Gefilte Fish

Parve

This recipe came all the way from Vienna with a Holocaust survivor who ultimately settled in Livingston.

6	pounds white fish	6	ounces (1½ cups) almonds, finely ground
6	pounds pike	1½	cups sugar
4	onions, quartered	3	tablespoons matzoh meal
2	carrots, quartered	2½	teaspoons salt
2	stalks celery, cut into pieces	1½	teaspoons white pepper
⅔	cup sugar	½	teaspoon black pepper
1	teaspoon white pepper	4	large eggs, lightly beaten
¾	teaspoon salt	1½	cups cold water
4	onions, finely ground		Fish Stock

Remove heads, skin, and bones from fish. (You may ask butcher to clean and grind fish for you, but remember to take head, skin and bones for stock.) Cover fish and refrigerate until ready to prepare.

Place fish heads, skin, and bones in a large soup pot or Dutch oven.

Add onions, carrots, celery, sugar, white pepper, and salt. Pour in water to cover fish and vegetables.

Bring to a boil, reduce heat, and simmer, partially covered, until ready to cook fish patties.

Place fish fillets in a food processor or meat grinder. Process until finely ground. Combine ground fish, onions, almonds, sugar, matzoh meal, salt, white pepper, black pepper, and eggs in a large bowl.

Add water, ½ cup at a time, stirring until the mixture is light and smooth.

Dip a large serving spoon in water to scoop up fish mixture and form a rounded shape with your fingers.

Slide the fish patty off of the spoon and into the simmering stock. Repeat, dipping the spoon in water and forming patties with remaining fish mixture. Add boiling water to stock, if necessary, to keep the fish patties submerged.

Simmer fish patties for 2 hours with lid partially open.

Gently remove the patties with a slotted spoon and place on a platter to cool. Cover and refrigerate.

Remove carrots from liquid; serve sliced or use as a garnish.

Strain fish stock into a large container, gently tapping some of the solids through the strainer. Discard remaining solids.

Cover and refrigerate until chilled and mixture has congealed. (If mixture does not congeal, reheat and combine with 1 or 2 packages of unflavored kosher gelatin. Refrigerate until chilled.)

Serve the gefilte fish cold, with horseradish, fish gelatin, and slices of carrot.

Yield: about 3½ dozen.

THREE MUSHROOM PILAF

Meat or Parve

6   tablespoons margarine
1   large onion, diced
1   cup sliced button
     mushrooms
1   cup sliced shiitake
     mushrooms
1   cup sliced portobello
     mushrooms (sliced same
     size as other mushrooms)

¾   teaspoon salt
⅛   teaspoon pepper
2   cups matzoh farfel
2   large eggs, lightly beaten
½   cup chicken stock
     (page 39) or bouillon
⅓   cup chopped fresh parsley

Heat margarine in a large skillet over medium-high heat. Add onion and sauté until transparent. Add mushrooms, salt, and pepper; sauté until tender. Transfer mushroom mixture to a bowl; set aside.

Heat farfel in the same pan over medium heat. Quickly stir in beaten eggs, stirring constantly, to coat and separate the pieces.

Add mushroom mixture and sauté, stirring gently.

Gradually add stock until desired moistness is reached, adding more stock if necessary.

Stir in parsley.

Yield: 6 servings.

**For Your
Passover Table,
May We Suggest . . .**

Rich, Golden Chicken Soup or Crystal Clear Chicken Soup

Light and Fluffy Matzoh Balls

Braised Short Ribs

Vegetable Medley

Crusty Garlic and Rosemary Potatoes

Flourless Chocolate Cake

Passover Peach Kugel

Parve

1 pound matzoh farfel
  Boiling water
1 (16-ounce) can sliced
  peaches, undrained
7 large eggs
1 cup margarine, melted

1 cup sugar
2 tablespoons vanilla
  extract or 2 packages
  vanilla sugar
Sugar
Ground cinnamon

Preheat oven to 350°.

Place farfel in a colander. Pour boiling water over farfel; drain and set aside.

Drain peaches, reserving liquid.

Beat eggs in a large mixing bowl until well blended. Beat in margarine, sugar, vanilla, farfel and reserved peach liquid. Cut in several peach slices.

Pour into a greased 13- x 9-inch baking pan. Place peach slices on top, pressing down slightly into batter to prevent burning. Sprinkle with sugar and cinnamon.

Bake, uncovered, for 1 hour.

Yield: 12 to 15 servings.

Flour Measurements for Passover

1 cup regular flour =
¾ cup potato starch
or
¼ cup matzoh
cake meal

½ cup regular flour =
6 tablespoons
potato starch
or
2 tablespoons
matzoh cake meal

CHEWY ALMOND DROPS

Parve

Parchment paper
3 cups (12 ounces) slivered
almonds
1½ cups sugar
3 large egg whites
1 teaspoon almond extract

Preheat oven to 325° with racks in upper middle and lower middle.

Line 2 large baking sheets with parchment paper; set aside. (You must use parchment paper. Cookies will spread too much on greased baking sheets and stick to ungreased baking sheets.)

Place almonds in the container of a food processor fitted with a knife blade. Process for 1 minute until ground. Add sugar and process 15 seconds.

Add egg whites and almond extract. Process until formed into a stiff, sticky paste similar to marzipan. If crumbly or dry, add a few drops of water and process 5 seconds.

Drop a scant 2 tablespoons of dough onto prepared pans or roll into balls 1½ inches apart.

Bake 20 to 25 minutes until pale golden brown. (Do not overbake.) Cool on parchment on wire racks. Store in an airtight container.

Yield: 2 to 3 dozen.

I CAN'T BELIEVE
THEY'RE PASSOVER COOKIES

Parve

2 cups Passover cake meal
2 cups matzoh farfel
1½ cups sugar
1 teaspoon ground
cinnamon
1 cup oil
4 large eggs, lightly beaten
1 cup Passover chocolate
morsels

Preheat oven to 350°.

Combine cake meal, farfel, sugar, cinnamon, oil, and eggs in a large bowl. Fold in chocolate morsels.

Form heaping tablespoons of dough into loose balls with wet hands. Place on a greased baking sheet and flatten slightly. (Cookies will not flatten during baking.)

Bake for 20 to 30 minutes until light golden brown (do not overbake).

Yield: about 5 dozen.

CHEWY CHOCOLATE ALMOND DROPS

Parve

1½ cups (6 ounces) slivered almonds

1½ cups sugar

¼ teaspoon salt

1 cup Dutch Cocoa

3 large egg whites

1 teaspoon almond extract

Follow directions for Chewy Almond Drops reducing almonds to 1½ cups (6 ounces) and adding 1 cup Dutch cocoa and ¼ teaspoon salt.

Yield: 2 to 3 dozen.

Shavuot

The dual-themed holiday of Shavuot, which falls on the sixth and seventh days of Sivan, celebrates the time of the giving of the Torah, and the harvesting and bringing of the first ripe fruits of the seven species to the Beit Hamikdash. *Shavuot* means "weeks," and relates to the seven weeks during which the Jewish people counted the days and prepared themselves to receive the Torah.

On Shavuot, we eat dairy foods such as blintzes, kugel, and cheesecake. One explanation for this custom is that when the Jewish people were receiving the Torah, they did not yet understand all the laws of kashrut relating to meat. Therefore, they abstained from meat, and ate dairy foods instead. It is also customary to decorate the shul and home with flowers and greenery on Shavuot to remind us of the holiday's harvest theme.

Strawberry Soup

Dairy

1 pint fresh strawberries, stems removed	1 teaspoon vanilla extract
1 ripe peach, peeled and chopped	5-6 tablespoons sugar
1½ cups pineapple juice	½ (8-ounce) container vanilla or plain yogurt

Combine strawberries, peach, juice, extract, and sugar in the container of a blender or food processor. Process until smooth. Stir in yogurt. Serve chilled.

Yield: 4 servings.

CHEESE BLINTZES

Dairy

Bite into this blintz and conjure up memories of a bygone era. This is the authentic blintz recipe eaten by generations at the famous Catskill resort, Grossinger's. Many of us remember holidays and vacations at the Grossinger's Hotel. The food was endless and never disappointing. Serve these blintzes for a holiday or any occasion and keep the Grossinger's spirit alive.

3	large eggs	¾	cup all-purpose flour
1	cup milk		Butter
2	tablespoons vegetable oil		Cheese Filling
½	teaspoon salt		Sour cream

Beat eggs, milk, oil, and salt together in a large bowl. Stir in flour.

Heat a small amount of butter in a 6-inch skillet over medium heat until melted.

Pour about 2 tablespoons of batter into pan; quickly tilt pan in all directions so batter coats the bottom of the pan.

Lift edges of crepe to test for doneness. When the bottom of the crepe is golden brown, carefully turn out onto a paper towel. Continue with remaining batter and butter.

Place blintzes, brown side up, on a work surface. Spread 1 heaping teaspoon of filling along one edge of the crepe; roll once to cover filling. Fold the right and left sides over the center and roll, jelly roll style, until completely closed.

Heat a small amount of butter in a skillet over medium heat until melted. Fry blintzes, 2 minutes on each side. Serve with sour cream.

Yield: 1½ dozen.

CHEESE FILLING:

2	cups farmer cheese	1	tablespoon melted butter
1	egg yolk	½	teaspoon salt
2	tablespoons sugar	½	teaspoon vanilla extract

Mash cheese with a fork in a small bowl. Add yolk, sugar, butter, salt, and vanilla; stir until well blended.

Yield: 2¼ cups.

COTTAGE CHEESE PANCAKES

Dairy

3 large eggs	¼ teaspoon salt
1 cup milk	Oil
1 cup cottage cheese	Sour cream
1 cup matzoh meal	Cinnamon-sugar
2 teaspoons sugar	Applesauce
½-1 teaspoon ground cinnamon	

Beat eggs and milk in a medium bowl; stir in cottage cheese.

Combine matzoh meal, sugar, cinnamon, and salt and stir into egg mixture.

Cover and refrigerate at least 1 hour to thicken.

Brush bottom of a griddle or heavy skillet lightly with oil; place pan over medium heat until just hot, but not smoking.

Spoon approximately 2 heaping tablespoons into pan; cook 3 to 5 minutes until tops are covered with bubbles and edges look cooked. Turn pancakes over and cook 3 to 5 minutes or until done. Serve immediately with sour cream, cinnamon-sugar, or applesauce.

Yield: 4 to 6 servings.

DAIRY RUGELAH

Dairy

1 cup butter, softened	1 cup chopped nuts
1 (8-ounce) package cream cheese, softened	½ cup sugar
2 cups all-purpose flour	½ cup raisins
Pinch salt	Ground cinnamon

Combine butter, cream cheese, flour, and salt, kneading until a smooth dough forms. Divide dough into 3 balls; cover in plastic wrap and refrigerate until well chilled.

Preheat oven to 350°.

Combine nuts, sugar, raisins, and cinnamon in a small bowl; set aside.

Place dough on a floured surface and roll to ¼-inch thickness in the shape of a 9-inch circle. Sprinkle filling on dough leaving ½ inch uncovered at the outer edge and a quarter-size circle uncovered in the center.

Cut into 16 triangles using a pizza wheel or knife. Roll each triangle, starting from the wide edge; place, seam side down, on a lightly greased baking sheet.

Bake for 22 minutes or until light golden brown.

Yield: 4 dozen.

DREAMY CREAMY CHEESECAKE

Dairy

Crust:

1¼ cups all-purpose flour
⅓ cup sugar
2 teaspoons grated lemon
   peel

¾ cup butter or margarine,
   softened
1 egg yolk

Filling:

5 (8-ounce) packages
   cream cheese, softened
1¾ cups sugar
5 large eggs
2 egg yolks
¼ cup milk

2 teaspoons grated lemon
   peel
3 tablespoons all-purpose
   flour
Fresh fruit (optional)
Apricot or apple jelly,
   melted (optional)

Combine flour, sugar, and lemon peel; add butter and egg yolk, stirring until well blended. Shape dough into a ball; cover with plastic wrap and refrigerate 1 hour.

Preheat oven to 400°.

Remove ⅓ of dough from refrigerator and press into the bottom of a 10- x 2½-inch springform pan.

Bake 8 minutes or until golden brown; cool on wire rack.

Increase temperature to 475°.

Remove remaining dough from refrigerator and press into sides of pan up to 1 inch below the top rim.

Beat cream cheese at medium speed with an electric mixer until smooth; gradually add sugar, beating well. Add eggs and yolks, one at a time, beating until blended after each addition. Add milk, lemon peel, and flour, beating until blended and smooth.

Pour filling into crust.

Bake for 12 minutes. Reduce temperature to 300° and bake 35 minutes.

Turn oven off and let cheesecake remain in oven for 30 minutes. Remove from oven and run a knife around edge of cheesecake. (This allows the loosened sides to contract without cracking the top of the cheesecake.) Cool cheesecake on wire rack, then refrigerate for 4 hours. Carefully remove sides of pan and place cheesecake on a serving plate. Arrange fresh fruit on top of cheesecake and brush with melted jelly.

Yield: 12 servings.

For Your
Shavuot Table,
May We Suggest . . .

Sun-Dried Tomato
Stuffed Mushrooms

Mini-Blini

Perfect French
Onion Soup

Baked Brie and
Raspberry Salad

Garlic Crusted
Whitefish

Penne à la Vodka

Crustless Spinach
Quiche

Green Beans with
Port Mushroom Sauce

White Chocolate
Mousse

BERRY AND FARMER CHEESE TART

Dairy

Crust:

1   cup plus 2 tablespoons
    all-purpose flour
3   tablespoons sugar
¼   teaspoon salt
¼   teaspoon baking powder
6   tablespoons unsalted
    butter, chilled and cut
    into pieces

1   large egg
1   tablespoon fresh lemon
    juice
2   tablespoons berry jelly
    (any kind), melted

Filling:

1   (7½-ounce) package
    farmer cheese
¼   cup sugar
1   large egg, lightly beaten
1   teaspoon cornstarch
¼   teaspoon grated lemon
    rind

½   cup heavy whipping
    cream
1½ cups mixed berries such
    as red or black
    raspberries, blueberries,
    or blackberries, divided
Garnish: fresh mint

Combine flour, sugar, salt, and baking powder in the container of a food processor fitted with a knife blade; pulse until mixed. Add butter and pulse until mixture resembles coarse meal.

In a small bowl, beat egg and lemon juice; add to flour mixture and stir just until mixture forms a dough.

Press dough evenly on the bottom and sides of a 10-inch tart pan with a removable bottom. Refrigerate 1 hour.

Preheat oven to 375°.

Brush bottom of pastry with jelly; prick all over with fork.

Bake 18 to 20 minutes or until golden brown; remove from oven.

Reduce heat to 325°.

Combine farmer cheese, sugar, egg, cornstarch, and rind in the container of a food processor fitted with knife blade; process for 1 minute or until smooth, stopping to scrape down sides. Add the cream and pulse until just blended.

Arrange ½ cup berries in the bottom of the cooked pastry. Pour cheese mixture slowly over berries.

Bake for 25 to 30 minutes or until custard is set; cool completely. Arrange remaining 1 cup berries over the top of the tart and garnish with fresh mint.

Yield: 10 to 12 servings.

The Kosher Palette would like to express its gratitude to the photographers and chefs who have supported this project with their professional expertise and in-kind donations. We appreciate their hard work and contributions which made this book possible. All photographs and recipes are printed with permission and protected under copyright.

PHOTOGRAPHY CREDITS:

©John Uher from Jacques Torres' *"Dessert Circus,"* published in 1998 by the William Morrow Company
  Cover photo: Chocolate Palette of Sorbets

©Scott Laperruque 1999
  Page 13: Salmon & Spinach Bonnet
  Page 21: Gravlax
  Page 24: Portobello Mushroom Napoleons
  Page 31: Lemon Topiary
  Page 46: Yellow & Orange Peppers
  Page 155: Three Tomatoes
  Page 80: Scallion
  Page 183: Checkerboard of Roasted Peppers
  Page 96: Autumnal Floral Arrangement
  Page 122: Vegetables and flowers in a bird's nest
  Page 125: Pesto Stuffed Veal Breast with Vegetable Ribbons
  Page 129: Chilean Sea Bass in Sun-Dried Tomato Vinaigrette
  Page 105: Braised Short Ribs
  Page 147: Bunches of Roses
  Page 269: Floral and Candle Arrangement
  Page 247: Chocolate Raspberry Thumbprints
  Page 286: Strawberries

©Jan Press 1999
  Page 54: Bok Choy Leaf
  Page 166: Vegetables
  Page 68: Terra Chips
  Page 273: Acorn Squash
  Page 111: Rosemary Sprigs
  Page 248: Mini Coconut Cakes
  Page 218: Apples
  Page 145: Spices
  Page 210: Rice
  All photos on special equipment pages

©Pamela Dennis
  Page 37: Antique Soup Terrine

©Tom Eckerle
  Page 50: Tri-Color Vegetable Soup

©Michael Lamotte from Judy Zeidler's *Master Chefs Cook Kosher,"* published in 1998 by Chronicle Books
  Page 53: Endive Salad with Tangerine Sections, Beets and Olives

©David Roth
  Page 72: Flavored Vinegar and Oil Bottles
  Page 160: Farfalle with Pesto & Tomatoes
  Page 259: Gefilte Fish
  Page 211: Blueberry Raspberry Tart
  Page 115: Stuffed Breast of Veal with Madeira Wine Sauce

©Allan Rosenberg from Williams-Sonoma Kitchen Library *"Grilling,"* published in 1992 by Weldon Owen for Time Life Books
  Page 73: Stuffed Turkey Breast

©Romulo Yanes/Gourmet
  Page 163: Feta Stuffed Eggplant Rolls with Salsa Verde
  Page 149: Pasta with Uncooked Tomato Olive Sauce

©Jack Anderson
  Page 176: Strawberries, Roses & Peonies Centerpiece
  Concept: Wayne Woods of *"The Woods Exquisite Flowers"* Los Angeles, California

©Jeff Sarpa
  Page 138: Sesame Encrusted Salmon with Spinach Watercress Sauce

©Jennifer Harper
  Page 257: Line drawing of Palette

©Rita Maas
  Page 239: Black and White Butter Cookies

©Iris Richardson
  Page 87: Chicken À L'Orange
  Page 198: Tri-Color Vegetable Soufflé

Courtesy of Foremost Caterers
Salmon and Spinach Bonnets p. 15
Braised Short Ribs p. 128
Chilean Sea Bass in Sun-Dried Tomato
Vinaigrette p. 129

Courtesy of Jeff Nathan of Abigael's Restaurant
Twisted Knish p. 19
Peking Chicken p. 82

Courtesy of Noah's Ark and NAOmni Caterers
Wild Mushroom Risotto p. 205
Apricot Glazed Stuffed Squab p. 102
Quesadillas p. 175

Courtesy of Petak's
Rotini with Artichokes and Sun-Dried
Tomatoes p. 161

Courtesy of Judy Zeidler from *Master Chefs Cook Kosher*" published in 1998 by Chronicle Books
Endive with Tangerine Sections, Beets &
Olives p. 55

Courtesy of Suzanne Maiorino Chef/Manager
Nordstrom Cafe*
Cream of Tomato Basil Soup p. 41

Courtesy of John Phillip Carroll adapted from
Williams-Sonoma Kitchen Library *"Grilling,"*
published in 1992 by Weldon Owen for Time Life
Books
Stuffed Turkey Breast p. 75

Courtesy of Mitchell Goldberg, Executive Chef of
Nero's Grill*
Pan Seared Yellowfin Tuna Steaks p. 143

Courtesy of Iris Richardson
Chicken à L'Orange p. 87

Courtesy of BON APPETIT Magazine "BON
APPETIT" is a registered trademark of Advance
Magazine Publishers Inc., published through its
division, The Conde Nast Publications Inc.
© 1996 by the Conde Nast Publications Inc.
Reprinted with permission.
Sesame Encrusted Salmon in Spinach
Watercress Sauce p. 138

Courtesy of GOURMET magazine "GOURMET" is
a registered trademark of Advance Magazine
Publishers Inc., published through its division, The
Conde Nast Publications Inc.

©1995 and 1996 by the Conde Nast Publications
Inc. Reprinted with permission.
Pasta with Uncooked Tomato Olive Sauce
p. 151
Feta Stuffed Eggplant Rolls with Salsa Verde
p. 164

Courtesy of Bobby Flay of MESA GRILL New York,
NY*
Chile Crusted Tuna Steaks with Tortilla Salad
and Orange Vinaigrette p. 144

Courtesy of La Maison, a French country inn in
Spring Lake, NJ*
Crème Brûlée French Toast p. 170

Courtesy of Sea Crest By the Sea in Spring Lake,
NJ*
Featherbed Eggs p. 172

Courtesy of The Barrow House Inn of Saint
Francisville, LA*
Bran Surprise Muffins p. 179

*These are not Kosher eating establishments. The
recipes were tested in strictly Kosher kitchens.*

INDEX

· · · · · · · · ·

C

· · · · · · · · · · · ·

D

Desserts

Cakes

Candies

Cheesecakes

Cookies

Frostings & Icings

Pies

Puddings & Desserts

Tarts & Tortes

Q

. . . .

R

. . . .

S

MEASUREMENTS AND EQUIVALENTS

1 tablespoon fresh herbs .... = ... 1 teaspoon dried herbs

1 tablespoon fresh ginger .... = ... 1 teaspoon powdered ginger

dash cayenne or red pepper ..... = ... few drops hot pepper sauce

1 teaspoon .... = ... ⅓ tablespoon

3 teaspoons .... = ... 1 tablespoon

½ tablespoon .... = ... 1½ teaspoons

1 tablespoon .... = ... 3 teaspoons or ½ fluid ounce

2 tablespoons .... = ... ⅛ cup or 1 fluid ounce

3 tablespoons .... = ... 1½ fluid ounces

4 tablespoons .... = ... ¼ cup or 2 fluid ounces

8 tablespoons .... = ... ½ cup or 4 fluid ounces

12 tablespoons .... = ... ¾ cup or 6 fluid ounces

16 tablespoons .... = ... 1 cup or 8 fluid ounces or ½ pint

⅓ cup .... = ... 5 tablespoons + 1 teaspoon

⅜ cup .... = ... ¼ cup + 2 tablespoons

½ cup .... = ... 8 tablespoons or 4 fluid ounces

⅔ cup .... = ... 10 tablespoons + 2 teaspoons

⅝ cup .... = ... ½ cup + 2 tablespoons

¾ cup .... = ... 12 tablespoons or 6 fluid ounces

⅞ cup .... = ... ¾ cup + 2 tablespoons

1 cup .... = ... 16 tablespoons or ½ pint or 8 fluid ounces

2 cups .... = ... 1 pint or 16 fluid ounces

1 pint .... = ... 2 cups or 16 fluid ounces

1 quart .... = ... 2 pints or 4 cups or 32 fluid ounces

1 gallon .... = ... 4 quarts or 8 pints or 16 cups or 128 fluid ounces

Source: *The New Food Lover's Companion, Second Edition*

THE KOSHER PALETTE

. . . .

℅ Joseph Kushner Hebrew Academy/Kushner Yeshiva High School
110 South Orange Avenue
Livingston, New Jersey 07039
(973) 597-1115 ext. 197

Please send me:

The Kosher Palette Cookbook	@ $26.95 each	Quantity _____	$ _____
Postage & Handling for first book	@ $ 5.00		$ _____
Each additional book	@ $ 2.00		$ _____
Sales Tax *(New Jersey Residents only add 6%)*	@ $ 1.62		$ _____
		Total Enclosed	$ _____

Ship to:

Name _____ Address _____

City _____ State _____ Zip Code _____

Make checks payable to *The Kosher Palette*

Charge to (circle one)   Visa   MasterCard   Signature _____

Account number _____ Expiration Date _____

All proceeds from THE KOSHER PALETTE will benefit the educational needs of the students
of the Joseph Kushner Hebrew Academy and Kushner Yeshiva High School.

Thank you for your order.

- -

THE KOSHER PALETTE

. . . .

℅ Joseph Kushner Hebrew Academy/Kushner Yeshiva High School
110 South Orange Avenue
Livingston, New Jersey 07039
(973) 597-1115 ext. 197

Please send me:

The Kosher Palette Cookbook	@ $26.95 each	Quantity _____	$ _____
Postage & Handling for first book	@ $ 5.00		$ _____
Each additional book	@ $ 2.00		$ _____
Sales Tax *(New Jersey Residents only add 6%)*	@ $ 1.62		$ _____
		Total Enclosed	$ _____

Ship to:

Name _____ Address _____

City _____ State _____ Zip Code _____

Make checks payable to *The Kosher Palette*

Charge to (circle one)   Visa   MasterCard   Signature _____

Account number _____ Expiration Date _____

All proceeds from THE KOSHER PALETTE will benefit the educational needs of the students
of the Joseph Kushner Hebrew Academy and Kushner Yeshiva High School.

Thank you for your order.